Narcissism

by Laura L. Smith, PhD

A Wiley Brand

Narcissism For Dummies®

Contents at a Glance

Table of Contents

Introduction

Ask anyone what kind of person a narcissist is, and they can quickly come up with an answer. Loud, brash, self-centered, obnoxious, superficial, entitled, and conceited are just a few descriptors that come to mind. And most people, myself included, can recall at least one or two narcissists who have played significant roles in their lives.

Narcissists generally make a lasting impression on those they come into contact with. Although they tend to be initially charming, once they catch someone in their web, the resulting emotional costs add up quickly. Partners, friends, coworkers, and family members suffer at the hands of narcissists who cheat, lie, manipulate, and sometimes become aggressive or even violent.

If everyone can pretty easily describe a narcissist and most people have met a few, why write a whole book about narcissism? The reason is that there is much more to the narcissist than the entitled exterior. For example, narcissists can be both overconfident and have very thin skins at the same time. Some of them can be surprisingly vulnerable to any kind of negative feedback. When backed into a corner, narcissists lash out, sometimes quite viciously and with surprising cruelty.

Also, narcissists can become firmly entrenched in your life, causing all sorts of hardship. If you are the child of narcissistic parents, you may have lasting emotional damage. If you get into a romantic relationship with a narcissist, your personality might change as you become embroiled in their manipulations. And if you work with a narcissist, you may be confused by their shifting allegiances and outright distortions of reality. Therefore, if you care about or have been touched by narcissistic manipulation or abuse, this book gives you ways to handle your present reality as well as changes you may need to make to establish healthy boundaries and maintain your sanity and safely.

About This Book

You may be aware that the word narcissist comes from the myth of a strikingly beautiful man who glances at a pond and falls in love with his own reflection. He is so enthralled that he cannot leave and eventually withers away and dies. This is a book that dives deeply into the pond of narcissism and gives you a close look at what lies beneath the shimmering surface.

Whether you are in a relationship with someone you suspect has narcissism or you are just curious about the topic, you'll find all you need to know about narcissism in the following pages, including down-to-earth, practical suggestions on how to protect yourself or deal with narcissistic maltreatment.

You'll notice a few other important things as you read this book:

>> For simplicity, I use the term *narcissist* to describe both people who exhibit narcissistic traits as well as those relatively fewer people officially diagnosed with narcissistic personality disorder (NPD), which reflects an extremely high level of narcissistic characteristics.

>> I try to keep the language simple and direct; when I do offer new vocabulary, I italicize and define it.

>> Sidebars are set off by a gray background. The material contained in sidebars may or may not interest you. Feel free to skim them or even skip them altogether. On the other hand, you might find them as interesting as I do (I admit to being a bit of a geek).

>> If you're reading a digital version of this book on a device connected to the internet, note that you can click the web address to visit that website, like this: www.dummies.com

Foolish Assumptions

If you've picked up this book, I'm guessing you have more than a passing interest in narcissism. Most likely, you fear you may be falling victim to someone you suspect is a narcissist, and you're looking for insight and ways to cope with this person. Or maybe you suspect you have some narcissistic traits yourself. Or possibly you're a mental health practitioner who just wants to know more about narcissism.

Whatever your reason, you've come to the right place. This book gives you a clear picture of the ins and outs of narcissism. It describes how insidiously narcissism disrupts the lives of those who are involved, whether families, friends, lovers, coworkers, or acquaintances.

Icons Used in This Book

Throughout this book, you may notice symbols in the margins. These icons designate a special type of material:

TIP

This icon provides bits of insight that may have practical relevance. Be sure to read and think about them.

REMEMBER

From time to time, you run into some material that is particularly noteworthy. You might decide to note it in your phone or put it up on your bulletin board to remind you of its importance.

WARNING

Narcissists can present special challenges or dangers. The warning icon reminds you to watch out and take care.

TECHNICAL STUFF

You may or may not be interested in these in-depth tidbits of information. Read them if you want, or feel free to skip them. Some of these icons refer to specific research findings.

Beyond the Book

In addition to the abundance of information regarding narcissism that I provide in this book, you can access more material online. Go to www.dummies.com and type "Narcissism For Dummies Cheat Sheet" in the search box. The cheat sheet gives you some quick tips and take-aways that can help you identify and handle a narcissist in your life.

Where to Go from Here

You don't have to read this book from cover to cover to get useful information. You can pick and choose what you want to find out more about. In fact, if you'd like to start at Part 6 and read those chapters first, that's perfectly okay.

If you're unsure where to begin, use the table of contents at the front of the book or the detailed index at the rear to find the topics that most interest you. If all else fails, start with Chapter 1, which provides an overview of narcissism and directs you to later chapters that provide more details.

Or feel free to browse. Wherever you land, happy reading!

1
Reflecting on Narcissism

Chapter **1**

Narcissism: The Big Picture

As I contemplated writing this book, I thought about the narcissistic people who have crossed my path over the years. I am a clinical psychologist and have treated a variety of people with narcissistic traits and some who've been diagnosed with narcissistic personality disorder, or NPD. (People with NPD have an extremely high level of narcissistic characteristics. Chapter 2 clarifies the distinction between narcissistic traits and NPD.)

I've also worked with partners and family members who were dealing with the trauma left by a narcissist in their lives. That trauma often caused lasting effects that impacted their functioning in many areas including work, family relations, and friendships. The destruction that a single toxic relationship delivers can be astonishing.

I also pondered the relationships that I have had with narcissists. I recalled the narcissist that I thought I fell in love with many years ago. Then there was a former narcissistic relative who wreaked havoc not only on his partner but on the extended family as well. I remember working with narcissists, some of whom were colleagues or supervisors. I had a good friend with narcissistic tendencies and neighbors who certainly could put on a narcissistic hat from time to time. In addition, there are the superficial contacts that everyone has had with narcissists, those entitled people who cut in front of the line with no regard for those patiently awaiting their turn, or the pushy salesperson who insists they alone have the perfect answer to their customers' needs. And who could forget the obnoxious politician or the grandiose celebrity who thinks surely everyone else recognizes their specialness and superiority.

The bottom line is that most people have had multiple interactions with narcissists. Because you're reading this book, you likely suspect someone in your life is a narcissist and would like to know more about what makes narcissists tick.

You've come to the right place. This book answers your questions about narcissism, from "What causes a person to become a narcissist?" to "Can narcissists change?" as well as "If I decide to end a relationship with a narcissist, how do I do it?" But first this chapter introduces narcissism and takes a general look at how these personality traits manifest in narcissistic individuals, groups, and cultures. It tallies some of the costs of narcissism for individuals, families, and society, and it provides some guidelines for dealing with narcissists. A brief introduction to treatment options is offered as well. Throughout this overview chapter you find references to later chapters in this book where these ideas are elaborated.

What's So Grand About Narcissism?

Narcissists usually feel pretty grand about themselves. After all, they are special, superior, unique, and highly successful. Or so they think. So, for many, in their minds, there's really nothing wrong with feeling grand about yourself. They tend to be self-centered and carefully construct realities in their minds that support their overly positive view of themselves.

In addition, narcissists are likely to be demanding, domineering, and entitled. If they don't get their way, they get angry. They seek power and control and can be extremely manipulative. Some narcissists are highly successful at work and able to maintain superficial relationships with others who provide them the validation they crave.

Spotting a narcissist

It's not always easy to spot a narcissist. That's because they often come across as socially skillful, charming, and friendly. If a narcissist wants to establish a relationship with you, watch out. They may offer excessive flattery, put you up on a pedestal, and shower you with gifts. Narcissists can also seem to be good listeners and appear extremely interested in hearing all about you. However, once a narcissist succeeds in captivating you, those interactions change.

Soon the narcissist seems like they are on stage, attempting to impress everyone with their uniqueness, importance, and greatness. Over time, they become tedious in their constant attempts to show the world how special they are. They no longer show interest in your life, only their own. They become less warm and agreeable and show their hostility and arrogance. If they experience failure or threats to their overly positive, inflated self-esteem, they blame others or react with anger or even rage. (See Chapter 2 for more information about the characteristics and different types of narcissists.)

TECHNICAL STUFF

Narcissists may not always be invisible. Raters (usually college students) were asked to look at the social media pages of various people. They were able to detect narcissism by looking at pictures posted (flattering and often seductive), messages (self-congratulating and flashy), and even email addresses (self-enhancing) of narcissists compared to non-narcissists.

Considering telltale narcissistic traits

Figuring out whether someone is a narcissist should be done by a licensed mental health practitioner. However, most folks with narcissistic traits have no intention of going to see a professional. The following questionnaire does not substitute for a professional opinion; however, it can help you identify and understand some of the typical traits of narcissists.

You can take the test for yourself, or think about the possible narcissistic person you are concerned about and answer as if you were that person.

Answer true or false for each of the following questions. Be honest. Don't worry; you don't have to show this to anyone.

1. I view myself as a superior human being.

2. Lots of people envy me.

3. I am an unusually successful person.

4. I am a born leader.

5. I like to show off my good looks.

6. I avoid spending time with those who are socially unacceptable to me.

7. I don't like associating with losers.

8. I enjoy having the best of everything.

9. I like people who tell me how great I am.

10. When I am the center of attention, I enjoy it.

11. I can manipulate just about anyone to do what I want.

12. People really enjoy hearing me talk.

13. I love what I see in the mirror.

14. I shouldn't have to wait like ordinary people.

15. I prefer associating with other high-status people.

16. I am capable and great at making decisions.

17. If someone is in my way, I'll push them aside.

18. I have achieved much more success than most people.

19. If there is trouble, I tend to blame others.

20. Someone should write a book about me.

The more answers that you endorsed as true, the more likely you have narcissistic traits. If you were taking this quiz as if you were someone else in your life, well, you may be dealing with a narcissist. Again, only a mental health professional can officially diagnose a narcissistic personality disorder.

Understanding how certain cultures foster narcissism

Cultures around the world differ in values. Although there are variations within a culture, generally Western cultures, such as the United States, are more individualistic. In other words, Western cultures emphasize success of the individual, freedom, and independence. Eastern cultures are more collective, valuing the success of the family or group over personal achievement.

How do individualistic cultures foster narcissism? What makes so many people in this culture more entitled and self-centered? I don't want to overgeneralize. The majority of people in the United States are not narcissistic. However, the trait of narcissism is likely higher here than in many other cultures because values in this culture reflect a narcissistic bent. Here are a few examples of cultural values that support narcissism:

>> Believing that high-status careers are more important than less flashy but meaningful work

>> Accumulating possessions for the sake of appearing better than others

>> Obsessing about looking good and staying young

>> Demanding immediate gratification

Consider this example of putting all of these cultural values on display. Imagine a commercial showing a 70-year-old actress (high status), lounging around her swimming pool (possessions), praising a skin care product that erases her wrinkles (obsessing about looking good and young), virtually overnight with one application (immediate gratification). It's pretty easy to imagine a commercial with such content. In fact, you've probably seen more than one or two.

Narcissistic cultures foster narcissism among individuals. What about the people who don't have the personal or financial resources to pursue high-status careers; obtain lots of flashy possessions; or purchase cosmetics, expensive clothing, or plastic surgery to stay looking young for as long as possible? Some in this group desperately want to achieve values that look suspiciously like narcissism. If unable to do so, they live lives of desperation or lash out in anger. Perhaps some of the strife people throughout western societies are experiencing is due to unsatisfied narcissistic dreams.

On the other hand, many people simply don't care about fame, fortune, or looking as good as clothes, makeup, cosmetics, or surgery can accomplish. For those folks, other values, such as being a good person, having a supportive social system, participating in a spiritual community, or being able to make a decent living makes their life quite satisfying.

Counting the Costs of Narcissism

When I've worked on books about anxiety, depression, or obsessive-compulsive disorder (OCD), I've easily accessed data about the societal costs and consequences of such mental health problems. I looked for information from the World Health Organization, the Centers for Disease Control and Prevention, and various other trusted sources. In my searches, I found plenty of charts and graphs displaying estimates of lost productivity; the portion of the population suffering from anxiety, depression, or OCD; and whether the rates of those disorders were increasing, decreasing, or staying the same.

The same is not true for narcissism. There simply isn't much information about the cost of narcissism in terms of lost wages, psychotherapy costs, or specifics on rates or rate changes over time.

There are reasons this data is so sparse and inconsistent. First, many people with narcissistic traits are never seen by a therapist or counted by a researcher. That's because they believe that they're special, superior, mentally healthy, and in no need of help. They're certainly unlikely to volunteer their valuable time for a research study. If they suffer, it's almost always viewed as someone else's fault.

A second reason that data is lacking has to do with the fact that the definition of problematic narcissism is inconsistent and unclear. In addition, narcissists often have overlapping mental disorders such as depression or histrionic personality disorder that make a precise diagnosis difficult (see Chapter 13). Therefore, an accurate count of narcissism and its societal costs is difficult or even impossible for scientists to tabulate. (See Chapter 2 for more information about definitions of narcissism.)

Despite the lack of hard data in charts and graphs, after reading a good portion of this book, you're very likely to be aware of who narcissists are when you encounter them and the costs to you or others. Narcissism, in its many variations, is quite common and costly in the United States and around the world.

Broken relationships

For those caught in a narcissistic web of abuse, the effects can be long-lasting. Partners of narcissists often lose a sense of who they are. They lose the confidence to handle daily life and struggle to make decisions. They suffer from bouts of anxiety and depression. They frequently feel similar to those suffering from post-traumatic stress disorder (PTSD), needing to be hypervigilant for possible danger and attempting to suppress memories of their abusive relationship.

Partners coming out of a situation of abuse struggle to set appropriate boundaries. They feel powerless to say no when necessary and allow others to use or abuse them again. Their self-esteem litters the floor with emotional debris. They have a desperate need to be liked and commonly go overboard in a frantic attempt to please others. (See Chapter 5 for more information about relationships with narcissists.)

Fractured families

A narcissist doesn't just affect their partner, they spread misery to other family members like a rapidly spreading cancer. One common tool of the narcissist is isolation. The narcissist attempts to control their partner by keeping them from meaningfully interacting with family members. This is especially true for family members who have the potential to give the partner of the narcissist helpful feedback about the abuse they are being subjected to. In addition, other family members usually recognize the lies, excuses, and other manipulations the narcissist uses to keep their partner in line.

Often partners of narcissists find themselves making excuses for the narcissist to other family members for rudeness, acting entitled, or deception. For example, the partner may declare that their partner is sick or too tired from work to participate in family gatherings. Relationships among family members and the victim of the narcissistic abuse can descend into a tangle of conflict and chaos.

Finally, children with one or more narcissistic parents rarely emerge unscathed. Their world is one of emotional uncertainty and turmoil. One day they may be the golden child, unable to do wrong. The following day, they are scapegoated and blamed for all the family's problems. However, if they are lucky to have a strong role model or parent who protects them and provides unconditional love, they may grow up to be surprisingly resilient and well-adjusted. (See Chapter 6 for more information.)

Conflict at work and in the neighborhood

Whether you work with one or more narcissistic colleagues or have the misfortune of being under the supervision of a narcissistic boss, the fallout can range from annoyances to career ending ruin. For example, narcissistic colleagues may claim credit for your ideas and accomplishments. A jealous, narcissistic boss, threatened by your talent, could sabotage your chances for advancement.

The same dynamic occurs across other settings such as neighborhoods and civic organizations. Conflict can erupt between narcissists and their victims. Arguments about vegetation growing over fence lines, parking spaces, or even the color of paint on a home provide ample fuel for narcissists to complain about. See Chapter 7 for more information about examples of encounters with narcissists around town and how to negotiate better outcomes.

Social unrest in group settings

When a group of people — whether a sports team, sorority, religion, fraternity, nation, race, or political party, or students of a particular college or high school — feels superior, special, entitled, and exceptional, it may or may not suffer from narcissism. It's perfectly natural to feel pride about being a member of a certain group. Many people feel positively about groups they're a part of.

However, when that pride is combined with the belief that the group is not sufficiently recognized as superior by other groups, then collective narcissism all too often raises its dragon-like head. Collective narcissism involves thinking that the superior qualities of one's group are not appreciated by others and other groups may be out to thwart their power. Social unrest occurs when people who are dissatisfied with something disrupt the regular social order to the detriment of others. It may be violent or nonviolent.

Collective narcissism has been linked to

>> Racism

>> Sexism

>> Homophobia

>> Prejudice

- » Fascism
- » Aggression
- » Violence
- » Nationalism

- » Religious fanaticism
- » Conspiracy theories
- » Terrorism
- » War

Those involved in a group that experiences collective narcissism are extremely threatened by perceived threats by another group. For example, white supremacists may believe that certain immigrant groups are out to get their jobs. People with these beliefs may respond to their imagined threats with revenge, including bullying, or attempts to intimidate the other group members. (See Chapter 3 for more information about collective narcissism.)

NARCISSISTIC PRESIDENTS AND WAR: 1897–2009

John P. Harden, while a doctoral student in political science at Ohio State University, studied 19 presidents, narcissistic traits, and days at war during each of their presidencies. The study, published in the *Journal of Conflict Resolution,* looked at the relationships between narcissism and length of war.

Experts and presidential historians reviewed historical biographies of the presidents. They then rated narcissistic traits of the presidents using a personality inventory. Just for your own information, during this time, Lyndon Johnson scored the highest on narcissism. Next in line was Teddy Roosevelt, and then Richard Nixon (note the most recent president rated was George W. Bush).

Using a database called the "Correlates of War," which measured combat between two countries in which at least 1,000 people died within a year, the research looked at how long wars lasted under high-scoring narcissistic presidents compared to low-scoring narcissistic presidents.

High-scoring narcissistic presidents tended to extend wars until they could declare at least some form of victory. Perhaps the humiliation of a loss is intolerable for narcissistic presidents. This study is obviously limited by the small sample size and other factors that could confound or complicate the results. However, the author concluded that narcissistic presidents, in their "desire to protect their inflated self-image," dragged out wars longer than necessary.

Dealing with a Narcissist: The Basics

Whether you interact with a narcissistic friend, coworker, parent, or romantic partner, a few strategies can help you handle their self-centered behavior. I introduce some strategies here and then explain each idea in more detail later in the book.

Responding thoughtfully rather than merely reacting

The most important technique for surviving encounters with narcissists involves awareness of your own reactions. When you experience a trigger, such as being mistreated, take a breath, step back, and analyze what you are feeling. Are you experiencing rapid breathing, tightness in the chest, a sick feeling in your stomach, sadness, or anger? If so, then consider what about the situation triggered those feelings.

Becoming aware of your responses and the triggering event in an encounter with a narcissist is the first step in understanding how to thoughtfully respond rather than simply react. Part 2 gives you more information about dealing with narcissists in interpersonal interactions.

Setting boundaries

Setting boundaries with narcissists can be difficult. They have spent many years mastering the art of manipulation and are exquisitely good at making unsuspecting people fall for their control tactics. Here are some brief tips on standing up for yourself; I offer many more ideas throughout this book.

>> **Stop making excuses for their behavior.** Family members and partners of narcissists often try to excuse rude or hostile behavior by making excuses. Narcissists show their too-frequent anger outbursts whenever it pleases them. Too often they do not face appropriate consequences for their bad behavior.

>> **Don't expect them to change.** Narcissists rarely change; if they do, it's usually because of some big loss, but you have no control over that change. Threats, pleas, and cajoling don't work. You can't change a narcissist no matter how hard you try.

>> **Demand respect.** What do you usually do when someone disrespects you? Do you tolerate it? If so, you may have been in an abusive situation so long that it has become a habit. Step back and think about how others would respond. Perhaps it's time for you to stop tolerating disrespect.

>> **Don't be afraid to say no.** Narcissists often make unreasonable demands on family, friends, and coworkers. Saying no sometimes leads to unwanted confrontations. However, if you don't say no, it will certainly result in an uptick of more unreasonable demands.

Recognizing gaslighting

Gaslighting is a form of emotional abuse that can make the victim start questioning their own sanity. Victims become increasingly confused, sometimes wondering whether they are losing their memory, their common sense, or their emotional stability. Narcissists often become experts at gaslighting. The abuse usually begins quite slowly, with small, insignificant suggestions that can lead to full-blown distortions of reality.

Here's an example of a somewhat common, mild form of gaslighting:

> Leo (the narcissist) asks his partner, Owen, "Did you pick up the drycleaning?"
>
> Owen replies, "No, you didn't ask me to. I didn't know it was ready."
>
> "We had that conversation last night. You promised me that you'd get it on the way home," Leo responds.
>
> "I don't remember either of us talking about that. Are you sure?" Owen queries.
>
> "Are you okay? Were you taking drugs last night? You really don't remember? We definitely talked about you picking up the drycleaning. You seriously don't remember?" Leo counters.
>
> "Okay, sorry, I don't usually forget things like that. You know I certainly wasn't on drugs! I'll go now and pick it up."
>
> "It's too late. They're closed, and I needed a clean shirt for work tomorrow. I'll make do," Leo says icily and walks away.

Owen feels untethered and uneasy. He searches his brain, going over the sequence of what happened the night before, but can't remember his promise. *Owen doesn't recall the conversation because it didn't take place.* This simple maneuver by Leo is the beginning of additional subtle but more serious attacks.

Narcissistic gaslighters feel free to lie; they simply make things up. Then later, they change the story, deny the original lie, or somehow blame it on someone else. This can be particularly frustrating to those around them.

Small instances of gaslighting make vulnerable people question themselves. Over time, the narcissist becomes more powerful and the victim weaker. Throughout this book, you can find many more examples of gaslighting and how to respond to it by recognizing gaslighting and staying focused on trusting your own feelings.

Maintaining your self-esteem

If you are in a relationship with a narcissist, whether casual or intimate, your sense of self may feel unbalanced. Keep a focus on who you are as a person, and be compassionate with yourself. You are dealing with a stressful situation, but you are still the same valuable person you were before encountering the narcissist in your life.

One ploy of the narcissist involves isolating you from others and filling your mind with their selfish, narcissistic realities. Finding other sources of information is critical in these situations. Talking to others can keep you from falling into the trap of believing the narcissistic reality. Consider working with a mental health professional to help you problem solve and navigate this type of grueling relationship. See Chapter 5 and Chapter 6 for more information about dealing with narcissistic abuse.

Keeping things superficial and brief

Narcissists love to be at the center of attention. They enjoy an adoring audience and tend to give lectures rather than have conversations. Once you really get to know a narcissist, you may not want to attend the show. Yet, because they work with you or live with you, or are your ex, your parents, your next-door neighbor, or the local grocery store clerk, you may have to make an appearance.

Prepare in advance. Make your interactions as brief as possible. Make sure you have a commitment ready as an excuse to leave (see Part 2 for more detailed information). Furthermore, as much as possible, put your feelings in your pocket when you experience narcissistic abuse. Narcissists can smell discomfort or distress and will use those feelings to manipulate any situation.

Cutting off or compartmentalizing hurtful relationships

Sometimes, the only safe alternative for your own physical and mental health is to leave a relationship with a narcissist. If it's the local grocer, that's probably pretty easy to do, but if you live in a small town, it can be more difficult. It's even more challenging when it comes to friends, but sometimes a breakup is inevitable. With bosses or coworkers, you probably need to maintain a cordial relationship in order to keep up with your responsibilities (see the Chapter 7 for more ideas).

Cutting off relationships with business associates, neighbors, and friends is hard enough. However, walking away from interactions with family members is even harder. But people do it, perhaps more than you realize.

Research on family relations in the United States suggests that well over a third of the population has been estranged from one or more family members for significant periods of time. Estrangement between parents and adult children are quite common. For some strategies to deal with these tough decisions, see Chapter 6.

Leaving an intimate partner may be the most difficult for some; for others it's just a relief. However, cutting off relationships with a narcissistic intimate partner is usually the most conflictual, dangerous, and draining of all. See Chapters 5 and 9 for help in managing and implementing this trying decision.

TIP

Be willing to calmly walk away from a toxic relationship. When facing an unwinnable battle, sometimes the best thing to do is to leave the scene. This is not surrender. It's another way to set appropriate limits.

Getting Help: Considering Treatment Options

Some treatments, such as psychotherapy (discussed in Part 5), have been found to improve the day-to-day functioning of narcissists. However, narcissists rarely seek help unless they are under some external threat such as an impending divorce, a job loss, or legal trouble. When they do engage in treatment, they tend to leave treatment prematurely or sabotage efforts by therapists.

For the most part, narcissists are not very likely to seek and benefit from psychotherapy. But that leaves their partners, families, and concerned others wondering what to do to decrease their own misery.

During an emergency in an airplane, it's important to put the oxygen mask on yourself before giving help to the other people in your row, and the same principle applies to narcissistic relationships. If you find yourself miserable or even in danger dealing with a difficult person, first put on your own oxygen mask.

Get yourself to a better space. Consider counseling for yourself before tackling the job of attempting to help a narcissist or leave the relationship. Therapy can be a tool that gives you the power and perspective to make wise decisions.

TIP

Interacting with a narcissist can be initially wonderful and more often, ultimately horrible. Long-term costs to your self-esteem can be significant. It's important to save yourself.

Chapter 2

Taking a Closer Look at Narcissism

I n ancient Greek mythology, Narcissus was a strikingly handsome young man. He knew how good he looked and held himself in exceptionally high regard. At the same time, Narcissus callously rejected those who sought his affection. His conceit and cruelty were noticed by the goddess Nemesis. She decided to take vengeance on Narcissus for his heartless dismissal of others. Nemesis condemned Narcissus to spend the rest of his life contemplating his own beauty. Walking by a pond, Narcissus stopped, captivated by his reflection. Unable to leave his own beautiful image, he remained at the pond staring at himself, in total despair. Eventually, he wasted away and died.

From this story, emanating from the ancient Greeks, emerged the modern concept of narcissism. Today, a narcissist is described as a person who thinks unusually highly of themselves, desires excessive attention and admiration, and believes that they are special and unique. This chapter further explores the characteristics of narcissism. In addition, it describes the different types of narcissism and discusses the criteria for diagnosing narcissistic personality disorder (NPD).

REMEMBER

The bottom line is not whether someone has NPD or one or more narcissistic traits; it's how their personalities affect those around them. If you are dealing with a narcissist, don't worry about the diagnosis. Look at the symptoms and how they affect you.

Recognizing Narcissistic Traits and Patterns

The *Diagnostic and Statistical Manual of Mental Disorders*, 5th edition, is published by the American Psychiatric Society. The book, widely used by mental health professionals, looks at emotional problems and describes the symptoms that are thought to be part of each mental disorder. For example, there are nine different symptoms of narcissism according to the DSM. The following sections take an in-depth look at these major symptoms and provide examples to further illustrate how the symptoms may manifest in an individual.

REMEMBER

The particular traits of narcissism lie on a continuum. They can range from mild to severe. And not everyone with relatively high levels of narcissism exhibits all the traits. However, someone who exhibits five of the nine symptoms of narcissism qualifies for an official diagnosis. In addition, the symptoms described in this section have considerable overlap. For example, if you feel grandiose, you're likely to also be arrogant.

Reveling in self-importance

Grandiosity is a particularly common symptom of narcissism. Like the word, people with this trait believe themselves to be grand. They believe in their self-importance, even if their lives don't reflect that. They overestimate their skills and capabilities. The following brief example illustrates this trait:

> Brent drops out of high school to pursue a career in tattooing. He's a good artist and makes what he thinks is a decent living. In reality, he brings in enough money to keep himself entertained. Brent believes he is a highly skilled businessman and that his decision to drop out of school was very intelligent.

> What Brent doesn't consider is that he lives with his parents who continue to enable him by providing shelter, feeding him, and paying for his health insurance. When Brent's business takes a downturn because he runs out of friends and relatives seeking tattoos, he asks his parents to give him some money to open his own shop.

> His father wisely asks Brent to write up a business plan detailing monthly expenses, income projections, and legal requirements. Brent produces an overly optimistic, simplistic, and incomplete plan.

> His father tells him that after he completes his GED and takes some business classes at the community college, he will discuss investing in his son's venture. Brent is furious with his father's response. He vows to find another investor who truly believes in his talents.

Brent exhibits grandiosity. He believes that he can run a successful business without the necessary knowledge or experience. He cannot take reasonable feedback and does not put in the work to develop a viable business.

REMEMBER

It's the gross overestimation of talent, competence, and importance that makes someone grandiose.

Seeking unlimited power and success — at any cost

Narcissists with this trait have big plans for now and the future. They often have schemes for making money that may be unrealistic to others. They're drawn like a magnet to anything that promises quick, easy power and success.

Theo's story is an example of narcissistic optimism taken too far. Many people with the desire for unlimited success can become victims of their own dreams, often taking others down with them.

> Theo is a firefighter in a medium-sized city. To pass the time between calls, he watches shows that feature house flipping. Always short of money, Theo is tempted to buy a run-down house, fix it up, and flip it. After all, his schedule gives him several days off every week. He's watched hours of house-flipping shows; it should be a piece of cake.
>
> Theo tells his wife his plans. She informs him that he is being ridiculous. First, they have no money to spare; second, he's always tired when he comes home from work; and third, they have four kids who need his attention.
>
> Theo puts his plans on hold, deciding to bide his time until an opportunity presents itself. He asks one of his firefighter buddies, who moonlights as a real-estate salesperson, to keep an eye out for a fixer-upper. Eventually, Theo finds his house. He goes ahead with the purchase without considering the risks involved or the impact this might have on his family. His wife is furious.

You can imagine what happens. Theo had not counted on the high cost of materials or the time and expertise it would take him to complete the remodeling. Eventually, despite working extra shifts, he realizes that he can't keep up with the additional payments. Another scheme lost. But undiscouraged, Theo continues looking for the next easy way to fame and fortune.

Believing in absolute uniqueness and worth

People with this narcissistic trait believe that they are different from others. That difference makes them unique and better than others. They feel like members of an exclusive club that only uniquely special people can belong to. These unique narcissists often seek out the company of other people they consider unique and special and shun those they feel don't belong.

The belief in uniqueness often brings with it a deep sense of entitlement. Charlotte's story shows both entitlement and the feeling of uniqueness.

> Charlotte is an overindulged teen living in an upscale suburb. She attends a prestigious private school, drives a new car, and dresses in the latest fashions. Her friends all attend the same school, and most are similarly spoiled.
>
> The requirements for Charlotte's Senior Experience class include volunteering at a food bank. Charlotte is appalled. She refuses to volunteer, saying that people in those places are disgusting. She states, "It will smell, and those homeless people are all lazy drug addicts. They don't deserve free food. They can easily get jobs at a fast-food joint. I won't do it."
>
> Charlotte demands that her parents excuse her from this unbearable task. Of course, her parents acquiesce and set up a meeting with the principal. The principal attempts to reassure Charlotte's parents that many students are surprised at how meaningful volunteering can be and that the requirement is nonnegotiable. Charlotte's father reminds the principal of the generous donations he has made over the years. Charlotte is given an alternate assignment.

Charlotte and her parents belong to an exclusive club, the wealthy. And some wealthy people think that they are better than others. Rules do not always apply to them, especially if they flash their money around. The club may be exclusive, but belonging to it can lead to narcissism.

Not all wealthy people feel unique. Many are humble and grateful. They do not have narcissistic beliefs of being distinct or special.

Demanding attention, approval, and praise

Narcissists often have an insatiable appetite for approval. They expect to be admired and given an uninterrupted stream of positive attention. When not given sufficient recognition, they pout, sulk, or get angry.

Scarlett and her husband have recently moved to a new town. She was previously very involved in nonprofit and charitable work. She knows it's a good way to get involved in the community and make new friends. She especially enjoys feeling appreciated.

Scarlett sees that the Historical Society meets on Wednesday mornings. She attends her first meeting. Everyone introduces themselves. Scarlett tells the others that she has been president of several nonprofits and is well known for her ability to raise funds.

Members of the board note her past experience and hope they've found a willing volunteer. At her second meeting, the president asks Scarlett if she'd be interested in co-chairing a committee. As is the case for most nonprofits, reliable volunteers are always hard to find.

Scarlett begins her work co-chairing the committee by taking it over. In her first week, she lectures other members about all the mistakes they are currently making. She informs others of her changes and implements them without getting input from more seasoned volunteers. She railroads her ideas through and waits for the expected accolades.

Many of Scarlett's ideas are great, and she does get lots of attention from members. However, the reliable volunteers feel a bit overwhelmed by Scarlett. The board members ask the president to intervene and counsel Scarlett to calm down a bit.

Scarlett does not like even a hint of criticism. When the president discusses some of the concerns, she searches for approval. Not finding enough, she immediately quits the organization.

Narcissists like attention and praise. However, they only perform for a friendly audience. If unable to get the approval they crave, narcissists move on to another theater.

Scarlett represents a common "do-gooder" narcissist. Although these types of narcissists often contribute to their causes, their basic motive is to get attention and approval. Individual narcissists who seek approval and attention through their community work are sometimes referred to as *communal narcissists*.

Feeling entitled: Expecting privileges and special treatment

The word *entitled* originated from the state of having a title to something. For example, you may have a title to your home (that is often shared with a mortgage company). Or a title to a car. But entitled also refers to having certain rights and privileges bestowed to you because of who you are, not because you've earned or deserve them. Like royalty (minus the wealth and power), narcissists believe they deserve to be treated better than others.

Years ago, I took my youngest son to a California theme park. Not wanting to wait in long lines, I bought an upgrade to some special status ticket that allowed us to bypass the lines. Excited, we rushed past people standing in the hot sun and joyfully jumped on the rides without waiting.

Most of that is true. The part that is a lie is the part about excitedly, joyfully jumping on rides. Actually, I was embarrassed to walk past sweaty, sullen people standing in line. I studiously avoided eye contact with the hundreds of people I imagined were glaring angrily at us as we made our way to the front of the line. I worried about getting spit at. I worried about bad karma. Obviously, I'm not a narcissist.

A narcissist would sashay their way past the peasants forced to wait for a rollercoaster. That's because a narcissist feels they deserve to be first and should never be kept waiting. They feel no remorse for stepping on a few toes. In other words, a narcissist feels and acts entitled.

Exploiting and controlling others

A common trait of narcissists, exploiting and controlling others is particularly damaging in intimate relationships. Narcissists view people as instruments used to get their needs met. They latch on to others who can fulfill those needs. Some prefer dependent partners who will do their bidding; others look for people who can provide them with additional status.

Here's an example:

> Levi has the idea that having a wife would help him further his career. He wants to find a beautiful woman whom he can show off and who will care for his home and his anticipated brood of good-looking children.

> Abigail met Levi through an online dating app. She's a college student finishing up her nursing degree. Levi's an airman first class and lives at the air force base near Abigail's school. On their first date, the two take a walk through a park and then have a long lunch. Levi describes his ambitions of rising quickly through the ranks, and Abigail is impressed. He asks about her dreams for the future, and she tells him about her lifelong interest in medicine. Levi notes that nursing is a flexible career that can fit in well with frequent moves.

> During the following weeks, Levi sends Abigail flowers and hundreds of texts. When she doesn't reply immediately to a text, he asks her if she is ghosting him. A few dates later, Levi asks Abigail to marry him. A bit overwhelmed but flattered, Abigail finds herself thinking about a potential future with Levi. She sort of likes the idea of traveling the world with a handsome young air force officer. But then she

realizes that she really doesn't know Levi, and although she feels strongly attracted to him, she isn't madly in love.

Abigail tries to explain her feelings to Levi. Instead of being understanding or sad, he becomes angered by her hesitancy. He tells Abigail that he'd thought she was the partner he'd always dreamed about. They'd make the perfect team. But he can't afford to wait around for her to make up her mind. "By the way," he tells her, "you'd be beautiful if you didn't wear all that trashy makeup."

Then, he coolly walks away. By putting her down, he maintains his sense of control. His attempt to exploit her failed. So, he moves on. Next time, he'll refine his pitch and take a bit longer to lead up to the conquest. Eventually, his seduction will work and his attempts at control and exploitation will succeed.

Lacking empathy

Empathy requires understanding a perspective other than your own. It's the ability to put yourself in another person's shoes. A narcissist who lacks empathy can only stand in their own shoes; no other shoes exist. They do not understand the experiences, emotional states, or desires of others.

A narcissist with impaired empathy is a bit like a young toddler. A toddler feels like the center of the universe and basically uses people to get their own needs met. "I want more milk. Play with me. I want to go outside now." On the other hand, normally developing toddlers certainly show love and the beginnings of concern for others.

In contrast, a narcissist with no empathy exists entirely in a self-centered world, coldly exploiting others to obtain what they want and feeling no guilt. Narcissists care about their own feelings and are less able to see the effect of their behavior on others. The next example shows a callous lack of regard for the pain of others.

Miles is a successful con artist. He has no preference for sex, targeting anyone who fits his needs. He looks for his victims online. The only criterion that matters to him is that they have money. It's an added bonus if they are lonely and looking for a companion.

Miles dresses well, stays in shape, and has the ability to charm just about anyone. He expresses deep interest in his prey, asking them personal questions, peppering them with flattery, and lavishing them with attention. Miles offers vague information about himself, insinuates that he is wealthy, and never brings the victim into his home.

The con happens after a personal connection is made. Miles changes his story to meet what he thinks will be the hardest for his victim to resist. He may say that he needs a few hundred dollars until his big check comes in the mail or offers an opportunity to invest thousands of dollars in a new lucrative business. Or perhaps he'll pretend that he has an urgent need to send money to a sick relative. He always promises a quick repayment. Once the transaction is complete, Miles vanishes.

Left feeling hurt, foolish, and ashamed, victims rarely report their losses to the police. They may not even tell their closest friends or family. Miles counts on that and continues with his chosen career. Miles does not empathize with his victims; in fact, he feels a sense of pride at his accomplishment.

A narcissist who lacks empathy does not consider the feelings of others. They rarely concern themselves with other people's distress. This particular characteristic can make any type of relationship difficult for those who interact with a narcissist who lacks the ability to feel another's pain.

Being immersed in envy and jealousy

When a narcissist feels superior to others, they become very threatened when someone else has something better than what they possess. A narcissist may envy those with more status, wealth, intelligence, friends, success, or whatever presents itself. The envy can be in regard to intangible things such as popularity, or tangible things such as a better car or a more handsome partner.

Envy and the feelings of discontent that accompany it can lead to deep feelings of resentment, hostility, fear, or anger. The reason a narcissist is particularly more likely to feel envy and jealousy is that having less than another is a threat to their inflated sense of self-esteem. These attacks on the narcissistic ego can lead to desperate attempts to obtain what others have or to diminish their success. This can result in some of the following responses by an envious narcissist:

>> Attempting to take credit for another's successful idea or plan

>> Exclusively surrounding themselves with high status people

>> Devaluing the attributes that make them jealous or envious

>> Refusing to acknowledge accomplishments of others

>> Becoming overly suspicious and controlling in a relationship

>> Stalking a former romantic partner

Narcissistic envy and jealousy can be very confusing. Imagine you achieve a goal in your life, like finishing school, getting engaged, losing five pounds, or running a marathon. You naturally feel a sense of accomplishment. The narcissist in your life may <u>pretend to support your success, but there's an undercurrent of envious</u> <u>hostility.</u> A narcissist wants to be the center of attention, getting all of the adoration. There's just not room for others to get what they want.

Exhibiting antagonizing arrogance

As I point out earlier, many of the characteristics of narcissism overlap. For example, how can someone feel entitled and not feel special? Or arrogant and not better than others? Arrogance is one such facet of narcissism. Arrogant people are overbearing and look down on others. They tend to be unpleasantly insolent and haughty, simmering with self-importance.

The following example likely resonates with many first responders working in difficult situations:

> Saturday night in the ER is always an unknown adventure. The medical team tonight is strong. Most staff are talented, experienced veterans. The 7 p.m. to 7 a.m. shift begins fairly slowly. A few suspected heart attacks, high fevers, and some drug overdoses start the evening off.

> As the night progresses, victims of various mishaps begin filling up the waiting room. All patients are triaged upon arrival and taken back in order of seriousness. Life-and-death matters are always dealt with first.

> For the most part, patients wait quietly, some moaning, some (especially kids) crying. Ambulances arrive, and some patients are wheeled directly into the ER, ahead of others. Frustrated, hurting, and disappointed by the long wait, a few come up to the front desk to ask how much longer the wait will be. Used to comforting the waiting, the medical assistant explains their priorities while validating their impatience.

> Around 9:30 the ER doors swing open and a man, woman, and young boy charge into the waiting room. The child is screaming in pain, the man is yelling for help, and the woman is weeping. Worried staff rush out to see what is going on. The child's arm is dangling at an odd angle, and the staff quickly ascertain that arm is likely broken.

> To avoid creating chaos, staff take the family back into a small room. They take the boy's vitals and confirm that he's stable. The attendant explains that an X-ray tech will be there shortly. Fifteen minutes pass, and the father leaves his sobbing son and loudly demands to see an orthopedic surgeon. An attendant calmly explains that an X-ray is necessary to make a diagnosis.

> "And just when will that happen? I need this now." His face is turning red, and he begins to raise his voice. "Let me talk to your boss. This whole place is incompetent. I demand action, or you'll be hearing from my attorney."

The attendant reassures the father that he will look for someone in authority. By this time, the ER is full of critical patients. The attendant begs the head nurse for a minute of her time. She explains to the parents that while she understands the discomfort and pain the child is in, she has people in the ER who will die without immediate attention.

The father screams at the nurse, red face now sweating profusely, "Do you not realize who I am?"

She replies, "I'm sorry; I'm afraid that I don't know you at all."

"I am the head reporter," he yells, telling her the name of a local television station.

"Sorry, I need to get back to my patients. You'll be seen as soon as we can spare a moment."

The father grabs the nurse's arm. "I'll ruin you and this hospital on tomorrow night's news if you don't attend to my son immediately."

Awful, right? Unfortunately, this behavior is not atypical in hospitals across the country. Overworked and understaffed healthcare providers deal with arrogant, angry patients on an almost daily basis. These haughty fools believe that they're better than others and deserve immediate care, while looking down their noses at those who attempt to intervene.

Displaying other telling symptoms

Many more symptoms are common in narcissistic people. Research on narcissism has uncovered some indicators that the DSM has left out. These signs include the following:

>> Excessive anger and hostility

>> Difficulty controlling emotions

>> Tendency to blame others

>> Frequent engagement in power struggles

>> Excessive competitiveness

>> Hypersensitivity to criticism

>> Flips between seeing others as all good or all bad

>> Dishonesty

>> Callous disregard for others

>> Little or no sense of humor

These symptoms may or may not be present in someone you are dealing with, but they can increase the suffering of anyone interacting with a narcissist.

Examining the Four Types of Narcissism

Narcissists come in a variety of flavors. Current thinking is that there are three major types of narcissists and then a fourth type that has bits and pieces of all three. There is a great deal of debate among social scientists on how these categories get defined, as well as what label they should have.

The next four sections describe the different types of narcissism that reflect current thinking. Truthfully, many mental health therapists find that narcissists often fluctuate between the three major types when faced with different life-challenges.

Grandiose

The grandiose narcissist is what most people think of when they hear the word narcissist. Grandiose narcissists consider themselves superior, distinct, and extraordinary. They tend to be domineering and manipulative, and they seek admiration from others. They feel entitled to special attention and privilege. Interpersonally, they can be aggressive, demanding, and lack empathy. Their narcissistic behavior is out in the open; in other words, it is *overt*. If they don't get their own way, they may just throw a temper tantrum. Basically, they act like spoiled children.

Vulnerable

Like grandiose narcissists, vulnerable narcissists also think very highly of themselves. Their narcissistic traits may not be as evident as those with grandiose narcissism; they may express their feelings of superiority indirectly or *covertly*. They can also be arrogant, conceited, cold, and uncaring. They tend to be highly jealous of others and resentful.

Vulnerable narcissists tend to be thin-skinned, easily insulted, and threatened by any hint of criticism. They are deeply vulnerable to threats to their overly positive self-esteem. Their positive self-esteem is quite fragile. They are terrified of others seeing them as weak or incapable. A small criticism can send them into despair. When their superior view of themselves is challenged, they may react with depression, anxiety, feelings of emptiness, and sometimes panic.

Vulnerable narcissists appear to be insecure, shy, and introverted. As a result of their vulnerability, they may be underachievers. Afraid of being humiliated, they may take job positions beneath their abilities and training. However, they harbor fantasies of grandeur. These visions are rarely realized.

Vulnerable narcissists may not act directly hostile, but when threatened by another can hold grudges, seek revenge, and act in a passive-aggressive manner.

Malignant

Like other narcissists, malignant narcissists believe in their unique superiority. Because of their superiority, they expect to have the best of everything and be treated like royalty. They tend to be arrogant, yet shallow, boasting of their accomplishments. They have a great need to control others, and often monopolize conversations.

What makes malignant narcissists more troublesome, and sometimes dangerous, is their total lack of regard for others. These narcissists see people as stepping stones to obtain what they want. They readily strike out with hostility, cruelty, and aggression.

Malignant narcissists have very fragile self-esteem. They must win every contest or race. Like vulnerable narcissists, their sense of superiority is easily threatened by others. When they encounter these threats, such as criticism, disagreement, loss, or failure, they react with rage and sometimes violence.

Malignant narcissists feel free to lie, cheat, or bully to obtain what they believe they deserve. They spread rumors and gossip about those whom they view as enemies. They are quick to humiliate. They have no remorse, rarely admit fault, and don't really care about those they have hurt.

Mixed

In reality, it's quite hard to put people with narcissism into the categories of grandiose, vulnerable, or malignant. Most narcissists display a mixture of all of these styles depending on the situation.

For example, a grandiose narcissist may suffer a great embarrassment and feel quite vulnerable. A vulnerable narcissist may have the opportunity to achieve a fantasized dream of success. When that occurs, the underlying insecurity may be replaced by a more stable sense of self-esteem.

Finally, either vulnerable or grandiose narcissists can potentially become malignant under severely stressful conditions.

People change over time. Always be cautious about labeling someone with a mental disorder. Only a trained mental health professional should be diagnosing narcissism. Nevertheless, knowing about narcissism and the major types of narcissism can allow you to be on the lookout for troublesome behavior.

Taking Traits and Patterns to the Next Level

You don't need to be a diagnostician to know whether someone you care about or interact with impinges on your life with obnoxious, narcissistic traits. However, it is helpful to understand how narcissistic traits can range from mild to extreme. If you have a relationship with someone with mild narcissistic traits, you may be able to establish a tolerable or even pleasurable connection. However, if your bond is with someone who has a diagnosis of NPD, it may be much less likely to find a way to tolerate or change their behavior.

Throughout this book, for simplicity, I use the term narcissist to describe both people who exhibit narcissistic traits as well as those relatively fewer people diagnosed with NPD.

Officially diagnosing narcissistic personality disorder

The *Diagnostic and Statistical Manual of Mental Disorders*, 5th Edition, (DSM) informs mental health professionals around the world on the specific symptoms that make up a mental health diagnosis. For example, to be diagnosed with narcissistic personality disorder (NPD):

>> A person must have a systematic way of thinking and behaving that is significantly different from cultural expectations.

>> They must demonstrate at least five of these nine symptoms of narcissism as outlined by the DSM (refer to the section, "Recognizing Narcissistic Traits and Patterns," earlier in this chapter for more info about each symptom).

- Exhibits grandiosity or excessive pretentiousness

- Fantasizes about unlimited success

- Feels special or unique

- Expects the best at all times (entitlement)

- Craves admiration by others

- Dismisses and exploits others

- Demonstrates a gross lack of empathy

- Manifests intense envy and jealousy

- Acts with arrogance and haughtiness

>> These characteristics must show up in the individual's interpersonal relations, emotional responses, and control of impulses. These patterns lead to distress in social situations, in work-related interactions, or other crucial areas of life functioning.

>> This pattern must be long standing, usually beginning in late adolescence or early adulthood.

Imagine a person who is arrogant and believes they are uniquely special. They have no empathy and see others as objects to be exploited. They have four significant characteristics of NPD, but do not technically have the five required for a formal diagnosis according to the DSM. Nonetheless, most people would probably consider such a person narcissistic. The next two sections describe the difference between a formal diagnosis of narcissistic personality disorder versus a person who exhibits significant traits of narcissism.

TECHNICAL STUFF

Both men and women can show narcissistic traits. Because narcissists rarely volunteer to be research subjects, there are no firm answers to the question of which gender has more narcissistic characteristics. Research about this issue usually involves giving undergraduate college students the Narcissistic Personality Inventory (NPI), a measure of narcissistic traits. Many studies using the NPI have discovered that men score higher than women on this test. However, considerable evidence exists that men are far more likely to have the more severe narcissistic personality disorder than women. Therefore, most researchers conclude that men are more narcissistic than women.

Taking a closer look at NPD

A person diagnosed with narcissistic personality disorder (NPD) is more severely impaired than those who simply exhibit narcissistic traits. Those with NPD have huge problems in everyday life such as getting along with others, fitting into society, following rules, and controlling impulses. Furthermore, they have at least five characteristics of the nine listed in the earlier section, "Officially diagnosing narcissistic personality disorder."

The following example is taken from my own experiences working with young people in jail and typifies some of the characteristics of a person with NPD (this is not a real person, just a character based on multiple interactions).

Tony is behind bars again for the fifth time. He spent most of that time in juvenile detention, but now he's turned 18 and is in the county jail for the first time. Tony is about to be interviewed by the jail's psychologist and looks forward to getting out of his cell for a half hour.

Dr. Davis greets him, "Hey Tony, how are you doing in here? I haven't seen you since juvie."

Tony replies, "I'm boss, no big deal. I've got this place under control; they know who I am, and nobody's gonna bother me."

"Really, do you know people here already?" Dr. Davis asks.

"I'm a special actor, known on the streets; people got to respect me. I be hanging with the top people by this afternoon. Hey, do you know when I'm getting out? I didn't do nothing."

"Well, Tony, it says right here that you were picked up for shoving an elderly woman down in the parking lot while you were snatching her purse. She ended up breaking her hip. There were multiple eyewitnesses, and the security guard caught you."

"Yeah, well, she shoulda just given me her purse and she wouldn't have gotten pushed down. Just shows you how stupid old people are. And this is my first offence."

"Sure Tony, your first offence as an adult, but you've been in and out of juvenile detention since you were 12."

"So what," Tony brags, "the court ain't gonna know that. I'll be out of here as soon as they have my preliminary hearing. I need to be out there doing the good work."

"Okay, Tony, I see you're still an optimist. Hope it works out for you. I'm here if you decide you want to work on staying out of trouble. Or if you just need to talk."

"Lady, I score twice as much money as you on a good weekend. I don't need advice from you. You are just a way to pass the time."

Earlier in my career, I worked with quite a few folks similar to Tony. In fact, it's estimated that over 20 percent of all incarcerated people have narcissistic personality disorder. Tony shows the necessary symptoms to qualify him for a diagnosis of NPD. He has a high degree of grandiosity and believes that he is unusually special. He has an exquisite sense of entitlement, cruelly exploits others, and certainly lacks empathy. Those represent five clear markers of NPD. In addition, these patterns endure over time, deviate from the expectations of society, and interfere with his ability to function. Tony is not someone you'd like to run into on the street.

Roaming the ranges of narcissism

People with narcissistic traits are not as severely impaired as those with NPD. However, their behavior can lead to toxic relationships with others, multiple breakups, problems at work, and difficulty getting along with people. The following example typifies someone with narcissistic traits.

> Vanessa is getting ready to go out with her latest boyfriend, Jason. She is doing her makeup and asks Jason if she looks good. He replies that she is beautiful as always. Vanessa beams, but then realizes that she is almost out of blush. "Honey, do me a favor and run down to the drugstore — it's about a half mile away — and get me some of this," she says, showing him the empty container.
>
> "But babe, we're already late for dinner. I don't want to keep everyone waiting."
>
> "Who cares? They'll just have to wait. I need that blush. Do you love me or what? Just go get it. You're wasting time fighting with me."
>
> "Hey babe," Jason implores, "we've kept our friends waiting before. You look great without blush. Let's just go now."
>
> "Oh, I get it," Vanessa says, suddenly cold. "You don't care about me or how I look. You just want to impress your friends. Screw you, I'm not going to your stupid dinner."
>
> Jason, confused, wonders what just happened.

Vanessa has traits of narcissism. She believes she is special and is certainly entitled, prioritizing her needs over others. In addition, she exploits Jason by making an unreasonable request. However, she does not have major problems with getting by in work, relationships with friends, or impulse control. Therefore, she does not have a diagnosis of NPD.

Chapter 3

Better Together? Considering Collective Narcissism

Think of all of the groups you belong to. Not much of a joiner? Doesn't matter. Consider that you're part of a generation. Are you a millennial, a Gen Z, or a boomer? What city, state, or country do you live in? What schools did you attend?

What race or gender do you identify with? Do you belong to a group associated with your religion or spiritual beliefs? Are you a member of a book club? How about a musical group? Who do you follow on social media? Are you a member of any online groups? Maybe you're a sports fan or you engage in certain hobbies or recreational activities. What is your political party preference?

People are born into certain groups, and they choose others. It's human nature to gather into groups. During early times, people formed tribes so that they could collectively protect themselves from potential enemies. Now, groups of people form countries with borders and militaries for protection.

You probably feel proud of some of the groups you belong to. For example, you may play softball with a team. You celebrate when you win and feel disappointed when you lose, but it's hardly the end of the world. If, on the other hand, after the game the losers hurl insults at the winners and push them around until an all-out brawl breaks out, there's a problem. The once benign softball team has evolved into a toxic, narcissistic stew.

This chapter introduces the concept of *collective narcissism*. Collective narcissism is a belief held by group members that their group is better than other groups and that other groups represent a threat to their group. Although many of the individuals of the group may not be significantly narcissistic, collective narcissism occurs when the group mentality turns narcissistic. This type of narcissism is associated with prejudice, revenge, violence, racism, terrorism, and war.

In-Groups and Out-Groups: The Benefits of Belonging

High schoolers of all generations have tended to gravitate toward students with whom they have the most in common, resulting in the formation of groups bearing various labels. From the hippies and greasers of the 1960s to the cheerleaders, mean girls, loners, jocks, band geeks, nerds, goths, and slackers of subsequent decades, kids of a feather have banded together.

These high-school groups offer kids a sense of who they are and where they stand. Whether a group is in or out is largely a personal perspective. If you are someone who sits in the back rows of the classroom playing video games on your phone (termed a *back of the class kid*, my high-school sources tell me), then you probably have an online social network of other kids who play video games. It's that feeling of belonging that keeps you feeling good about yourself. It doesn't really matter to you that your teachers are frustrated by your lack of interest in school. You return to your network of online friends for validation.

TIP

In-group or in-crowd, out-group or out-crowd are expressions that vary across time and cultures. Their meanings are based on the perception of the members. Some feel that they are "in" while others feel excluded or "out."

Not all groups necessarily display collective narcissism. They generally feel no need to put down or denigrate other groups.

On the other hand, some groups, such as gangs, exhibit collective narcissism. For the most part, they believe that they are superior to outside gangs, feel mistreated, and anticipate attacks by rival gangs. The collective narcissism felt by gang members often leads to physical violence and even murder.

Group membership is neither inherently good nor bad, it depends on what it does for individuals within the group and for society. Whether the group has a religious, recreational, or national affiliation, as long as it is founded on positive social values, there are benefits and little potential for harm exists. However, some groups conduct illegal or immoral actions or promote antisocial values, such as racism, sexism, prejudice against people from countries other than their own (*xenophobia*), or extremist thinking.

REMEMBER

People need to belong to groups to feel safe and validated. Humans are essentially a social species. Group membership increases confidence, and people derive purpose, meaning, and a sense of belonging from participating in various groups. Being part of a group can be emotionally supportive, offer strong social connections, and even lead to a longer life.

On the other hand, some groups can become narcissistic incubators for the development of aggression or bullying behavior, even leading to violence. For more information about narcissistic bullying and violence, see Chapter 11.

Understanding the Appeal: Narcissism and Groups

Remember that *collective narcissism* involves two components. The first is that people in a particular group feel superior to one or more out-groups. In fact, the group culture has many of the characteristics of a narcissistic individual, including

>> Feeling self-important

>> Craving power and success

>> Believing in uniqueness

>> Demanding approval

>> Expecting special privileges: entitlement

>> Exploiting and controlling others

>> Behaving in an arrogant way

>> Feeling envious and jealous

>> Lacking empathy for others

The narcissistic group may display many of these same characteristics. Arrogance, exploitation, and lack of empathy for those in the out-group are especially common attributes.

The second component that makes a group collectively narcissistic is the belief that other groups are out to get them. By contrast, lots of groups feel superior and have intense pride but do not denigrate or criticize their competitors. They feel that their group is special and exceptional but have no ill will against other groups.

What makes people in the superior group think that others intend to hurt or attack them in some way? One factor that has been identified is low self-esteem among members.

The low self-esteem factor

Low self-esteem among group members increases the risk of collective narcissism. You may wonder how low self-esteem fits in with collective narcissism.

Research suggests that people with low self-esteem make fun of, throw insults at, lie about, and may even become aggressive with people in outside groups. Simply put, by putting down others, the person with low self-esteem hopes to feel better by pumping themselves up in relation to others.

In addition, individual narcissists can participate in and sometimes even lead collectively narcissistic groups. In other words, "If I am the greatest, smartest, and most popular person," it only follows that, "my group is the most exceptional, special, and powerful group."

The pull of puffed-up groups

People who are vulnerable and fragile are particularly drawn to groups that display collective narcissism. They feel profoundly insecure and driven to find sources of approval and validation. Other factors that may make people vulnerable to joining collectively narcissistic groups include

>> Loneliness

>> History of significant rejection

>> Feeling like an outcast

>> Feeling unappreciated or undervalued

>> Previous experience of abuse

>> Lack of clarity about identity

>> Being oversensitive to criticism

>> Lack of emotional or social support

Leaders of collectively narcissistic groups are highly skilled at identifying and recruiting members who lack emotional resilience and security. They use many tactics to recruit members. One common tactic is an appeal to emotions, especially fear. If people can be convinced that the world is a dangerous place, that others are out to get them, and that membership in a certain group will provide them with a safe haven, then membership becomes more desirable.

They also use the same strategies that advertisers use to sell products. For instance, when messages are repeated frequently, they become more believable. That occurs even when the message is blatantly untrue. Numerous studies have confirmed the potency of the repetition phenomenon. A collectively narcissistic group may repeat lies over and over until members stop questioning their validity.

It's not surprising that collective narcissistic groups often form in times of trouble and social turmoil. For example, historians connect the Great Depression to the formation of fascism before the outbreak of World War II. Economic stress can also lead to religious, racial, ethnic, or political extremism. Both the recession of 2008 and the accelerating discrepancies between rich and poor may be leading to rapid growth of collective narcissism in today's world.

REMEMBER

A group that exhibits collective narcissism can fulfill some of the unmet needs of the lonely, isolated, and disadvantaged, and those who crave a sense of purpose and belonging.

Evaluating whether a Group is Collectively Narcissistic

Have you ever wondered if a group that you are a member of may have some collective narcissism? Remember that a group could be a club, social group, sports team, religious group, political party, or another organization with shared interests. The questions in Table 3-1 may give you some idea whether one of your groups has become collectively narcissistic. Focus on one group that you're involved in as you answer the following questions.

TABLE 3-1

Indications of Belonging to a Collectively Narcissistic Group

Check each of the following statements that you agree with or apply to your group.	
Being part of this group is a huge part of my life.	
I get really mad when anyone criticizes my group.	
If my group were in charge, the world would be a far better place.	
My group doesn't get the respect we deserve.	
People don't understand how special my group is.	
My group deserves special treatment from others.	
My group is more important than people realize.	
My group stands out and is superior.	
My group often doesn't get fair treatment.	
My group should take center stage.	
I can't stand it when my group is disrespected.	
My group should win everything and be number one.	
People are jealous of my group.	
People should show my group more respect.	
Only special people belong in my group.	
People in my group are better than others.	
My group has a divine purpose.	
When someone disrespects us, we never forget.	
When another group wins something, we get angry.	
My group is far better than other similar groups.	
Other groups don't deserve respect and are basically losers.	

Count how many check marks you made. While this is not a scientifically based survey, it is similar to ones that have been researched for many years. There's no formal cutoff point, but the more checks you have, the more likely your group demonstrates collective narcissism. Even more than a few checks can suggest a problem related to collective narcissism is at play in one or more of your groups.

With an understanding about the characteristics of collective narcissism in groups, you can watch out for it in any group you belong to.

Even groups that carry seemingly innocent or benign-sounding names such as "Apple Pickers of America" or "Citizens for a Clean Country" can use their names to recruit members into a narcissistic, cult-like group.

Concerning Outcomes of Collective Narcissism

Narcissists are often described as thin-skinned. Their fragile egos are easily punctured, and they require frequent reassurance from others to confirm their superiority. When that sense of superiority is threatened, they lash out. Think of a collectively narcissistic group as you would an individual narcissist. The group is thin-skinned, constantly hypervigilant, and looks for signs of disrespect or threats. The narcissistic group may also lash out, become violent, and seek revenge for even imagined slights.

Racism and anti-Semitism

Two of the most disturbing results of collective narcissism are racism and anti-Semitism. Racists believe their race to be superior, entitled, and threatened by other races. People who are anti-Semitic discriminate against Jewish people and believe them to be inferior. Both racists and anti-Semites are hypersensitive to perceived threats, including the worry that others are conspiring to replace them. Those beliefs lead to prejudice, hostility, incivility, and discrimination as well as violence.

Sexism

Sexism can also morph into collective narcissism. One particularly dangerous form of sexism can be found in the "incel" community. This mainly online movement believes that women are genetically inferior to men. This perceived inferiority drives women to reproduce with attractive, so-called superior men. Men whom women find unattractive label themselves as involuntarily celibate or "incel."

This male-driven, misogynist movement has two elements of collective narcissism: They believe that their group is superior and that they are being threatened — in this case, by women. Those who buy into this movement have become more hateful and extremist over time. Multiple instances of threats, intimidation, violence, and even murder have been linked to individuals in this group.

WARNING

These collective narcissistic groups are far from benign. Elliot Rodger became a hero of the "incel" movement in 2014. He targeted women and men he perceived as sexually successful. Prior to killing 6 and wounding 14 around the University of California Santa Barbara campus, he published a manifesto extolling his hatred of women for rejecting him, his jealousy of couples, especially biracial couples, and his desire for retribution. The Hague International Centre for Counter-terrorism called this an act of misogynistic terrorism.

Extreme devotion to sports teams

Even some sports fans become narcissistically obsessed with their favorite team. Soccer (football) has been particularly marred by violence over the years. Fans and players have been injured when teams lose or a referee call is challenged. Violent incidents have prevented some games from being played in front of fans and resulted in others being cancelled.

World Series wins are frequently followed by violent rioting in the streets. Interesting research looked at the effect of upset losses in the National Football League (NFL) on domestic violence. Independent of other factors (such as holidays or hot weather), there is an increase of about 10 percent of intimate partner violence following an upset loss of a favored team in a football game. Clearly, losses threaten the fan who is a member of a collectively narcissistic fan group and can also lead to violence.

Blind patriotism

Social scientists have identified two types of patriotism: *blind* and *constructive*. A constructive patriot, although loyal to their country, is aware of problems and able to listen to criticism. Blind patriots, on the other hand, do not welcome thoughtful criticism and are completely devoted to an overly idealized version of their country.

Violence between nations can result from collective narcissism. Extreme nationalism, led by blind or malicious patriots, is a form of collective narcissism. When a nationalistic country perceives a threat from an outside group, the potential for dangerous outbreaks of hostility greatly increases. The hostility excessively pumps up the self-esteem of the nationalistic country. When hostility breaks out into war, it may be fueled more by collective narcissism than an actual menace.

TIP

Populism is a term that sometimes refers to a belief in the good sense and rights of the common people. However, it has frequently become a method used by powerful politicians to manipulate the need for acceptance and validation that regular citizens believe they lack.

Indeed, many ordinary individuals feel that they are not getting enough attention and concern from those in political power. *Populist leaders* attempt to exploit those ordinary people by promising them the power they desire. They use the resentment and frustration of the people to attain control and power. Populist leaders fan the flames of hostility toward the allegedly elite politically powerful so that they can redirect support to themselves. These leaders and their top cronies benefit, whereas the promises to vulnerable, ordinary people are rarely fulfilled.

Members of collectively narcissistic groups also easily fall victim to conspiracy theories. These theories often involve shady, malevolent plots of others attacking innocents or their own group. They exaggerate the threat of the out-group and enhance the importance of the collectively narcissistic group. These theories are based on little or no evidence. Some of the plots are literally fantastical, but they justify the constant effort necessary to promote fear in their members. Thus, the fear helps to maintain interest in the collectively narcissistic group.

Identifying Ways to Decrease Narcissism in Groups

Research clarifies the dangerousness of collective narcissism. Outcomes such as terrorism, war, racism, sexism, and violence are certainly undesirable. But what are the antidotes to collective narcissism? And why does it appear to be such a problem throughout the world?

Interestingly, little research has been done to address the specific issue of decreasing collective narcissism. However, relatively more research has been conducted on attempts to decrease individual narcissism. Two remedies have been suggested that are worthy of consideration.

Increasing solid group self-esteem

Once again, I want to turn to the benefits of group membership. Is it possible to turn a group that is collectively narcissistic into a group that has solid, non-narcissistic self-esteem? (See Chapter 10 for more information about the relationship of self-esteem to narcissism.)

It may be more useful to start with individuals of the narcissistic group. Leaving a narcissistic group is difficult. They often have cult-like power over their members and may look to take revenge on anyone who leaves the group, especially if the person criticizes the organization.

Membership in alternative groups that promote positive social values can be encouraged. The individual will likely need support from a friend or family member in order to integrate into a new group. The collectively narcissistic group offered the member a sense of identity that needs to be replaced in a healthier manner.

Communities can offer ways to integrate people into meaningful groups. Volunteer activities, civic groups, and interest groups may help people leave the grip of collectively narcissistic ties.

Increasing values such as gratitude, forgiveness, and acceptance may help decrease collective narcissism. Much of this work may begin at the community level.

Finding commonalities

Sometimes great disasters or tragedies lead collectively narcissistic groups into altruistic actions. For example, after a deadly hurricane in Florida, people gathered resources to help each other. Prior to the storm, political parties had enormous animosity toward each other.

However, political parties made no difference in who was affected by the storm. Party differences were largely forgotten in the efforts to save lives and clean up in the aftermath. Too bad the newfound fellowship was fleeting.

It is often necessary to remind people of the similarities in the human condition rather than highlight differences to find common ground. For the most part, people want to live happy, meaningful, and calm lives surrounded by others who care about them.

Chapter **4**

Tracing the Roots of Narcissism to Parenting

The vast majority of people do the best they can in life with whatever resources they possess. In the case of parenting, with very few exceptions, most parents want what's best for their children and do their best to raise them well.

Although there are probably hundreds of thousands of sources of parenting advice, the average parent doesn't have access to that advice consistently in their head — especially when they're exhausted after countless sleep-deprived nights and their 10-month-old starts wailing at 3 a.m. Nor do they have the perfect patience preached in parenting advice columns when their 5-year-old throws a tantrum at the grocery store.

Parenting today is difficult. There are many more single-parent households, more families in which both parents work, problems in the schools, and childcare challenges. In addition, the influence that modern media has on children is undeniable.

So, it is with kindness and empathy that I write this chapter. Although specific parenting practices appear to be associated with higher levels of narcissism, parents may engage in these behaviors with little knowledge of the long-term effects.

This chapter explains these main problematic parenting practices, offers some solutions, and ends with a quiz for those parents who may be wondering, "Am I raising a narcissist?"

Growing a Narcissist

How do people become narcissists? Is it an inherited trait? Or is it taught and modeled? The answer is both.

The limited link to genetics

Most personality characteristics and emotional disorders are known to be partly genetic. For example, if you have a lot of family members with anxiety or depression, you're at some increased risk for reacting to stress with anxiety or depression.

Does narcissism run in families? At least one small study has supported that idea, *to a point*. Researchers looked at two factors of narcissism:

>> The first factor, relating to how narcissists feel about themselves, was *grandiosity*, the belief of being greater than others.

>> The second factor, relating to how people interact with others, was *entitlement*, the belief that one should get special treatment and privileges.

The study looked at two samples of twins, identical and fraternal. All sets of twins were raised together in their parents' homes. Results indicated that identical twins were more likely to share the characteristics of grandiosity and entitlement than fraternal twins, supporting the hypothesis that at least a portion of narcissism is inherited.

TECHNICAL STUFF

The reasons that twin studies answer questions about inheritability is because identical twins share almost identical genetic material and are raised in the same environment. Fraternal twins are also raised in similar environments but share less DNA. Therefore, differences are assumed to be due to genetics as opposed to learning or environmental influences.

Although the study of inheritability of narcissistic traits suggested some role of genetic influence, the study has limitations. One limitation is the use of a small sample size. In addition, I as the mother of identical twins, know that look-alike twins get a lot of special attention from others that fraternal twins don't. So, perhaps it's at least partly the extra attention rather than genetics that make identical twins more narcissistic.

Even if genes are in play, that doesn't leave parents off the hook. The bottom line is that most evidence points to particular parenting practices that are thought to contribute to the development of narcissism.

There are competing theories on how narcissism develops: the social learning theory and the psychoanalytic theory. Although I present both theories, I lean toward the *social learning theory* because that theory is based on empirical evidence, including formal research studies. *Psychoanalytic theory* on the causes of narcissism has been primarily based on clinical evidence derived from working with patients. Clinical evidence is gathered from individual interactions with patients and is not considered as reliable or valid as empirical evidence. However, both theories provide rich explanations for how narcissism may develop in children.

The significant role parenting plays

The way children are treated by the people who take care of them greatly influences their development.

REMEMBER

I refer to parenting in a broad manner. Parenting means taking care of children. Parents can be mothers, fathers, grandparents, adoptive parents, cousins, siblings, close friends, or even teachers. The influence any of those caregivers have on a particular child is determined by the time, quality, and the intensity of the interactions.

Giving gold stars for breathing: Damaging overvaluation

Children are born pretty special and should basically get whatever they need as infants. If they are wet, change them; hungry, feed them; tired, let them sleep. It they're fussy, rock them or distract them. During the first months of development, it's hard to go overboard with care.

REMEMBER

As children grow, their world gradually begins to widen. As they're exposed to more people, have more experiences outside of the home, and eventually have to relate to a variety of people and environments, damaging overvaluation often begins, and overvaluation of children is the greatest predictor of narcissism.

How exactly do you overvalue a child? The caregivers/parents start by treating their children as perfect and therefore entitled to special privileges. Not only do they feel that their children are special, but they're also convinced their kids are better than other children. It's the *better than others* part that is especially troubling because it implies superiority, a key component of narcissism.

Parents often advertise their little one's special qualities by dressing them in T-shirts with logos such as the following:

>> I Am Special

>> Mommy's Prince

>> Daddy's Princess

>> Chick Magnet (with a picture of a chicken, cute)

>> Once in Awhile Someone Amazing Comes Along and Here I Am!

>> Grandma's Favorite Human

>> I love me!

This overvaluation is also present in elementary schools and beyond where kids are involved in "I am special" activities, such as collages entitled "Everything That's Great About Me," or are given stickers and praise by their teachers for their classwork regardless of quality. As described in Chapter 12, the influence of overvaluation may be partially responsible for the grade inflation that has been occurring in schools over decades.

Parents who overvalue their kids do not take kindly to other adults who dare to criticize their precious babies. Parents like these often complain to teachers, principals, or coaches if their child is not getting the kind of positive feedback they feel their Little Johnny or Sweet Suzie "deserves."

This overvaluation leads to what is known as helicopter parenting. *Helicopter parents* are overinvolved with their children. They supervise every activity and hover over their children, protecting them from even minor hardships and ultimately, the realities of the world. Examples of helicopter parenting include

>> Supervising all playdates (never trusting others to look after young ones)

>> Excessively worrying about child safety even with low-risk activities

>> Fighting their kids' battles

>> Giving trophies for merely participating

>> Not keeping score in sports for fear of hurting someone's feelings

>> Doing homework for kids starting in early grades

>> Intervening to keep a child from experiencing frustration

>> Coaching coaches and insisting on more play time for their child

>> Telling teachers what to teach

- » Complaining to teachers about their child's grade
- » Driving kids even when walking is safe and easy
- » Writing college entrance essays for their high-school graduates
- » Complaining to college professors about their adult child's grades

Unfortunately, all of these activities done by loving parents and guardians give their children no opportunities to experience real life. By overvaluing and overprotecting children, parents doom their children to being unprepared for the realities of adulthood.

TIP

Children need opportunities to fail when the stakes are low in order to learn how to handle inevitable frustrations later in life.

Never saying no: Permissive parenting

My youngest precocious two-year-old grandson loves to play with remotes. He is sometimes allowed to play with remotes at other locations (not naming any specifics here). However, my smart house has remotes for all sorts of gadgets, and if any of them get reset, my not-so-smart self sometimes struggles to reconnect them with the other inanimate smart gadgets.

When I saw him playing with a remote given to him by another unnamed source, I was slightly, okay, *very* concerned. Not wanting to interfere with someone else's parenting, I held my tongue.

The next time my grandson came over, he headed straight for the first remote he spotted. He asked me to get it for him. I cheerfully told him that at grandma's house, remotes were a "No" and that was the rule at grandma's house.

He made a little sound of complaint, which I ignored, and he simply gave up. He often looks longingly at the remotes but doesn't touch them.

Oh, if it were only that easy for caregivers to consistently implement rules. It can be surprisingly difficult to hold the line. Children are exquisitely adept at training their parents to give them what they want. They use sophisticated manipulation as soon as they are able to whine — which is a skill that they use with ease. And parents don't like to see their children unhappy. So, they give in.

Unfortunately, the inability to set limits and say no has terrible consequences. In my role as a psychologist, I can't tell you how many kids I saw over the years that had complete control over their parents. How did they manage to do that? Usually by making noise. A lot of noise. Horrible noises, like fingernails-on-a-chalkboard horrible.

Have you ever been on an airplane while a baby was screaming? There is something extraordinarily grating about that sound. Humans have an instinct to be disturbed by a baby's crying. It's a distress signal that keeps babies alive.

So, it's understandable why parents give in to their kids' crying, especially in public. But when children are always given what they want and never told no, they are at risk of becoming obnoxious, narcissistic teens and adults.

When parents ignore their children's objectionable behavior, they fail to give their children the skills necessary for learning self-control. Considerable research supports the idea that self-control and the ability to handle frustration are critical to healthy development.

Permissive parenting has been linked to the following outcomes in children:

>> Lower academic achievement

>> Aggression

>> Substance abuse

>> Increased risk for delinquency

>> Poor self-control

>> Emotional outbursts

>> Narcissism

TIP

Permissive parenting does not just mean giving into temper tantrums (although that is certainly one aspect); it also involves avoiding all confrontations with the child, having few rules, and enforcing no consequences. The worst offence of a permissive parent is when they allow their children to infringe on the rights of others. Sounds like a narcissist in the making!

Adding Fertilizer to the Narcissism Seed: Other Contributing Factors

Although overindulgence and overvaluing children have been linked to narcissism by empirical research, other factors have been identified that may contribute to the development of narcissism. These factors, derived largely through clinical evidence, include child neglect, overvaluation of prestige, muted emotional connectedness between parents and children, and abuse.

Furthermore, these factors likely interact with each other to cause some children to think too highly of themselves, which paves the way to grandiosity.

Neglecting children

Children need nurturing to grow into well-adjusted adults. Positive needs include safety, warmth, and nurturance. However, not all kids get what they need. Being deprived of these basic needs can result in narcissistic behavior. That's because the state of deprivation leads to the child craving for power, control, and care. To obtain those things, the child may react by demanding special treatment. Unfortunately, their efforts often fail.

REMEMBER

Neglect is the most common form of child maltreatment. Neglect involves a failure to provide adequate amounts of food, shelter, care, connection, and guidance. Child abuse consists of more active, harsh, and punitive behavior by the caregiver. Abuse can be physical and/or emotional.

>> Physical neglect involves not providing sufficient food, clothing, or shelter.

>> Medical neglect involves not getting appropriate preventative care as well as neglecting illness.

>> Educational neglect is not taking care to see that children attend or do well in school.

>> Emotional neglect is rarely reported but may be the biggest risk factor for later emotional developmental problems such as depression, anxiety, behavior problems, poor school achievement, and narcissism.

Children require interactions with adults in order to develop normally. When not given feedback and left alone for long periods of time, they look to other sources to soothe themselves or find comfort. Self-soothing takes many forms, for example:

>> Sucking on fingers or thumbs, blankets, or clothing

>> Rocking back and forth

>> Biting nails or cuticles

>> Pulling or twirling hairs

WARNING

Most young children engage in one or more self-soothing activities. It's only when these behaviors occur for long periods of time that they can be of concern. Excessive self-soothing behaviors may be indicative of developing emotional problems. As teens, those children may seek drugs or alcohol in order to sooth themselves.

Neglect appears to be associated with the vulnerable type of narcissism. Vulnerable narcissists are hypersensitive to criticism, self-absorbed, and inhibited, but have grandiose fantasies that are unlikely to be realized. (See Chapter 2 for more on the various types of narcissism.)

Valuing prestige over decency

Another source of narcissism derives from parents teaching their children that winning is the most important goal in life, and how you get there is of no consequence. Parents model these values by showing off with expensive cars, even when they can't really afford them; taking advantage of others; cutting in line; and lying about their kids' ages to get cheaper tickets.

These parents believe that when their children go to school, getting a good grade by cheating is okay, as long as you get away with it. Similarly, stealing attractive clothing from the lost-and-found locker makes a kid look smart, not guilty of thievery. Bribing officials and using fraud to get your child into a prestigious college is also a signpost of privilege over decency.

Parents who prioritize prestige also see plagiarizing as fine, but if you can't get away with that (some schools have software that detects plagiarizing), they rationalize that you can pay someone else to do your work. Just go online and search for "pay someone to write my essay."

TECHNICAL STUFF

One of the greatest parts of writing a book is that I get to endlessly research related aspects of the topic, and I inevitably find some fascinating trivia. For example, I knew that you could pay someone to write an essay, but I didn't realize just how many sites blatantly advertise this horrible form of cheating. Prices start at around $10 a page; unbelievable. With the proliferation of artificial intelligence technology, the opportunities for cheating may skyrocket.

Turning a cold shoulder to kids

Emotionally cold and distant, but demanding parents may foster vulnerably narcissistic children. Such parents lack warmth and use their children to promote their own narcissistic needs. These children often are used to show off for the benefit of the parent.

For example, a musically talented child may be asked to perform for their parents' friends and then be told to disappear after the performance. The performance is totally a show for the parents' ego, not a way to cherish the talent of the child. If the child does not perform up to expectations, the parents may become angry or rejecting. The child learns that their status in the family is tied to their ability to perform perfectly and impress others. They do not receive the unconditional love that gives children security and safety. Thus, they form the seeds of later narcissism.

REMEMBER

Unconditional love is not the same thing as lavishing excessive praise or overvaluing a child. It means that the child is loved regardless of behaviors. Behaviors can be applauded or criticized; the child is still loved.

Being abusive

Although overvaluation of children is the most potent contributor to the development of narcissistic children, the opposite extreme sometimes produces similar results. This seems somewhat counterintuitive; however, it makes sense. Narcissistic behavior can be an attempt to bolster negative self-views developed as a result of abuse.

Abused children often have a faulty belief that they somehow deserve to be punished. This belief results in a deep sense of shame. That shame motivates behaviors designed to prop up their fragile sense of self in an attempt to avoid feeling vulnerable. Ultimately, the abused child becomes dismissive of others in order to escape more feelings of shame.

There has been some research on college students which discovered that early childhood abuse is associated with vulnerable narcissism. Students who were physically abused by their caregivers showed more reactive aggression when their egos were threatened. In other words, they showed the thin skin and quick anger of a vulnerable narcissist.

Fending Off Narcissism: Arming Your Child with Healthy Self-Esteem

This is not a parenting book; it's a book about narcissism. However, most research directly ties narcissism to child-raising practices. And most people when asked don't want to raise a narcissistic child.

The following list provides child-raising strategies for encouraging resilient, non-narcissistic children who have a solid sense of self-esteem. These points are basic, common sense child-caring practices. When applied consistently, they help keep kids' egos in check.

>> **Teach empathy.** Talk to your children about how other children must feel and how adults feel under difficult circumstances. When your child

misbehaves and hurts someone else, thoroughly dissect the situation and talk about how both sides must feel.

>> **Allow small frustrations.** Encourage your child to experience waiting, doing unpleasant tasks, and encountering challenging situations. Discuss how it feels to deal with frustration and how to get through it. Model dealing with frustration by talking to your child as you wait in traffic. For example, say, "I get frustrated when I have to wait, but then I think it's not that bad; I'll still get where I want to go eventually."

>> **Criticize actions, not children.** All children misbehave. When your child messes up, criticize the misbehavior, not the whole child. Action-specific feedback does not indict the whole self of the child. Don't say "Bad boy for drawing on the wall," say "I don't like it when you draw on the wall; it makes a mess. Please help me clean it up."

>> **Celebrate failures as opportunities to learn.** When you or your child experiences a failure, point out how you can grow from the experience. For example, if your child fails a test, you can review what led up to that failure, and then help your child prepare better for the next test.

>> **Learn to say no and mean it.** Tone of voice matters. Be kind but firm. Don't be fooled by your child's whines and tears. Stand resolute. "No" is one of the most important words for parents to master.

>> **Set and consistently enforce house rules.** Try to establish a few rules in your home and stick to them. Rules should reflect the values of kindness, respect, and cooperation. Everyone fails to enforce rules on occasion, but consistency is the goal.

>> **Help with household chores:** Even preschoolers can learn to pick up their toys. The home is a place of cooperation; everybody helps. Later, chores can be tied to some reward such as an allowance, simple praise, or choice of a pleasurable activity. However, some families prefer to expect kids to help out just because doing chores is a part of being a responsible member in a caring household.

>> **Provide appropriate supervision.** Children need to be monitored, especially in the early years. Little kids need clearly defined boundaries on where to be. For example, they can play in the yard. As they get older, those boundaries can be broadened. In addition, monitor their friendships and get to know parents of children they play with. Decrease monitoring as your child develops skills, but if they fail to be responsible, increase monitoring as needed.

>> **Teach self-control.** Never tell a child that it is not okay to feel a certain way. However, offer the child strategies to manage strong feelings in an appropriate manner. For example, it's okay to feel frustrated, but it's not okay to hit or

scream at others (unless it's a clear case of self-defense). It's perfectly normal to cry at times, but loud crying at a restaurant may mean a brief time outside to calm down. In addition, teach coping strategies like taking deep breaths or saying that bad feelings are temporary. You can also model how you handle strong feelings when you have those opportunities.

» **Praise effort over outcome.** When you notice your child trying hard, take the time to praise their effort. Overemphasis on outcomes encourages overvaluation of success over persistence. Persistence has been found to be a highly significant predictor of positive emotional development and later success and happiness in life.

» **Teach your children manners.** Early on, talk about saying please when asking for something and thank you when something is given to them. As they get older, show them how to hold a door open for someone, greet people politely, avoid bossing people around, and play cooperatively. In addition, since most American kids have a phone by age 12, phone etiquette should also be taught. *Phubbing,* which means snubbing with your phone, should be limited. Children need to learn how to have conversations in order to be successful adults. Phubbing, whether done by children or parents, is simply rude behavior and has a strong flavor of entitlement.

» **Teach your child to apologize when they are wrong.** (And model this behavior yourself!) Everyone makes mistakes. Use those as opportunities for self-reflection. Teach your child to apologize when they hurt someone's feelings, whether intentionally or not, or when they break a rule. Also make sure the apology is sincere as opposed to blaming others for feeling bad.

» **Love your child.** Love is attention, hugs, nurturance, and warmth. Love is not giving in to your child or providing every comfort. Love is consistent care. Warmth in parenting is associated with high self-esteem, not narcissism.

» **Teach your child to be humble.** I know that your child is special and important to you; however, overvaluation is the most significant cause of narcissism. Model how you feel grateful for the gifts of life. Gratitude walks hand in hand with humility. Yes, your child is special and may have incredible qualities, but humility is a strength that will serve your child well in the future. Humility is highly undervalued as an emotional strength.

There are many factors that are out of your control when you raise your child. For example, heredity may predetermine some of your child's characteristics. In addition, sources such as social media, technology, the neighborhood, and schools influence your child's development. Also, random events that happen in the world, such as wars, accidents, natural disasters, recessions, or pandemics, can impact child development. Nevertheless, parents retain a powerful position in childrearing. Use that power wisely.

Are You Raising a Narcissist? An Eye-Opening Quiz

Children are naturally self-centered little humans. Depending on age and stage, a bit of narcissism is normal. But as they grow and mature, they should begin to see others as humans too.

Are you worried that you may be raising a narcissist? Take the quiz in Table 4-1.

TABLE 4-1 **Parent Practices That Lead to Narcissistic Kids**

Check off the questions that sound like you as a parent.	
1.	My child is always entitled to the very best of everything.
2.	As much as I can, I completely ignore my child's misbehavior.
3.	If my child does something special, like graduate from kindergarten, I go overboard with praise and presents. After all, they're only children once.
4.	I consider my child to be superior to other children.
5.	I don't make my child say please and thank you.
6.	I basically give my child everything they want.
7.	I give my child lots of special attention, probably more than most kids get.
8.	When my child cries, I can't stand it and usually give in.
9.	I let my child interrupt and monopolize the conversation.
10.	When my child gets into a conflict, I step in and fix it.
11.	If I screw up in front of my child, I try to cover it up or ignore it. I never admit fault.
12.	My kids are always part of the decision making in our family. In fact, they usually win on what we get or where we go for dinner or a vacation.
13.	I tell my kid that it is babyish to cry.
14.	When my child is upset, I try to ignore them. I don't want to get into any conflict with my child.
15.	My child comes from a very successful family, and I expect them to be successful as well.

16.	I try to shield my child from all frustrations.
17.	I want to always be my child's best friend.
18.	I let my kids run wild in the neighborhood.
19.	I honestly let my child play video games so I don't have to deal with them.
20.	I don't feel comfortable with hugging, kissing, and telling my child that I love them.

Count the check marks you made on the quiz. There is no official cutoff score, but the more statements you endorse, the more likely it is that you may be raising a narcissist.

Don't despair; it's never too late to start doing things a bit differently. Pick one or two items that particularly grab your attention. For example, vow that you will pay attention to how many hours your child is spending on screens and try to decrease it by a bit. Or try giving more affection to your child every day.

Don't try to change everything at once. Change slowly and see what happens. There's no point in getting overly critical of your parenting practices; that will only make you feel worse. I'm sure that you want what's best for your kids.

WARNING

If you don't adjust your parenting techniques away from the parenting practices that lead to narcissism in kids, you may suffer from being the parent of a self-centered, grandiose snob who demands attention and applause without putting forth much effort. Not really that much fun for you — or anyone else for that matter.

2

Interacting with Narcissists

IN THIS PART . . .

Discover some coping skills for handling narcissistic partners.

Find out what narcissistic parents can do to their kids.

See how narcissism can taint the workplace.

Explore how narcissists draw others to them.

Open up a tool box to help you get through abuse.

Chapter 5

Dealing with Narcissistic Partners

Have you ever wondered why the expression "falling in love" has the word "falling" in it? Falling seems like an odd word to be associated with love. Falling is dangerous. When you fall, you can hurt yourself, you lose control, and you become vulnerable.

But loving someone should be joyful and uplifting, not scary or dangerous. Or maybe, there really is a risk you take when you become enamored with someone. In effect, you become captured and dependent on that person to treat you kindly. Falling in love is always a gamble, *particularly* with a narcissist.

This chapter is all about falling for someone who thinks of themselves as grand, superior, entitled, and special — in other words, a narcissist. It shows you the probable early stages of the relationship and how the dreamy honeymoon often turns into a nightmare. It details some of the devious ways a narcissist seeks to maintain control. In addition, the personal costs to the partner of the narcissist are examined.

A powerful technique to help you decide whether to leave or stay is described. Finally, coping skills are offered to help the partner who resolves to stay as well as to assist the partner who decides to leave a narcissistic relationship.

Charming, Charismatic, and Considerate: What's Not to Like?

People with narcissistic characteristics usually make great first impressions. Multiple research studies indicate that first impressions of narcissists in social settings, academic settings, or at work tend to be positive. People see narcissists as outgoing, charming, and physically attractive. They are often chosen to be leaders. These positive first impressions, however, are short-lived.

Over time, people are more likely to view narcissists as self-promoters, arrogant, difficult, and often hostile. They begin to see through their early charm and start to perceive manipulation, deception, and condescending behaviors. Quite a dramatic change.

In intimate relationships, this pattern is repeated. However, the narcissistic person may manage their behaviors a bit differently in order to captivate their potential partner. Their charm lasts just long enough to snare their unsuspecting prey.

Connecting too quickly

A narcissist stands out in a crowd. Most narcissists present themselves as attractive, successful, and self-assured. You may notice and be attracted to a narcissist without knowing much about them. Narcissists have the ability to look at you with intensity, make you feel special, and start the grooming process as soon as they identify you as a potential partner.

Although the narcissistic person is self-centered, they can turn on the charm and seem fascinated by you. Finally, someone shows deep interest in your experiences, your life. You may feel incredibly listened to and deeply understood. You go on wonderful dates, they send sentimental texts, and give you thoughtful gifts or flowers.

Do you hear any warning bells going off? Maybe not; maybe you are blissfully happy at this stage. But things are moving a bit fast. Is this too good to be true?

Do you notice the conversation turning more and more toward subjects about the life of your narcissistic partner? Does it seem that you try to start a conversation and the topic changes unexpectedly? These may be red flags. Most people with narcissism are only able to engage in the flirtation process for a short time. Their needs for attention, privilege, and adoration begin to emerge early in the relationship.

WARNING

Although you've heard stories of love at first sight, the truth is, most healthy relationships take time to establish. There may be an instant attraction. And although physical attraction may be necessary to get things going, it's usually not sufficient to sustain a good partnership. Go slow and steady; get to know someone in multiple settings before committing to a long-term relationship.

Love bombing

Love bombing usually starts at the beginning of a relationship with a narcissist. Within a matter of mere days or weeks, the narcissist wants to spend every minute with you. When apart they want constant communication through calls or texts. Love bombing is over-the-top, too much, too soon. Narcissists may say things like the following:

>> I can't stand to be away from you.

>> You're an unbelievable person.

>> I love everything about you.

>> I feel so close to you.

>> We share so much in common, we're soulmates.

>> We belong together.

>> You're everything I've dreamed of and more.

>> I'm falling in love with you.

>> You're the sexiest person I've ever known.

>> You're perfect for me.

Wonderful words, but you've only been with this person for a short while. Come on, you just met! Love bombing is definitely a red flag. The narcissist uses it to lure you in and increase your dependency. At this point, a narcissist wants to create a strong tie to you, a tight bond. It's like being psychologically zip-tied.

WARNING

Love bombing can be difficult to detect. It's perfectly normal to shower someone you care about with affection, attention, and even small gifts. But in the case of love bombing, the intent is to gain the ability to manipulate and control. The attention is over-the-top and not expected at that stage of the relationship.

TIP

If you worry that someone may be love bombing you and you're not sure what's really going on, ask a few trusted friends or family members their opinions. They have a distance from the relationship and can be far more objective than you.

The following example is based on clinical experiences of those who have been victimized by love bombing. However, as in all examples in this book, the details have been changed and do not represent any specific individuals.

Harper meets Eva in the break room at work. Both medical technicians, they work the night shift in different units in a large hospital. Their first date is over coffee following a shift. Harper talks about her interest in hiking and camping. Eva says that she always wanted to do more of that. Eva asks Harper what kind of music she listens to. Harper says country. Eva tells Harper that she loves country music too. Eva also talks about the big career plans she has and hints at getting a considerable amount of money from her family.

Harper finds herself surprisingly attracted to Eva in a short time. It seems that everything Harper is interested in, Eva likes too. They enjoy several more outings.

But Harper has a feeling in her gut that Eva is too good to be true. She seems to agree with everything Harper says and spoils her with treats and gifts. Eva starts to talk about moving in together, and Harper hesitates. Her instincts tell her this is too fast. She has a funny feeling that she can't explain. She tells Eva that they need to get to know each other a bit more.

That night a huge bouquet of flowers and balloons is delivered to Harper at work. The staff tease Harper about having a secret admirer. After her shift, Harper spots Eva standing next to her car. She grins and thanks her for the flowers. In a few weeks, the two agree to move into Harper's apartment. Harper's healthy defenses have been overwhelmed by Eva's love bombing.

Shortly after Eva moves in, the relationship changes. The gifts and flowers stop. They start arguing about money. Harper realizes that Eva has huge balances on her credit cards in spite of her earlier suggestions that she had family money. When Eva doesn't have enough money to pay her share of the rent, she angrily blames Harper's need for gifts and flowers for her financial difficulties.

Harper doesn't know how this happened to her. She's usually so practical and down-to-earth. She feels unsettled but also uncharacteristically paralyzed. She's not sure how she's suddenly in this relationship or what to do.

Love bombing usually occurs during the early parts of a relationship with a narcissist. It's hard to resist positive attention, affection, and flattery. But there is often a cost when you realize what you fell for — the cost is loss of self-confidence and a sense of control.

Love bombing can also occur after a relationship has been firmly established. It usually happens when the narcissist is in trouble. For example, if the person with narcissism is caught cheating, becomes overly abusive, or engages in long periods of silent treatment, the partner may consider leaving the relationship. At those times, a person with narcissism may experience deep vulnerability and respond with more love bombs. As time goes on, the love bombs are likely to become less effective.

TIP

However, for some, the pattern of love bombing followed by deception can last many years. Frequently, abused partners of narcissists hang on with renewed hope after each breakup that the relationship may be salvageable. Unfortunately, the damage done to the abused partner can last long after the final door shuts on a narcissistic relationship.

TECHNICAL STUFF

The term "love bombing" was described in the book *Cults in Our Midst* by Margaret Singer (published by Jossey-Bass). She wrote about the way religious cults recruit new members by providing them with a steady flow of excessive flattery, companionship, and attention. Interestingly, some view being entangled with a narcissist as similar to being drawn into a cult.

Taking trophy partners

A person who thinks of themself as grand, superior, and special prefers to have a partner who can add to that grandiose belief. It's almost like a drug addiction; narcissists can never get enough. *Trophy partners* are usually younger than their partners, physically fit, and stunningly attractive. They are used as status figures by their older, richer spouses or partners.

The trophy wife is probably a more common phenomenon; however, young handsome men can also serve as trophies. When a narcissist has their eyes on finding a trophy, they usually use love bombing to nail the conquest.

WARNING

You may not know that you are a trophy to the narcissist with whom you have a relationship. A narcissist may want someone who has a prestigious occupation, a certain address, or an important lineage. You also may be an innocent, attractive person who happens to think you and your partner have a loving relationship. You may also think that although they cheated in the past, they would never cheat on you. Unfortunately, trophies tarnish over time and often end up neglected or packed away in the attic or garage.

TIP

If you are a trophy partner, you may feel unloved or uncared for. Your partner may show you off but seem uninterested in what you're thinking or feeling. Pay attention to how you're treated and get feedback from close friends, family, or counselors if you are unsure of your status.

Going from g.o.a.t. to ghost

The early days of a narcissistic romance usually fade over time. You may have started out feeling like the greatest of all time, but before long, the person's narcissistic behaviors such as arrogance, lack of empathy, and grandiosity bubble to the surface. The change may be subtle; those long talks or walks slowly disappear. Your narcissistic partner becomes more self-absorbed and less interested in your life.

They may suddenly become more arrogant, demanding, and critical. You lose your sense of stability and security. You, the person you thought was loved, begin to disappear. It's as if you're not even there.

If you have a busy life, you may be able to ignore the signs of loss for some time. You may turn your attention to your career, hobbies, studies, visiting with friends, or spending time with family. But the beginning signs are clearly evident, and narcissistic abuse likely follows.

WARNING

Some people with narcissistic traits may want to stay in a relationship for a variety of reasons. Perhaps they want to avoid an expensive divorce or the public embarrassment of another breakup. Or the narcissist may like the power and control that ghosting gives them over their partner.

So, sometimes the narcissist minimally remains with their partner while leading their own lives, cheating when they feel like it, and putting a minimum of effort into keeping things peaceful. When their partners demand more, they may go back to a quick period of love bombing, hoping to maintain the sham relationship. Nevertheless, partners of narcissists become less and less themselves — ghost-like.

If you've gone from the best ever to almost invisible in a relationship, consider some of the tips in the section, "Coping Skills: Keeping Your Sanity While Dealing with a Narcissistic Partner," later in this chapter.

Entitled and Egotistical: So Much for the Honeymoon Phase!

Narcissistic partners demand attention and care. They want to be in control of important decisions and expect their desires to be affirmed. You, who recently stood on a pedestal, start to lose your self-confidence. You feel demeaned and devalued. The very foundation of your essence begins to crumble.

Embarrassed by your predicament, you may try to fix the relationship, but your efforts are shunned. The narcissist has many ways to control the relationship that are both obvious and subtle. Few egos are strong enough to withstand the onslaught.

All's well on social media

There is a clear connection between frequent social media posting and grandiose narcissism. Grandiose narcissists have a platform to brag and show the world how wonderful they are. Self-promotion and narcissism fit like hand and glove. Narcissists post frequently but are rarely truly engaged with others on social media. In other words, they don't really communicate with others; rather, they simply enjoy the imagined spotlight.

Narcissists show themselves on social media dancing, smiling, sexy, happy, and engaged in life. Narcissists thrive, posting pictures of their so-called perfect lives. Partners of narcissists are required to put on a happy face when the narcissist wants the perfect picture. The example of Hanna and Matteo illustrates the false face of a narcissist on social media.

> Matteo fumes beside his wife, Hanna. He's not happy to be at her cousin's wedding; he doesn't really approve of any of her relatives. To him, this event is a complete waste of time. The chicken is rubbery, and the bar is cash. What a bunch of cheapskates.
>
> Hanna leans over to Matteo and attempts to start a conversation. He turns his head away from her and reaches for his phone. She sits uncomfortably conscious of his obnoxious behavior. She notices a videographer filming the guests seated at the table. When he gets closer, Hanna nudges Matteo who grunts, "Leave me alone. This is crap."
>
> Then he notices the camera about to film their table. Matteo suddenly beams, puts his arm around Hanna, and waves at the camera. When the videographer leaves, Matteo returns to sulking with his phone.

WARNING

Thin-skinned, vulnerable narcissists use social media to anonymously voice their rage. (Turn to Chapter 2 for the lowdown on vulnerable narcissists.) When a relationship doesn't work out, they can switch from love bombing to cyberbullying quickly and easily. See Chapter 11 for information about narcissists, aggression, and cyberbullying.

If you are in a relationship with a narcissist who posts phony self-promotion on social media, I have two suggestions. First, don't waste your time analyzing the truthfulness of their posts. Second, don't feel that these posts reflect accurate information about you or those you care about.

Gaslighting

Gaslighting is a common form of emotional abuse in which the abuser lies or distorts reality to confuse or manipulate the victim. The purpose of gaslighting is to degrade someone's self-esteem and increase fear or instability. Gaslighting begins slowly in a relationship and usually intensifies over time.

Signs of gaslighting

Gaslighting can be hard to nail down. Some attempts seem so trivial that they are easy to dismiss as miscommunications, coincidences, or simple forgetting. However, over time, gaslighting by a narcissistic partner can cause you, their victim, to become confused and isolated, wondering whether you're going crazy. Here are a few signs to consider if you suspect you're being gaslighted:

>> **You feel overly sensitive.** Your partner always has a semi-plausible reason for their behavior. For example, they may say they're three hours late because there was a huge traffic jam.

>> **You feel like you're always making excuses for your partner.** For example, they never attend the kids' sports activities because they work so hard.

>> **You can't do anything right and feel increasingly insecure.** For instance, your partner's standards are so much higher than yours that you think you're not putting in enough effort.

>> **You are always apologizing to everyone to keep the peace.** You feel like you dance around trying to please everyone and can't seem to manage your life like you used to.

>> **You are confused by what is going on but can't figure out what is real.** Sometimes you think your partner is lying, but they always have slick explanations that make you look and feel absurdly jealous, petty, or stupid.

>> **You have lost your sense of competence and confidence.** You seem much more unsure of your thinking and problem-solving skills.

>> **You don't tell your best friends about a lot that goes on between you and your partner because you're embarrassed.** You know deep inside that you're being emotionally abused but aren't ready to admit it.

>> **Friends and relatives warn you about your partner's behavior, but you keep on enduring it.** You've been made to feel emotionally ill-equipped to make it on your own.

>> **You feel like you're being put down all the time.** Your partner tells you that you're being too sensitive, says they didn't mean to put you down, or claims to have been joking.

» **You doubt yourself and begin to question your memory and judgment.**
So many times, when you confront your narcissistic partner, they tell you that
what you remember never occurred or that you totally misinterpreted it. The
constant repetition begins to change what you believe.

» **You think your partner may be cheating, but you can't prove it**. You don't
want to confront your partner because they'll have some excuse and make
you feel worse for suspecting them.

Early gaslighting

Narcissists who gaslight are master manipulators and well-practiced liars. They
wait until the relationship has been established before beginning the abuse.

Gaslighting can be subtle or overt, but the narcissist knows how far they can reach
depending on their victim's state of mind. For example, early in a relationship,
gaslighting may be almost unrecognizable. You may recall an event in the past
when your narcissistic partner made fun of you and hurt your feelings. Your partner told you that they were just kidding and questioned your lack of a sense of
humor.

Or your narcissistic partner blatantly flirts with someone else in front of you.
When you confront them about their inappropriate behavior, they say that you are
overreacting and reading into things — that the events you think you saw are
simply not true.

Those early signs of gaslighting can evolve into much more sophisticated and
cruel forms. Consider the story of Isabelle, a narcissist, and Noah, her victim, as
an illustration of a subtle but devious form of gaslighting.

After a whirlwind courtship, Noah and Isabelle elope. Noah, recently divorced and
the father of two children, is a bit hesitant about not including his children in the
wedding. But Isabelle, who almost always gets her way, convinces him.

Upon returning, the news of their marriage spreads quickly through the small town
they live in. Cards and gifts of congratulations arrive. One evening, Isabelle tells
Noah that her former boyfriend is stopping by that evening with a gift.

Isabelle greets her ex with a hug that lasts a bit too long. Not being the jealous
type, Noah shakes the ex's hand. He's beginning to let his guard down when they
open the present to find a watercolor painting that's obviously not new; in fact, the
back of the picture is dusty. Isabelle doesn't seem phased and instead eagerly
wants to hang the picture over their bed. Noah reluctantly agrees.

Days later Noah is going through paperwork on his desk when he finds a photo-
graph of Isabelle that he's never seen. It's Isabelle, scantily clad, sitting on an

unmade bed — not theirs. Noah is shocked when he realizes that the picture her ex just gave them for a wedding present is hanging over the bed in the photo.

Noah realizes that the painting was intentionally regifted by her ex, so he confronts Isabelle with the photo. He's confused about the significance of the watercolor. She denies ever noticing the picture but admits the photo was taken at her ex's home. She tells Noah that he's overly sensitive and to just forget it. After all, she and her ex broke up almost a year ago, and her ex has been going through tight times and wanted to give them a gift to show his support for her relationship with Noah. Still feeling upset and uneasy yet wanting his otherwise perfect relationship with Isabelle to be true, Noah wonders if he really is overreacting.

This scenario reflects an early stage of gaslighting. In reality, Isabelle and her ex are having an affair, and they are cruelly taunting Noah. Both narcissists, they enjoy playing games and have no empathy for poor unsuspecting Noah.

Gaslighting usually has a purpose, but that purpose almost always is sinister. In the case of Noah and Isabelle, it's simply cruelty and manipulation, which increases Isabelle's power and control over Noah.

Later gaslighting

Gaslighting can also be used to promote a vulnerable narcissist's feeling of superiority and specialness. When that grandiose self-concept is threatened, such as during or after a breakup, gaslighting may be part of a strategy to get a former partner back. The narcissist's gaslighting weakens their partner's confidence and resolve and sets them up to potentially be lured into returning to the relationship.

Gaslighting can seem easily detectable to an outsider, but when narcissistic abuse takes root, the victim becomes more and more bewildered and gullible. The following story illustrates that point.

After enduring years of cheating and conflict, Mia finally tells Cole that he must move out. Cole drags his feet, but ultimately, he moves into an apartment close by, supposedly so that he can see their kids more often. After an initial burst of attention, Cole stops visitation under the guise of better focusing on pressing work assignments, but really, he wants more time to attend to his busy social life.

Mia finally feels better about herself after a few months of Cole stepping back and not constantly berating her. She's gaining confidence about her parenting skills, even though her three boys are quite boisterous. They, too, seem to be fighting less and getting along better since their father has been less involved.

On the first day of school, Mia has the arduous task of shepherding the kids out the door and into the car. Her hands full and her mind preoccupied with details, she doesn't realize that she didn't get the front door of the house closed. A neighbor notices the open door but assumes that someone must still be in the home.

Mia drops the boys off and comes home to find Cole parked in the driveway. Mia, shocked by Cole's unexpected and uninvited visit, gets out of her car and starts up the drive. "Mia, stop," shouts Cole. "The door is open. Someone must have broken into your house. I'll go check; you stay here."

Mia waits tensely while Cole enters the house. She hears crashes and Cole shouting, "Get out, get out!" As Mia frantically dials 911, she hears more crashes, and then Cole appears, breathless.

"I chased him out. I don't think he got anything. He went out through the back. You're safe, Mia, you're safe."

She hears sirens in the distance, and soon three patrol cars skid to a stop in front of the house. The police jump out, guns drawn, and start a search with Cole directing them to the now open back door.

Neighbors in the usually quiet neighborhood come out, including the neighbor who had noticed the open door earlier. The police find no evidence of a burglary except overturned chairs that Cole said were upended while he was chasing the burglar. Still, they interview the neighbors.

Since there is no evidence of a theft or even an attempted burglary, the officers feel there is not much to be done. One wise police officer takes Mia aside and asks her whether she and Cole are having problems. She admits that they recently split up. The officer, having seen many strange domestic dramas during his career, shakes his head and tells her to be careful and report any further problems. He shouts to the other officers that it's time to leave.

Mia suddenly feels sick to her stomach. She isn't sure what just happened, but she feels afraid. Did this really happen, or could it possibly have been one of Cole's manipulations? Cole approaches her and gives her a hug saying, "It's going to be okay, honey. I'll make sure we get better security. I'll protect you and the kids."

Mia begins to sob. Cole pulls her closer. He's grinning inside but keeps his serious, comforting face on. He had decided earlier that he couldn't afford his apartment and wanted to move back in. This lucky accident of conducting this con worked out great.

WARNING

Gaslighters use the vulnerabilities of their victims to their advantage. They make up fantastic stories and turn to slick lies when they need to. Their end game is to maintain power and control.

Gaslighting can sometimes seem outrageously unbelievable to outsiders. However, the victims of gaslighting have usually been groomed over time to set aside logic and fall for the manipulation. If you are a possible victim, it's time to ask trusted others for their perspectives.

Cheating and deceiving

As the research suggests, narcissists enjoy initial popularity. They present as outgoing, attractive, and to some, sexy. Narcissists certainly believe that they are good looking, powerful, and entitled to special privileges. They enjoy conquering others and showing their dominance, sometimes sexually.

Research about people with narcissistic traits indicates that they tend to be less committed to relationships and are open to short-term mates and multiple sexual partners over a lifetime. In addition, studies have found that narcissists in committed relationships are more likely to repeatedly engage in infidelity.

Therefore, if you are in a serious relationship with someone with narcissistic traits, watch out. There is a greater than average chance that your narcissistic partner may be on the lookout for opportunities to show their ability to seduce and dominate someone else.

The narcissist is unlikely to feel guilt or remorse while cheating. Unfortunately, the fact that they may be hurting someone who loves them doesn't matter or even occur to them. Infidelity is simply a game of entitlement, sensation seeking, and winning.

Not all narcissists cheat on their partners; they may have other ways to pump up their egos. And people without narcissism also cheat for many different reasons. However, the odds go up if you are in a relationship with a narcissist.

The following are warning signs of possible infidelity and how your narcissistic partner may take them a step further:

>> **Unexplained absences:** These vary from hours to days to weeks. One person claims to work multiple overtime hours. Funny thing though, somehow those hours never show up in bigger paychecks. Others claim to have emergency trips out of town to attend to sick friends or relatives. Long business trips are opportunities for affairs. Some simply don't answer their phones or texts for extended periods of time with no explanation. Narcissistic partners become angry or indignant if their excuses are questioned.

>> **Cancels plans at the last minute.** Because narcissists tend to feel entitled, if something better comes along, they have no guilt about cancelling plans. The

reason may seem slightly off or even like a flat-out lie, but challenging them only firms up the excuse.

>> **Spends a long time on social media and is secretive about it:** Your narcissistic partner may be flirting with someone else, browsing dating apps, planning a hook-up, or watching pornography. They are likely to keep their phone away from you and possibly have the phone password protected. Social media is a tempting playground for a cheating narcissist.

>> **Being warned by someone who was previously in a relationship with your partner:** Sometimes you have a chance encounter with your partner's ex, or someone reaches out to you about a cheating narcissist. If you check with your partner, they will likely dismiss these accusers as having a desire for revenge or being an unstable alcoholic, a drug addict, or a stalker. Don't be quick to dismiss these past victims. It's quite common for a narcissist to degrade former partners by spreading malicious rumors or rewriting their history.

>> **Changes in behavior:** These vary from changes in their work hours or sexual behavior to spending more time in front of the mirror or getting a better wardrobe. Another sign may be a sudden increase in love bombing such as flattery, more overt affection, or giving unexpected gifts to distract you.

If you suspect your partner is cheating, what can you do? If you calmly confront them, even with clear evidence, they're likely to deny all responsibility. Narcissists lie, cheat, and manipulate without remorse. Listen to your feelings. Ask yourself if what you are being told makes logical sense. When something feels like a lie, it probably is.

However, don't expect your partner to confess. You can have all the evidence you want. Part of the narcissistic joy of having an affair is the excitement of getting away with it. However, you don't have to simply accept it. See Chapter 23 for more info on leaving the relationship when you're ready.

The silent treatment

The silent treatment is an exquisitely cruel form of emotional abuse. It is used by people with narcissistic traits to punish and control their partners. When used, all lines of effective conflict resolution cease. The victim of silent treatment may not know what they did to displease the narcissist or there may have been an argument, but whatever happened, the result is stonewalling silence.

Early in a relationship, the victim of silent treatment may reach out, try to apologize, and attempt to resolve the conflict that started the dismissal. Over time, using the silent treatment leads to a breakdown of trust and faith in the relationship.

When Luke met Delilah, he believed he had found his true love. They had many mutual interests and for the most part got along great. However, early on, Luke noticed that Delilah seemed to get easily annoyed by minor frustrations. Sometimes she resisted working out simple conflicts by pouting and refusing to talk. But, like many hopeful people early in relationships, Luke justified and excused her behavior. He really wanted the relationship to work out. The following narrative shows you how the silent treatment confuses and devastates Luke later in their relationship.

Luke, a public-school teacher, meets Delilah, an attorney, through mutual friends. Both divorced, they date for about six months, seeing each other most days and spending their evenings and most nights together. After a year, the two decide to live together because they're wasting money on maintaining two households.

Luke is a people person who enjoys talking about relationships, his future goals, and how he has grown as a person following his divorce. Delila finds his musing entertaining, but she usually doesn't respond with details about her own struggles in her previous marriage. Perhaps that's because her first husband divorced her after discovering Delila's multiple affairs and getting put off by her constant demands for adoration.

One evening, over a glass of wine, Luke tells her that his main goal in finding a permanent relationship is finding true intimacy. Delila becomes frightened. In her mind, she believes that intimacy with another person is suffocating. Then she's mad. Luke is demanding more than she can possibly give. This is his fault.

Delila stops talking. Luke asks her if she is confused or hurt about something he said. Delila doesn't reply but leaves the room. Luke follows her. "Hey, Delila, let's talk this through. I'm sorry if I said something hurtful; tell me what just happened."

Delilah walks away, turns on the television and sits silently. Luke is stunned and asks several times for clarity. Delila sits stonily silent. Frustrated, Luke turns off the television. Delila saying nothing, gets her coat, and leaves the house. Luke runs after her, "What's going on? I don't understand. Let's figure this out."

Delilah is having a narcissistic temper tantrum. She's an accomplished attorney and extremely intelligent, but she's acting like a toddler. Her ability to have empathy, to negotiate during emotionally arousing situations, and her level of emotional intelligence are not well developed. She has no desire to problem solve; she'd rather dramatically jump up and down and stomp away. Delilah is likely a vulnerable narcissist who both fears and disdains people who try to understand her. (See Chapter 2 for more information about vulnerable narcissists.)

This is totally new territory for Luke. Although Delilah has been sulky and pouty at times, she's never acted out in this extreme manner. Luke has never experienced this kind of reaction before from an adult. He is reminded of the conflicts his fifth-grade students have when they sullenly refuse to talk to each other. But here he is dealing with an adult, one whom he thought was mature.

TIP

Narcissistic anger and abuse often erupt suddenly in a relationship. Partners are frequently stunned by the new, intense behaviors. Consider these unexpected shifts a red flag.

The silent treatment is a gigantic red flag that you're dealing with a narcissist or another type of severely damaged person. These strategies are means of manipulation and abuse. They are almost impossible to break through. If you have a new relationship and this happens, proceed cautiously and consider your options including those provided in Chapter 23.

Isolation from family and friends

If you are in a relationship with a narcissist, you may find yourself more and more isolated from family and friends. Why does a person with narcissistic traits want to accomplish this? They want complete control over you. They need you to feel totally dependent on them. They do not want you to get support from others who may confront you with the truth about your relationship. How do narcissists manage this form of emotional abuse?

>> They tell you not to talk about private issues to others.

>> They complain that others are a bad influence on you.

>> They overwhelm you with tasks and take away your free time.

>> They talk about the faults of friends or family.

>> They act rude in front of others.

>> They give you the silent treatment after you have seen others.

REMEMBER

When you are isolated from people who may be able to help you understand what you are going through, the narcissist is free to continue their abuse, uninterrupted. Check out my advice for handing this issue in the section, "Coping Skills: Keeping Your Sanity While Dealing with a Narcissistic Partner," later in this chapter.

All take and no give: Lacking empathy

When you are in a narcissistic relationship, your partner demands constant attention and adoration. They may want you to respond to their problems with deep empathy and understanding. And of course, they always expect you to take their side. Therefore, you may concentrate great amounts of time and attention to listening to your partner with narcissistic needs. It's basically a one-way street. If you need someone to share your own feelings or difficulties with, well, there's no one home.

The narcissistic person lacks the desire to empathize. After all, empathy requires taking the focus off themselves. Although they may seem to be quite empathic during the courtship, once the conquest is over, the spotlight of empathic attention must be returned to the narcissist.

Oliver and Amelia have been married for five years. Over time, Amelia has become numb to Oliver's narcissism. The following example describes a common occurrence in their relationship.

Oliver calls Amelia almost every night he's on duty as a security manager at a large corporation. Amelia answers her phone while she is cleaning up after dinner. *Imagine only being able to listen to Amelia's part in a phone conversation.* The call lasts about 45 minutes.

> "Hi Oliver, how are you doing tonight?"
>
> "Oh, really."
>
> "Umm."
>
> "Huh."
>
> "Nice."
>
> "Oh."
>
> "Yeah."
>
> "Oh, no."
>
> "Ah, ha."
>
> "Love you too, bye."

Amelia's phone call with Oliver was not a conversation. Oliver talks while Amelia provides supportive sounding noises and affirmations. While having this conversation is perfectly normal from time to time with someone who needs to vent, in their relationship, this is always the pattern. Oliver talks and Amelia listens.

This one-way style of communication leaves someone in a relationship with a narcissist feeling empty and alone. After many years of emotional abuse, a person can feel battered, numb, and unable to find their way out.

If you are on a phone call like Amelia's, be sure to find a few truly supportive people who care about you and your life and who'll give you supportive feedback.

The Debris of Emotional Abuse: Longing for Intimacy and Coming Up Short

Whether victimized by the silent treatment, gaslighting, or being isolated, the partner of a narcissist suffers. The narcissistic person is engaged in emotional abuse. Emotional abuse consists of the tactics used by the abuser designed to diminish the victims' sense of competence, independence, value, and worth. It creates fear and dependency. Emotional abuse is not always recognized by the person who's being abused or by others. There are no black eyes or bruises to see, but nevertheless, there is significant damage.

When emotional abuse is obvious, outsiders may wonder why someone puts up with it and why they allow it to happen in the first place. Narcissists are clever manipulators. They take the time necessary to groom their prey into submission. They do that by degrading self-esteem and self-confidence until the victim becomes passive and unable to defend themselves. The victim emerges helpless and hopeless. And the narcissist lands on top.

You no doubt went into the relationship hoping it would work out. You were initially enticed by a friendly, captivating, warm, and charming person. That person made you feel special and loved. You thought you'd finally found the one!

Then things changed, slowly at first, but gaining in intensity and frequency. The intimacy you searched for was nowhere to be found. Gradually, you realized that things were not as you expected.

You reach out, try to reason, to negotiate, to bring back that person you thought you loved. But you can't find them. You try talking and more talking. Maybe you work on the relationship in couples' therapy. Nothing seems to get better. You are shunned, ignored, and then cruelly dismissed.

Your self-esteem dwindles as you sacrifice yourself, and feelings of helplessness and hopelessness intensify. The following sections describe this progression.

Losing your self-esteem

During the process of loving a narcissist, you lose your sense of who you are. You experience a strange feeling that there is something wrong with you. You always seem to be messing up. You find yourself questioning your own competence.

Even when you experience a sense of accomplishment, that accomplishment is somehow diminished. You are not allowed to forget that your partner must be more successful and always superior, looming over you.

Sacrificing yourself

Your narcissistic partner usually tells you loud and clear that their needs come before others, especially yours. Or they may be less overt, simply expecting immediate agreement with what they want.

For example, narcissists may demand their partners drop everything to do the following:

>> Run an errand for something that actually could wait

>> Pick up the kids even when you're busy (narcissists rarely take on chauffer duties)

>> Miss work for a special date (even when work offers limited time off)

>> Do things for the narcissist and neglect their own responsibilities

The partner of the narcissist walks on eggshells, worried about not doing enough. These partners run themselves ragged trying to keep the peace in the house by doing everything their narcissistic partner asks of them. But the narcissistic partner is never completely satisfied. No gratitude is expressed. The narcissist believes that they deserve to be served by others to punch up their feelings of entitlement.

The narcissist's partner keeps hoping that if they do just a bit more to please, life will get better. They become desperately subservient hoping to return to the early stages of the relationship. Alas, nothing is good enough.

Feeling helpless and hopeless

When you try and fail, and your self-esteem has crashed, you may feel helpless and hopeless. Depression can follow. Depression is a treatable disease, and you should seek help. Your primary care provider is a first, good stop. Don't try to diagnose yourself. Signs of depression include

>> Feelings of sadness and gloominess most days

>> Loss of pleasure or interest in activities that were once enjoyable

>> Feelings of worthlessness

>> Changes in appetite (increases or decreases)

>> Changes in sleep (either too much or insomnia)

>> Feeling agitated or slowed down

- **»** Poor ability to concentrate or be attentive
- **»** Feeling spiritless or tired all the time
- **»** Worthless or guilty feelings
- **»** Feeling flat and emotionally exhausted
- **»** Recurrent thoughts of dying or suicidal thoughts

WARNING

When you are depressed, it's not a good time to make important decisions. Get help for yourself first, whether through medication or therapy. See the section "Consider individual therapy" for more information.

Coping Skills: Keeping Your Sanity while Dealing with a Narcissistic Partner

If you are in a relationship with a narcissist, you've probably already experienced many challenges and frustrations. However, sometimes you have good reasons for staying in the relationship. Perhaps you aren't able to independently function on your own for the time being. Or you lack confidence in your ability to find a better living situation. Or maybe, despite the narcissistic tendencies, you believe there is hope in saving your relationship. Then there is love: Despite all the trouble, abuse, and flaws, there's something about your narcissistic partner that you continue to love.

Whatever reasons you have for staying, the following strategies may help you cope and keep your sanity while dealing with the narcissist in your life.

Be knowledgeable about narcissism

The more you understand about the tricks of the narcissistic trade, the more you are able to defend against them. Narcissists believe that they are superior and entitled. For the grandiose narcissist, that's all there is to it. Those with grandiose narcissism do not struggle with demons of shame. They are the greatest, and they know it.

However, the vulnerable narcissist may start with a deep sense of shame. Their narcissism blooms in an attempt to keep that feeling of inferiority at bay by projecting their shame onto others. Other people are made to feel shameful so that the narcissistic person can remain superior.

When you understand gaslighting, isolation tactics, the ability to easily lie and deceive, love bombing, and other forms of manipulation, it makes it a bit easier to recognize these schemes and step away when they're happening to you. However, don't expect that knowledge to always protect you from abuse.

The narcissist knows your weaknesses and preys upon them. It may be when you are in public, or around your family or kids. You don't want to make a scene or start a fight. So, the manipulation continues.

TIP

Knowledge is powerful but doesn't cure the challenge of dealing with a narcissist.

Don't expect your partner to change

People often engage in imagining a better future. It's an adaptive strategy to motivate people to move forward in the act of obtaining goals. For example, you may study hard in school inspired by the thought of graduating with a degree that will improve your financial life. Or take a regular morning jog to improve your long-term mental and physical health.

Narcissists engage in projecting better futures as well, in what is known as *future faking*. Future faking involves promising positive outcomes, hopes, and dreams that are unlikely to materialize. For example, a narcissistic person may promise to stop being so demanding as soon as they get the promotion they are expecting. Or that their crabbiness will stop once the kids get older. *Or next year, the whole family will take a fabulous trip to Hawaii.*

Don't fall for future faking. The real, sad news is that narcissists rarely change — as in almost never. Your partner won't get better if the stock market goes up or when you finally lose those 20 pounds.

REMEMBER

Narcissists don't feel the need to change because they are grand, superior, entitled human beings. They believe if there are problems, it's because everyone else is somehow screwing up. Certainly not them.

Do an honest cost/benefit analysis

A cost/benefit analysis is one of my favorite tools for making any important decision. Usually, by taking a closer look at both sides, you can start to plan for the future or readjust your thinking about your current situation. A cost/benefit analysis is also a good strategy to help focus your attention on what's important and move ahead.

You can use this analysis to decide about a career choice or to help you decide what car to buy. Or you can use this strategy to help you decide whether you want to stay in a relationship with a narcissistic partner.

The following example of Autumn and Lincoln shows how a cost/benefit analysis helps Lincoln decide whether to stay with or leave his girlfriend.

Lincoln has been living with Autumn for about three years. Lincoln was initially overwhelmed by Autumn's outgoing personality, her good looks, and her enthusiasm for life. Autumn loved to party, dance, and drink. Lincoln entered her social world and had a lot of fun. They were both in college, and somehow, despite their partying, managed to get degrees.

That was three years ago. Now Lincoln feels ready to have a more stable life. Since graduating, he has started a good job at a financial services company, and he sees a promising future at that company. Autumn is keeping her job in retail for now, not really thinking about the future. She still wants to go out to clubs and fights with Lincoln when he tells her he has to work in the morning.

Lincoln has been struggling with the relationship for some time. He finds Autumn somewhat immature and superficial. Autumn doesn't seem to care about his success at work or his desire to move into adulthood.

Lincoln is talking over his problems with a work friend who suggests, "Lincoln, you know how we're trained to do cost/benefit analysis on business moves — why don't you do one on you and your girlfriend? You know getting it out of your head and onto paper sometimes clarifies things."

Lincoln takes his friend's suggestion. He realizes that he sort of wants to break up with Autumn. Here's what he comes up with.

Benefits	Costs
I could move on before the relationship. gets too serious.	I really enjoy going out with Autumn.
I'm pretty bored talking to her. She doesn't really have any interests in common with me.	I'd miss seeing some of her friends.
I could find a more mature partner.	We have good sex and I'd miss that.
I don't really love her enough to want a life with her.	She's a great dancer.
This year when I took off a month from drinking, she was not happy or supportive.	Most of the time she's in a good mood.

Benefits	Costs
When she gets angry, she gets mean and says horrible things to me. Then she doesn't speak to me for days.	It's going to be an ugly breakup. She won't take it well.
I think she cheats on me when she gets mad and doesn't talk to me.	
I deserve better. I'm not about partying anymore.	

Lincoln finishes his cost/benefit analysis and realizes he's been unsatisfied for a long time. Autumn is all about having a good time on her terms. She was a good match for him while he was in college. But now, he's ready to move on.

The cost/benefit strategy is simple and straightforward. You make two columns. Label the left column "benefits" and the right column "costs."

Take your time and consider each response. It's okay to put something down and change it later, but give yourself the freedom to open your mind to all possibilities.

I encourage you to use pen and paper for this exercise. If you are worried about privacy, simply tear it up and throw it away when you're finished.

Expand your relationships

Get out of the house and meet some new friends. This may be a perilous journey. Your narcissistic partner often finds these activities threatening and can become jealous. Remember that narcissists use isolation as a tactic to keep your focus turned to them. Resist the temptation to stay at home. Keep trying to find opportunities to be out and about with other people.

Spending time with friends allows you to be in low-stress situations. You can feel the weight of living with a narcissist lighten, at least for a short time.

Enliven your interests

In many cases, exercise works just as well as — and sometimes even better than — antidepressants or antianxiety medication. Take a yoga class or join a gym. Being with others is a bonus. Get out into nature; take a walk.

It may be time to take up a new hobby or begin taking classes at an adult education center. Volunteer. Helping others improves mood and can take your mind off of your own problems.

Consider individual therapy

You've probably spent considerable time thinking about your relationship problems. You may have had long conversations with friends or family. Those are good things to do. Others may have good perspectives that haven't occurred to you.

However, relationships with narcissists can do serious harm to your emotional well-being. It's a good idea to seek help from a professional mental health therapist who can assist you in restoring a sense of confidence in your own ability to make decisions.

Going to a therapist does not mean that you are crazy or mentally ill. Rather, it's a sign of strength. It takes courage and openness to be able to ask for help. Lots of perfectly healthy people get tangled up in situations that challenge their ability to cope.

WARNING

When you are in a relationship with a narcissist, you may feel very stressed out. The strain may lead you into abusing substances or developing eating problems. Don't blame yourself for these reactions, but please talk over any problematic use with your therapist.

Give up the dream

You entered this relationship dreaming of true love and hoping for happiness. The loss of the dream is like losing a loved one. You naturally feel grief. Just as when you lose someone you care about, you may go through many phases. At first, you try to deny the shortcomings of your relationship. Then you try everything you can think of to fix the relationship. You may fight and get angry; you rage against the unfairness of your situation.

Then come feelings of hopelessness and helplessness. You give up trying. But, given time and help, you may finally reach a point when you are able to understand what happened. Yes, with a bit of bitterness and regret, but eventually you can go beyond the pain, to a place of acceptance.

Chapter **6**

The Effects of Narcissistic Parenting

This is a chapter about love: love of self and love of children. By definition, narcissists believe themselves to be the center of the universe. They definitely love themselves. But think about a narcissistic parent: Is that parent capable of loving their children? I have no doubt that if anyone were to ask a parent who has narcissistic tendencies if they love their child, they would, of course, answer yes. But is it love or something else, like a need for admiration and attention?

The very qualities of a narcissist — including grandiosity, entitlement, lack of empathy, desire to exploit others, need to control others, arrogance, and constant seeking of admiration — interfere with good parenting. Considering the personality characteristics of narcissistic parents, growing up as the child of a narcissist is usually quite challenging.

This chapter describes the possible effects of narcissistic parenting on a child's development, from infancy through adulthood. The chapter delves into how narcissistic parents raise their children. It also offers hope and provides skills for coping with being the adult child of a narcissist.

Note: Narcissistic parenting can only be measured by recollections of children of narcissists, which is not really the best way to do research. At the same time, you couldn't really design a study that assigned infant A to a narcissistic parent and infant B to a non-narcissistic parent, and then follow their development over time. I'm quite positive that study would be unethical. So, we are left with these retrospective studies as well as a whole bunch of common sense and clinical experience to understand the effects of narcissism on children.

Taking a Look at Attachment Styles

A critical task of childhood is becoming attached to a caregiver. *Attachment style* refers to the way children relate to their caregivers. These styles begin in the early months and years of a child's life and often remain somewhat stable through adulthood.

Many factors influence how a child attaches to their caregiver such as the child's genetics, temperament, health, and the environment. Nevertheless, most research looks at how interactions between the primary caregiver and the child establish particular attachment styles.

Attachment starts during infancy and early childhood. During this period of development, babies and their caregivers have predictable interaction patterns. The following four attachment styles have been identified and studied for decades:

» **Secure attachment:** Those with secure attachment feel distress when separated from their caregivers but are easily soothed when their caregiver returns. Secure attachment occurs when the caregiver is consistently available and safe. Babies and their caregivers form a team of loving communication. Babies are touched and held; caregivers and babies make eye contact. When babies are distressed, caregivers respond with soothing voices and appropriate action (feeding, changing diapers, or snuggles).

» **Anxious attachment:** When separated from their caregivers, those with anxious (sometimes called ambivalent) attachment become very distressed. When the caregiver returns, they are not easily soothed and sometimes even show anger to their caregiver. Anxious attachment is linked to inconsistent early care. On some days, the caregiver may be warm and available, and at other times, caregivers are emotionally undependable. Babies cannot depend on getting their needs met.

>> **Avoidant attachment:** Those with avoidant attachment are less likely to become upset when separated from their caregivers, and pretty much don't care or get angry when the caregiver returns. Caregivers who reject or abandon their children are associated with avoidant attachment in children. Little two-way communication happens, and there is a lack of emotional bonding. Although these babies get fed, think of a propped bottle in a crib as the normal way of feeding.

>> **Disorganized attachment:** This style is one of inconsistencies. Sometimes the child is distressed, other times fearful, still other times avoidant. Babies depend on adults to care for them. When they associate the potential of danger with their caregiver, they become fearful and anxious. Disorganized attachment is usually related to caregiver mistreatment or abuse.

Why is attachment style so important? Securely attached infants develop into secure adults. They tend to have higher self-esteem, more resilience in the face of adversity, more academic success, and better relationships with others. They have good control over their emotions and are more optimistic.

Anxious, avoidant, and disorganized attachment are all insecure attachment styles. They suggest a high likelihood of disrupted parent/child relationships or abnormalities caused by events such as accidents, trauma, illness, unexpected separations, war, and/or genetic abnormalities.

Insecurely attached babies have more difficulties as they grow up. They tend to be needy, with low self-esteem. They lack good self-control and usually perform poorly in school. Insecurely attached adults may also struggle with relationships, and they don't hold up well when under stress.

TECHNICAL STUFF

Most children of narcissists do not end up with secure attachments. However, some children are genetically and temperamentally resilient and capable of withstanding a moderate degree of inconsistent or distant parenting and establish secure relationships. At the same time, in some families, the baby is taken care of by a caregiver who models a secure attachment style. The narcissistic parent is less involved in day-to-day caregiving and thereby exerts less influence.

TIP

You can, in effect, earn secure attachment as an adult, even if you had anxious, avoidant, or even disorganized attachments early on. Earned secure attachment comes to those who work through their early experiences and develop more self-awareness. Security can also come from a long-term relationship with a stable person who gives you validation and emotional support. Much of this work can be accomplished with the guidance of a professional mental health provider.

Considering How Narcissistic Parents Approach Their Child's Life Stages

Of all the characteristics of narcissism, lack of empathy is probably the most damaging to the child of a narcissistic parent. A parent who cannot take the perspective of a crying baby, demanding toddler, or surly teen is likely to respond to those challenges in ways that are dismissing, diminishing, or even cruel.

Some children of narcissists may be emotionally abandoned. Understandably, they're not capable of fulfilling their parents' constant need for attention, adoration, and special treatment. Other children become part of, or extensions of, their parents. As an extension, the child must give constant admiration and support to their narcissistic parent. This overly controlled child's purpose is to reward their parent with status. These kids must overperform so that their parents can bask in glory.

Sometimes narcissistic parents choose one child to be the favored or golden child. This child is given special treatment and escapes some of the narcissistic abuse. Another child in the family is labeled as the family scapegoat, being blamed for all that goes wrong. Whether a child is favored or not, narcissistic love is always conditional, never dependable, and easily withdrawn. In essence, it's a transactional relationship: "I will love you as long as you meet my needs."

REMEMBER

Bringing up a child requires effort on the part of the caregivers. Like a healthy plant that is watered, fertilized, and provided sunlight, children who are given proper care grow up emotionally healthy. Narcissistic parents are not always present to care for children. They are self-absorbed, unavailable, and entitled. It's no accident that the children of narcissists, like neglected plants, do not always grow up to be healthy adults.

Caring for babies: "What's in it for me?"

Anyone who has taken care of an infant knows how time consuming, exhausting, and frustrating it can be. Infants are demanding, and in the early stages, they don't do much to reciprocate. But if you are madly in love with your baby, eye contact, snuggling, and those early smiles are more than enough reward to sustain you during all the hard work.

When things go well between an infant and their caregiver, the baby becomes securely attached. That care includes being responsive to the infant's signals of discomfort and providing a soothing, safe environment. A narcissistic parent may not be equipped to put forth a steady stream of comfort and love. An entitled parent may resent the effort needed to adequately care for a baby. A baby is not able to give the narcissistic parent attention, gratitude, or praise.

THE STILL FACE EXPERIMENT AND NARCISSISM

Back in 1975, Edward Tronick, Ph.D., presented research about the effect of nonresponsive parenting on infants. The experiment involved having a mother interact with her baby for about three minutes. Then, during the experiment, the mother is told to make her face blank, devoid of emotion for two minutes.

The babies in these interactions frantically attempt to reengage their mother. They squirm and whine. Finally, they break down and begin to cry. You can see the original study by searching for "still face experiment." This study has been replicated with older children and with fathers. Children have a need for interaction with their caregivers.

What does this study have to do with narcissism? When a narcissist withdraws from interactions because of their own need, in effect giving their children the silent treatment, those children show considerable distress. A child's early attachments are likely to be insecure. This process begins during infancy and continues throughout a child's life with a narcissist.

Consider caregivers of babies who in effect replicate the still face by paying excessive attention to their phones while feeding and caring for their babies. Instead of a dance of looking and cooing at each other, the baby is faced with a "still face." I know caregivers are overwhelmed with responsibilities, but face to face interaction is critical to forming good bonds and healthy attachment styles.

Some narcissistic parents choose to have children to fulfill their own unrealized dreams. Thus, they may provide adequate care or get others to care for their infant. The child becomes something like the trophy partner to the narcissist, something to show off and take credit for.

WARNING

When care is inconsistent, attachment may be anxious or avoidant. In the worst case, if there is abuse or neglect, the child may develop a disorganized attachment.

Taking on toddlers: "Too much trouble!"

As babies grow, so do their abilities to get into trouble. A narcissistic mother or father can leave their crying baby in a crib for a long period of time. But when that baby becomes old enough to crawl out, life changes. Around the same time, toddlers learn how to manipulate their caregivers by crying for things other than food or a diaper change.

Toddlers' quickly growing language skills allow them to express their own opinion on what is happening around them. And they learn the most dangerous word of all, "no."

Narcissistic parents do not tolerate frustration very well. When toddlers start to express themselves, conflict begins. The narcissistic parent may lash out with rage, and the child may become submissive and afraid. Or the narcissistic parent may simply escape and let the child be, ignoring any misbehavior and giving the toddler freedom to never master self-control.

A securely attached toddler with an unusually resilient nature, or who has been taken care of by other effective caregivers, may be able to weather the narcissistic storms. However, those kids who are anxiously attached may become extremely worried and easily frightened. They are overly dependent and seek attention from adults. Those with disorganized or avoidant attachments can become withdrawn, with bursts of aggressive acting out.

Sending kids to school: "You're my best friend"

To make narcissists content, everything must revolve around them, and that includes their children. Children are typically seen as possessions to further glorify their narcissistic parents. If they are not seen as capable of doing that, they are often emotionally abandoned or abused.

Narcissistic parents may use their children to gain prestige, pushing them into activities that then reflect positively on the parents. When the child achieves something of note, the narcissist is rewarded. But when the child does not measure up, blame must be found. The parent may punish the child or someone else (such as a teacher or coach) for the failure.

One of the most damaging aspects of being a child of a narcissistic parent is sometimes called reverse parenting. Roles are reversed: Emotionally, the parent becomes the child, and the child becomes the parent. The narcissist demands that the child become responsible for comforting and taking care of the parent's emotional well-being.

Obviously, this role reversal can be confusing for children. When narcissists are upset by any frustration, they turn to their children to take charge. This impossible task leaves children feeling responsible for keeping everyone happy. At this stage, children are not mature enough to handle the demands and may become extremely anxious.

The following example of reverse parenting is quite common when a narcissist is going through a breakup.

> Zachary, one more time, is caught cheating on his wife, Zoe. Zoe discovers the truth when the woman he's having an affair with actually sends a text to her with details about the when and the where of their relationship. She's done (again) with his repeated affairs and vows to talk to an attorney (again).
>
> Zachary's 13-year-old daughter, Willow, witnesses this fight just as she has witnessed fights between her parents for as long as she can remember. Willow quickly retreats to her room. Later that evening, her dad asks her to take a walk with him. Fearful of saying no, she agrees.
>
> Zachary tells Willow how he and her mom have been having sexual problems for years. He explains to Willow that her mom just doesn't want to have as much sex as he needs, and that is why he's had to turn to other women to satisfy his extraordinary sexual desires. Willow, extremely uncomfortable, doesn't know how to respond. Her father puts his arms around her and says he just needs her to be understanding and on his side. Willow cringes in his grasp.
>
> Willow has had to deal with her parents' marital problems over the years. They each reach out to her and try to make her agree with one or the other's side. This puts Willow on edge, and she becomes hypersensitive to any emotion in her home. She tries to keep peace in the house by agreeing with both sides. Instead of dealing with her own issues of finding herself, learning, and developing relationships with others, she is consumed by her parents' problems. In the process, Willow loses something of herself.

Narcissistic parents often put their children into roles that they are too immature to deal with. Just as Willow's father did, they break the normal boundaries between parent and child. Selfishly, narcissistic needs come before their children's needs.

A possible healing experience for children of narcissists is school. For the first time in their lives, children in school experience a different reality. A warm and supportive teacher can help children transform from feeling worthless to finding authentic self-esteem. If children experience success in school, they have hope of escaping some of the worst effects of narcissistic abuse. Of course, if children with avoidant or disorganized attachment styles act out in school, their deep-seated feelings of worthlessness are only reinforced when they receive consequences from schoolmates or teachers.

Children also begin to develop friendships that can provide additional comfort and affection. They may observe interactions in their friends' families that make them more aware of what they are not getting at home. Sometimes, kids can develop relationships with other adults that give them that needed support.

Although those early attachment styles are still part of children's emotional functioning, these positive experiences outside the home can provide them with new skills and strategies, such as disengaging with their narcissistic parent, setting boundaries, and avoiding conflict. These new perspectives can help to protect them from narcissistic abuse.

Emerging adulthood: "Two can play that game!"

Adolescence is a time of developmentally normal narcissism. Do you remember how self-conscious you were as a teen? You worried about every possible blemish, stumble, or shortcoming, sure that the whole world was watching. Teens are almost completely self-absorbed.

They are at a stage where they shift their attachments from the family to friends. They struggle with changes in hormones and body. Many have insecurities and overconcerns about their body image.

They worry about who they are and what they will become. They may try out new identities, rebel, and experiment. Narcissistic self-absorption is a normal developmental stage of adolescence. Eventually, most teens grow out of this self-conscious stage.

However, this normal part of adolescence is particularly threatening to a narcissistic parent. The following characteristics of teens are especially challenging to narcissistic parents:

>> **Teens shift focus from family to friends.** Narcissistic parents desperately want and need to be the center of attention. They may even feel jealous of their kids' friends or try to establish their own friendship with their kids' friends.

>> **Teens begin to form their own identity.** Narcissistic parents want to consistently feel in control. When their children exert their independence, parents may respond with anger and criticism.

>> **Teens have strong, fluctuating emotions.** Narcissistic parents have little empathy for their children and may ignore them or get angry that they are trying to get attention. After all, attention focused on teens takes attention away from parents.

>> **Teens express opinions that conflict with their narcissistic parents.** Narcissists believe that they are right about everything. Teens having

different opinions from their parents is very normal, but it's not acceptable to narcissistic parents.

>> **Teens may start to realize that their narcissistic parents are entitled and begin to question and challenge them.** Teens may resist unreasonable demands on their time and attention. Narcissistic parents cannot tolerate this imagined rejection and often react with rage.

>> **Teens believe that they know more than their parents.** Expressing this belief threatens and enrages narcissists, who demand unquestioned approval and power.

The narcissistic parent uses the common tools of their trade on their teens. They may stop speaking to them, manipulate them, attempt to gaslight them, or sabotage their dreams. The narcissistic parent does not easily relinquish power. Their arrogance and sense of superiority can be impossible for a teenager to handle.

As teens become young adults, the damage of having a narcissistic parent follows them. They may lack confidence, feel unreasonably guilty, be hypersensitive to criticism, and struggle with identity. They may be at higher risk for substance abuse, eating disorders, or self-harm. Alternatively, some children of narcissists follow in the footsteps of their narcissistic parents, becoming budding entitled, grandiose copies of their parents. For more information about the outcomes of narcissistic parenting, see the section "Viewing Possible Outcomes of a Narcissistic Upbringing" later in this chapter.

Also, take a look at the section "Coping with the Fallout from Narcissistic Parents" for help in overcoming narcissistic abuse.

Focusing on Narcissistic Mothers

While gender roles have evolved and blended over time, there are still fragments of traditional stereotypes reflecting differing parenting behaviors of mothers and fathers. Parents of any gender taking on the mother role tend to be more tied to day-to-day caregiving. That special role has consequences when the mother is narcissistic.

Narcissistic mothers come in different flavors. The first type is the narcissist who is not able to share the spotlight with her little ones, so she discards and *emotionally abandons* them to someone else. Finding her children too needy, she pushes them away. The mother then looks for adoration and attention from others while her children fend for themselves.

A second type of narcissistic mother *emotionally swallows* her children so that they become parts of her. Emotionally swallowed children become enmeshed with their mothers. *Enmeshment* occurs when boundaries are unclear. The children must be able to give the mother additional ego-boosting material to continue to be accepted. This mother expects the mother/child relationship to be centered on her own needs. In a role reversal, she expects the child to assume responsibility for her own happiness. Thus, the child's ability to develop emotional independence is thwarted.

The third type of narcissistic mother vacillates between abandonment and enmeshment. The mother depends on the child for emotional support. When the child performs and increases the mother's status, the child is welcomed. However, when the child does not perform well, the child is abandoned.

Unfortunately, most narcissists lack empathy, warmth, and compassion, and their children end up victimized. However, since a narcissistic mother is "perfect," there is no acceptance of responsibility or blame. The invisible abuse children suffer usually has long-lasting effects.

Note: In this section and the ones that follow about mothers, daughters, fathers, and sons, I use traditional gender pronouns to ease reading clarity. This does not imply that other genders or identities are not equally valid or important.

Daughters: Walking a tightrope

Daughters of narcissistic mothers have to walk a perpetual tightrope. They must work to constantly please their mothers or face their fury. Narcissistic mothers push their daughters to succeed, but when they achieve success, the mothers take the credit. What's even more distressing is when mothers become jealous of their daughters' successes and shun or dismiss them. The mothers must always retain their superiority.

In the following example, narcissistic mother Judy unleashes her wrath on her daughter Sophie when Sophie doesn't live up to Judy's expectations.

> Sophie is a good swimmer who competes with a local club. Sophie's mother, Judy, attends all practices and swim meets. Judy makes sure that her daughter attends all the special skill-building sessions and every optional practice. Swimming consumes every morning, afternoon, and weekend.
>
> Sophie often comes in first place because of her intensive training. When that happens, she sees her mother beaming and talking with the other parents. But when she doesn't come in first, her mother turns to ice. And that is happening more and more often. Judy blames Sophie for not putting in enough effort and tries to make her eat more protein to help boost her endurance.

As she's gotten older, Sophie starts to lose interest in the sport. She'd like to have more time to spend with her friends. She's even thinking of trying out for the school play. Sophie is terrified of broaching the subject with her mother, but after each meet in which she doesn't win every race, her mother screams, puts her down, or simply stops speaking to her, obviously furious. It's getting to be too much for Sophie.

One afternoon, feeling discouraged after another lackluster performance, Sophie tells Judy, "I think I need a break from swimming. It's just not fun anymore."

Judy, beyond angry, grabs Sophie's arm. "Do you know how much I've sacrificed for you? How dare you disrespect me? I've put my life on hold for you, you ungrateful piece of trash. You don't deserve a mother like me."

The daughter of a narcissist is often groomed to be successful or attractive to others. This process involves the mother invading her daughter's privacy, autonomy, and boundaries. Again, the purpose of the grooming is to provide more adoration and attention to the mother. If the daughter does not measure up, the mother typically becomes vicious or abandoning.

As a result, a daughter may feel that love is conditional. If she is doing what pleases her mother, she feels loved or at least approved of. She becomes overly concerned about what her mother expects and doesn't develop a solid sense of who she is. These beliefs follow her into adulthood, leading her to always look to others for a sense of worthiness.

Sons: Serving as saviors

Sons, like daughters, also may be emotionally swallowed or abandoned by their mothers. A narcissistic mother may use her son to support her emotionally, demanding he become a companion and supply her with admiration. She may idealize her son, pushing him to serve as her savior. The son may become a favored companion to his mother; she makes him her best friend and confidant.

This favored status of the son can become dashed when the son does something to displease his mother. She can abandon him in an instant if his focus shifts to something outside of her sphere. If he expresses sadness or displeasure, her manipulations can turn vicious.

Ten-year-old Steven wakes up early on Christmas morning. He can't wait to see what he got, but he's also looking forward to giving his mother her gift. Steven earned money shoveling snow, and he's proud that he can finally pay for her present on his own. His parents are already up drinking coffee. Before opening his own presents, he takes his gift to his mother. "I paid for it myself, Mom," he says proudly.

She opens the box and inside finds a toaster oven. "Are you kidding? This is no present. I can't believe you would waste your money on an appliance. What do you think I am? Kitchen help? Women like jewelry or perfume."

His mother storms out of the room and slams her bedroom door. Steven begins to cry, his Christmas ruined. He doesn't know what he did wrong. His father steps outside to smoke, leaving Steven alone, sitting under the tree with his unopened presents.

Being the son of a narcissistic mother is confusing. Boys try to please unpleasable mothers who expect their sons to be able to read their minds and fulfill their every desire. Steven's mother wanted something more personal than a toaster oven, but how would a 10-year-old know that?

These boys who have enmeshed mothers may struggle with their own emerging independence as they become adolescents. Their mothers may become jealous of friends or romantic partners and attempt to sabotage normal relationships. The mother's constant state of neediness may make the son feel guilty and torn between his desire to keep his mother happy and his own need for autonomy.

Considering Narcissistic Fathers

A father role, like a mother role, involves a fluid, ever-changing set of expectations. However, historically, fathers have been less involved in child-rearing and more concerned with breadwinning. These stereotypes are far less typical in today's world, but the remnants of the traditional style can be found in some households.

A narcissistic father, like all narcissists, is self-absorbed, superior, and entitled. Like a narcissistic mother, he may simply be unavailable to his children, essentially leaving them for others to raise — but arrives in time to bask in their glory when they succeed.

The narcissistic father may be quite popular with other people. He can be a good storyteller, have fantastic ambitions, crave excitement, and enjoy lots of attention. But to his children, he's aloof and easily irritated. When he gets angry, either all hell breaks loose or he disappears. Cold, distant, and only approving when his children do something special to inflate his own ego, the narcissistic father offers little support.

At times, a narcissistic father can become overly involved with his children. He can control all of their activities, dominate their decision making, and take away all autonomy. These enmeshed fathers raise vulnerable, insecure, and anxious children.

Daughters: Riding an emotional roller coaster

Daughters of narcissistic fathers may experience confusing lives. Their fathers may be affectionate to them in public but dismissive in private. Daughters may also be used as surrogate partners. Fathers may cruelly act in subtly seductive ways to make their daughters pay attention to them, and then turn on them when they become too needy.

Many have rigid gender stereotypes, expecting their daughters to be quiet and submissive. They may be very critical of any physical flaws such as being even slightly overweight or not conforming to their impossible standards. Daughters may feel unworthy despite their achievements.

The following example of Daisy characterizes an overachieving daughter of a narcissistic father.

> Daisy, a junior in college, receives a letter inviting her to join Phi Beta Kappa, an honor given to students who take a variety of science and arts classes and have high grade point averages. She and her parents are invited to a celebration at the school. When she shows the invitation to her father, he says, "You can't possibly have gotten that; it must have been a mistake. But, anyway, it's not like you go to an Ivy League school. And the ceremony is in the middle of the day. I'm not going to miss work for that."
>
> The next day at work, her father tells all of his coworkers about his daughter's amazing achievement. By the end of the day, everyone in the office knows about Daisy's Phi Beta Kappa award. But when he returns home, nothing is mentioned about Phi Beta Kappa again. Daisy continues to do well in school but feels like she'll never measure up to her father's standards.

Daughters are important when they can be bragged about to others, but they're not allowed to become a bigger star than their narcissistic father.

Sons: Always competing, never measuring up

Narcissistic fathers easily slip into competition with their sons. They may scornfully reject sons that don't meet their expectations but feel jealous when they do meet their expectations. Sons often grow up believing that they will never be good enough.

Tomas won a regional bodybuilding championship in the category for those over 40. He posed for multiple pictures, his buff body almost naked, holding up his trophy. Recently divorced, he had no trouble getting into brief sexual relationships with both men and women. Tomas is self-centered, easily bored, and believes he's entitled to have fun. His marriage lasted 15 long, tumultuous years, and he's ready for some action.

Unfortunately, Tomas has a son, Logan, who misses his dad. Logan is a thin, lanky teen who has no interest in bodybuilding. Tomas encourages Logan to bulk up but doesn't offer to take him to the gym. His dad criticizes his physique, his lack of drive, and his laziness. When Logan attempts to defend himself, his father loudly lectures him on all of his faults. Once launched, Tomas shifts to blaming his ex-wife for all of Logan's deficiencies. He becomes more and more enraged, throws Logan against the wall, and declares, "You're no son of mine."

This rage was all because Logan failed to pump up Tomas's already buffed-up ego. Logan, frightened, sad, and scarred, wants to go back to his mom's.

Some sons work hard in order to measure up, but never receive praise or recognition for their efforts. Others give up in despair. Still others model their fathers and become narcissists themselves. What sons miss out on is a sense of security, love, and worth. They may be lucky enough to have another parent or other important person in their lives to help limit the effects of their father's narcissism, but the loss is never really erased.

Viewing Possible Outcomes of a Narcissistic Upbringing

Adult children of narcissists take several different paths. These diverging paths may be because of genetic factors, the presence or absence of a normal parent or understanding adult, empathetic friends, or an effective therapist. However, some characteristics are particularly common.

Even after reaching adulthood, the child of the narcissist is often expected to be under the influence of the parent. They are often called on to be emotionally available, to sacrifice their needs, and to stand ready at the beck and call of their still demanding, entitled parents.

REMEMBER

Some kids are exceptionally resilient even while growing up with a narcissistic parent. Somehow, they manage to grow up to be happy, well-adjusted adults. However, many other children of narcissists struggle with various emotional patterns or problems.

Putting others first: Pleasers

Adult children of narcissists have been brought up in a minefield of emotional abuse. During childhood, they become skillful at dodging being blasted by anticipating their demanding narcissistic parent's needs. As adults, they maintain that habit by looking for ways to make others happy.

People pleasers cater to others. They always send birthday cards, bring food for the break room, or visit others in the hospital. They find it hard to say no. People pleasers want to avoid conflict and will agree with anyone to keep the peace. They may apologize for something that wasn't even their fault.

They are overly sensitive and on the lookout for other people's emotions. They may be desperate to cheer people up or calm people down. They feel responsible for other's negative feelings even if they are not involved in the situation that caused those feelings. They worry about others and not about themselves.

Pleasers are at risk for getting involved in abusive relationships. Because they grew up learning that their needs come after those of their narcissistic parents, they may find themselves repeating the pattern with an abusive partner.

Pleasers don't ask for help or support when they need it, but they spend their time taking care of others. People pleasers hope to divert attention from their own sense of inadequacy and feel some sense of control. By helping others, they attempt to make up for their own deprivation in childhood.

Suffering self-doubt: Never good enough

Because completely satisfying a narcissistic parent is impossible, many children of narcissists grow up thinking that they are somehow inherently flawed. Brought up to believe they're defective and unworthy, this feeling spills over into their present lives.

As adults, they may have difficulty achieving what they are capable of because they doubt their own abilities. They may underachieve in school or at work. They may allow others to take advantage of their insecurities. They sometimes give up potential positive experiences because of that deep sense of unworthiness. They don't take on new opportunities because they don't believe they are capable enough. They avoid opportunities out of fear of failure.

Some children of narcissists manage to achieve success. However, because they were trained early on that moving the spotlight off of their narcissistic parent was dangerous, they may downplay their own accomplishments. Instead of feeling pride, they become fearful. They distrust their achievements and often consider themselves to be frauds. Despite external praise, they consistently judge themselves and their performance to be inadequate.

Feeling anxious and fearing abandonment

Adult children of narcissists that endured an anxious attachment may be extremely vulnerable and worried about abandonment (see the earlier section "Taking a Look at Attachment Styles" for more information about attachment). During childhood, they lived under constant threat of emotional outbursts and became hypervigilant to any potential danger.

Because they learned to be afraid of speaking up in their homes, they may avoid expressing themselves as adults. They feel on edge and fearful of any conflict. They yearn for relationships that can overcome their own insecurities. They look to others for safety.

But when they are in a relationship, they constantly fear abandonment and become overly dependent and clingy. They may expect to be hurt or cheated on and constantly nag their partners about their activities. They may search for clues of disloyalty, overstepping boundaries. This desperate search for stability has an undercurrent of hostility. Their dependency may, after some time, drive away their partners.

Thus, their original fear — that of abandonment — is once again realized. These anxious adults blame themselves for this failure and reinforce their anxiety.

Turning disagreeable and avoidant

The adult children of narcissists who have avoidant or disorganized attachment styles have learned that no one is to be trusted. After all, when they had emotional needs during childhood, they were ignored or rejected by their caregiver.

They see the world as a cruel place, and they react by refusing to get close to others. When avoidance does not work, they are disagreeable and easily angered. They tend to be defiant and aggressively defend against any real or imagined criticism.

These disagreeable adult children believe that others are out to get them. They are overly suspicious of others and tend to view the world cynically.

They may engage in manipulation, charm, and cheating to get what they want. These avoidant adults think nothing of using others because they really don't care about anyone except themselves. However, under that veneer is a wounded child, who has had insufficient love.

Following a parent's lead: Learned narcissism

Some adult children of narcissists take on the characteristics of their narcissistic parent. Perhaps as a coping mechanism to thwart the trauma of being rejected and dismissed by the narcissistic parent, these children are able to assume the same disdain for others that their parents had for them. Thus, they become grandiose, entitled, and self-absorbed.

Some research has suggested that certain traits of narcissism can be inherited. But possibly this learned form of narcissism is a more likely reason for the passing on of narcissism from one generation to the next.

These grown-up children may be somewhat more vulnerable narcissists who are prickly, easily insulted, and viciously revengeful. However, these vulnerabilities are strong defenses against attacks on their overly inflated yet highly fragile egos. They retain their superior, entitled self-views but remain on vigilant guard. Meanwhile, they use others as objects designed to surround them with adoration.

Other children of narcissists seem to act more like the grandiose narcissist. They have no worries about potential attacks on their egos because they are confident in their greatness, uniqueness, and specialness. They lack empathy and manipulate others to get what they please. Even if they experience a significant failure, they dismiss it by blaming others. See Chapter 2 for more information about vulnerable and grandiose narcissists.

Coping with the Fallout from Narcissistic Parents

A first step in coping with a narcissistic parent is educating yourself about the many facets of narcissism. It's hard to fight an invisible enemy, so take some time to look at how narcissism works and how it impacted your childhood. Spend time thinking about these issues.

WARNING

Looking back at childhood trauma may cause you to have strong emotions. If you feel overwhelmed, or if this task seems too difficult, consider seeing a mental health professional to help you explore these memories and feelings and how to deal with them.

Consider the following questions and write down your answers:

>> What did your parent do that made you believe them to be narcissistic?

>> Was your parent an overt, grandiose narcissist — entitled, flashy, arrogant, manipulative, and demanding attention and approval?

>> Was your parent more like a covert, vulnerable narcissist — self-absorbed, needing attention, hypersensitive to criticism but quietly grandiose?

>> On the other hand, like many narcissists, did your parent have characteristics of both types?

>> How was narcissism played out in your family?

>> How did interactions go between your parents and the children and among the children?

>> Were there favorites among the children?

>> Has a brother or sister of yours taken on any narcissistic tendencies?

>> How was conflict in the family handled? Was there yelling, gaslighting, silent treatment, overreactions to minor incidents, or other abuse?

>> What are some of the memories you have of being a child or teen interacting with your narcissistic parent?

>> Is the parental narcissistic abuse continuing today? If so, how do you deal with it?

>> Do you feel loved and appreciated by your parents today?

>> Do you believe that you have taken on some of your parent's narcissistic tendencies? Which ones?

>> How are you emotionally coping today?

After considering these questions, decide what you want to do looking forward. Your narcissistic parent and their demands for power, control, attention, and total agreement may have felt traumatic while growing up. How do they feel to you now, as an adult?

Some adults of narcissistic parents remain enmeshed in their parents' self-absorbed world, still catering to their every demand. A few try to change their narcissistic parents but rarely succeed. Others cut off all contact. Some attempt to maintain brief, superficial contact. Any way you decide to go, it's a difficult world to navigate.

Setting boundaries

A boundary is a dividing line. It can be physical, such as a fence, or the line that designates different states or countries. You have a boundary demarking your own home. You may welcome your family or even a few close friends to walk through your front door without knocking, but if a stranger arrives, opens the door, and steps inside, you'd consider calling 911 and getting out your bear spray. Boundaries can also be emotional lines that limit what behaviors are acceptable.

People with narcissistic personalities tend to step over other people's boundaries without a thought. Their entitlement may allow them to walk over people's beliefs of fairness. Or their arrogance can hurt other's feelings.

When dealing with parents with narcissism, it's critical for adult children to set firm boundaries to protect themselves from further emotional abuse. The following guidelines help you establish your own boundaries:

>> **Learn to say yes or no and mean it.** If your narcissistic parent asks you to do something, decide whether it's something that will be too burdensome or emotionally dangerous. If it is, say no. Don't let yourself be cajoled into changing your mind. If, on the other hand, the favor is easily incorporated into your life and you want to do it, say yes. Whatever your response is, stick to it. Don't back down.

>> **Don't let yourself get trapped into arguing.** You can never win an argument with a narcissist. They will lie, gaslight, or belittle you. It's best to stay calm and carry on. Agree to disagree. Limit the potential disagreement to a few sentences and no more. Stop.

>> **Don't let narcissistic rage threaten your boundaries.** Your narcissistic parent may display unpleasant emotions in an attempt to blackmail you into doing their bidding. Plan your escape route ahead of time.

>> **You are now an adult and responsible for taking care of yourself.** Understand that your emotions are something to be protected. Do not let your narcissistic parent continue to abuse you. Walk away.

TIP

Setting limits and boundaries can be painfully difficult, especially for someone with a history of trauma or abuse. If you find yourself unable to stick with your plan, consider seeing a mental health professional.

There are many more boundaries and strategies you may need to create with your narcissistic parent. Be as clear as you can when enforcing your boundaries. Explain the boundary and what the consequence will be if it is breached.

The following example illustrates this process.

> Eddie's mother is jealous of Margo, Eddie's beautiful girlfriend. His mother, like many narcissists, doesn't like attention being drawn away from herself. She finds devious ways to put down Margo. She deliberately makes Margo feel uncomfortable whenever she can.
>
> Eddie confronts his mother, who, of course, denies that she is doing anything wrong. She uses gaslighting to suggest that Eddie and Margo must be imagining something. Eddie knows all about this trick and simply states, "If you want to continue seeing us, then you will have to treat Margo with respect. If you do not, there will be no arguing or discussing. Margo and I will leave. We may try to get together after a few months, but if it happens again, then we won't be seeing you."

This may not go well, but discipline can sometimes be a learning experience for narcissists. And if it doesn't go well, you are protecting yourself from more narcissistic abuse.

Achieving healthy, resilient outcomes

The goal of good parenting is to love, nurture, and teach children to become well-functioning adults. Parents love their children so that they can eventually leave them. A good enough parent is not perfect, nor do they need to be. They are able to recognize their parenting mistakes are not catastrophes and that parents can always get back on track.

The goal of good-enough parenting does not often happen smoothly in homes with a narcissistic parent. The narcissistic parent generally has ambivalent feelings about the emancipation of their adult child. The narcissistic parent may continue to demand attention and adoration, and as always, their needs must come first.

Therefore, the adult child may struggle with leaving the nest. Staying stuck under the spell of a narcissistic parent leads to more abuse and pain.

TIP

The hurt of narcissistic abuse will always be with you. You can't erase intense emotional experiences. Sit with that truth. Acknowledge the pain.

Thus, understand that your parent will not change, and you cannot change your history. However, you do not have to remain a prisoner of abuse. You can acknowledge and accept the reality of what happened. You can move on, knowing the pain, but moving forward in your life.

One silver lining of growing up with a narcissistic parent is the possibility of changing the pattern in your own life. Your narcissistic upbringing provides you a guide for how not to reproduce that dysfunctional template with your own children.

Giving up the dream

Having reached the point of understanding and accepting what you went through, you may experience deep sadness for all that you lost. Everyone wants to have a happy childhood, in which families gather around dinner tables. In that idealistic family, parents play with their children, and people laugh and love.

That idyllic scene of family life was probably not yours if you grew up in a family with a narcissistic parent. It's appropriate for you to grieve your loss. So, let yourself mourn the loss of what should have been.

However, know that you are not alone. Many have suffered as you have. And they have lived. Dust yourself off, decide what you want out of life, and discover how to fly on your own.

Chapter **7**

Close Encounters with Narcissists

N arcissists are everywhere — at home, in the neighborhood, and at work. You may have a narcissistic neighbor that makes you feel unsafe in your own home. You may be friends with a narcissist who continually takes advantage of you. You may work with a narcissist who engages in deception and gaslighting. Or you may have a narcissistic boss who makes your life miserable.

This chapter is about the relationships you have with narcissists in the community. Narcissists among us share the same characteristics as those you encounter in close relationships. They feel entitled, superior, lack empathy, and seek control over others. When threatened, they tend to react with rage. At times, these encounters escalate and lead to dangerous situations.

Having to "Live with" Narcissistic Neighbors

If you have a neighborhood social media site, you probably see frequent posts from complaining neighbors. Their grievances may be perfectly legitimate, such as too much noise, boundary violations, dangerous driving, off-leash dogs, or grossly overgrown weeds.

However, in the hands of a narcissistic neighbor, even everyday irritations can fuel narcissistic rage. A narcissistic neighbor may take inconsequential grievances, such as garbage can placement or grass length, greatly exaggerate them, and then make extensive written complaints to social media, the neighborhood association, and planning and zoning committees, or they may even call police.

Watching for warning signs

Obviously, you can't diagnose your neighbor with narcissism. However, some of the warning signs include

>> Excessive and consistent anger over small issues

>> Constant complaining

>> Exerting control over neighborhood activities

>> Feeling entitled to special privileges and attention

>> Frequent harassment of neighbors

>> Feelings of superiority and being a know-it-all

The following example of Matthew, a narcissist, and his neighbor Nick illustrates the point.

Matthew believes that he is entitled to have a parking spot in front of his house. Matthew has a garage and driveway but likes to keep that spot available in case he has a visitor. It's his house, so he feels he should have that spot.

However, Matthew lives on a public street with no parking restrictions. His neighbor Nick's family has three drivers and three cars. They occasionally park in front of Matthew's house when there are no other spaces available. When Matthew recognizes one of Nick's cars pulling into the spot in front of his house, he goes out and yells at Nick's son, saying that he can't park there. Nick's son says okay and parks around the block.

Nick tells his son that he can park wherever he wants on the street, including in front of Matthew's house, because there are no laws restricting access to street parking. Next time, Nick deliberately parks in front of Matthew's house. The following morning Nick gets to his car and notices a long, narrow scrape on the passenger side of his car. He goes to Matthew's house, and Matthew says that he knows nothing about the scrape. He reminds Nick that it's his parking spot, and Nick starts to argue about public parking. Matthew gets loud and threatens legal action.

Nick is confused by his neighbor's behavior. He knows it's public parking. The next time one of Nick's family members parks in that spot, they later find excrement smeared across the front windshield.

Matthew is showing significant warning signs for being a narcissist: He feels entitled to special treatment, has no empathy, and becomes enraged over his lack of control over the public street in front of his house. Neighbors such as Matthew can wreak havoc on those living in the area. Neighborhood narcissists sometimes escalate into violent rages, affecting the safety and mental health of their neighbors.

When you live right next door

Although narcissistic neighbors may make living nearby uncomfortable, when a close-by neighbor targets you, watch out. A next-door neighbor can truly make your life at home virtually unbearable.

Usually, narcissistic neighbors, like other narcissists, can be initially charming and likable. Small events may happen that seem insignificant, until the abuse grows. The following example reflects that pattern.

Anna and her family buy a home in a neighborhood with large lots. Most people have small backyard courtyards and leave the rest of the lot natural. On moving day, they're welcomed by friendly folks, including their next-door neighbor, Oscar.

Anna hires a landscape maintenance crew to clean up the weeds on the lot surrounding their home. One of the crew members knocks on the door and tells her that her neighbor (Oscar) is very angry because they accidentally pulled some weeds on his property.

Later that afternoon, Oscar stops by and tells Anna to keep her workers off his property. Anna apologizes and invites Oscar in for a cup of tea. Oscar brusquely leaves without acknowledging Anna's invitation.

In the first year of living in their home, Anna and her family put in a fountain and several bird feeders around the property. One day when she is working on her garden, she notices Oscar on his roof, putting up spikes to keep the birds off. He then starts swearing, very loudly, about people feeding birds and bringing more of them to the neighborhood. He is waving his hands about his head yelling at the birds to "stay the f*** away from my house."

Anna works hard to avoid Oscar after that incident but remains cordial and waves to him when they cross paths. The next summer, she adopts a rescue dog. The dog barks a lot, and Anna has a trainer come to work with her for several months.

Over time, Anna is able to walk the dog in the neighborhood without too much trouble. The dog lunges and barks at a few dogs while on the leash, but for the most part, behaves.

One day when she's out walking, she passes by Oscar with a dog he has apparently just adopted. Oscar's dog barks at Anna's dog, who returns the bark. Oscar launches into a verbal assault on Anna and her dog. Stunned at his vulgarity and anger, Anna walks away.

From that point on, Anna tries to completely avoid Oscar when she walks the dog. However, she inadvertently runs into him one day. Oscar carries a 6-foot-long broomstick and starts swinging it high in the air as she walks by on the other side of the street. He stirs up Anna's dog, who starts pulling the leash and barking. Oscar mutters obscenities under his breath.

Anna, frightened by the incident, asks another neighbor about Oscar's behavior. The neighbor recalls an incident in which Oscar sat in his drive with a rifle, pointing it at anyone driving by that he thought might be speeding. The police were called and talked to Oscar, who told them he was out cleaning his gun and they had no right to tell him what to do on his own property.

Oscar is likely a malignant narcissist. He has no empathy and feels superior to others. His rights are never to be questioned, and he uses intimidation to get his point across. Anna should be careful in her interactions with Oscar. He obviously has an aggressive streak. (See Chapters 2 and 11 for more information about malignant narcissism.)

Handling challenges

If your neighbor is a narcissist, use your knowledge of narcissism to survive. First, remember that a narcissistic person always wants attention. Try to ignore and stay away from them the best you can, but when that's impossible, the following tips should be considered:

>> **Put a Mona Lisa smile on your face.** You can do it. Pretend to be friendly and always be polite in order to minimize triggering their narcissistic antics. You don't need to allow them to step on you, but stay calm when assertiveness is called for. Narcissists usually crave drama, so don't give it to them.

>> **Recognize the narcissist and don't take it personally.** This goes along with being cordial. It's easier to stay cool when you know that the narcissistic person you are dealing with probably treats everyone the same way.

>> **Never confide personal information.** Narcissists can act very friendly and ask lots of personal questions, seemingly concerned. Be wary — they're likely to use that information against you. Be cautious about your personal privacy.

>> **Document all events.** Hopefully, you won't need those notes, but you can't tell how far the narcissistic neighbor might go. Put a couple of notes in your calendar so that if things escalate to the point of legal involvement, you'll have records of previous incidents.

>> **Evaluate your home security.** It's a sad commentary on our society, but more and more people are turning to security cameras as an inexpensive way to keep track of what is going on around their home. Security doors allow you to answer your door without letting someone in. In addition, you may need to beef up your home alarm system.

>> **Stop all contact and communication.** This is a step up from ignoring the offender. You may have to send a text, letter, or email telling your neighbor, in polite language, that you do not want to have any more communication. Don't go into lengthy explanations. Then sign your note with something positive like, "wishing you well." Keep that document (or a copy of it).

>> **Report significant threats or illegal actions.** Hopefully, it won't come to this, but neighbor conflicts have escalated into destruction of property, abuse of pets, physical threats, assaults, and infrequently, even murder. File a restraining order. Even if there is no police action, at least you have documented the conflict.

Figuring Out Your Friend Is a Narcissist

Friends are chosen people with whom you share your interests, passions, achievements, disappointments, and inner insecurities. You should be totally comfortable with a true friend. You may have work friends, neighbor friends, acquaintance friends, and especially close friends.

Being authentic and honest makes close friendships blossom. Close, deep friendships involve give and take, acceptance, and trust. These friendships remain strong without expectations or work. They remain constant over time. Deep friendships can last a lifetime and be a source of great security and support.

When you were a child, you probably chose your friends from a limited source, those you played with in your neighborhood or your classmates. Your best friend in elementary school may remain your best friend forever, but your paths have likely diverged.

Adults have more challenges with establishing close friendships. With work and family responsibilities, it's sometimes difficult to find the time to find compatible friends. Friendships among adults take time to form, and trust builds slowly.

Along the way of building adult friendships, there may be some attempts that don't work out. Because many adults are open to new friendships, it's natural that some attempts will result in getting involved with a narcissist.

Watching for warning signs

Narcissistic friends may fly under the radar in the beginning. They come across as fun, interesting, and entertaining. Their stories amuse you, their extensive connections in the community impress you, and their initial generosity moves you. You may quickly feel close and engaged.

REMEMBER

Narcissism lies on a continuum. There are some people who have a few narcissistic traits and can be "good enough" friends. You understand and forgive them. Their positive qualities balance out their negative ones. However, the more narcissistic an individual is, the more likely they are to quickly become a toxic friend.

The level of intimacy between friends is less intense than that of parents and children or romantic partners; therefore, signs of narcissism can often be ignored or easily forgiven between friends. It's not that important when a friend forgets an important day in your life or your birthday. Narcissism may sneak up in small doses that over time build into toxic overdoses. Some signs that you may be in a relationship with a narcissistic friend include the following:

>> **Conversations are one-sided.** Your friend may gossip about others, tell great stories, and fish for praise and attention. Interactions are all about the narcissist. Skilled narcissists will allow you a bit of attention so that they can move on to what counts, their own agenda.

>> **Boundaries are pushed.** You may schedule something with your friend, but if something better comes along, they will cancel at the last moment.

>> **They use or exploit your relationship.** Narcissists like to hang out with important people. They may use your connections to others or your skills without reciprocating. Reciprocity is a foreign concept to most narcissists.

>> **They expect more from the friendship than you can reasonably give.** Narcissists view people as objects that fulfill their needs. As friends, they may expect you to do unreasonable chores for them, such as watch their children for long periods of time, loan them money, or drive them around when they know you're working.

>> **They may promise to help you out or listen but may instead use you for gossip purposes.** Narcissists like to have details about people so that they can use that information later or amuse others with great gossip.

>> **They may stop the friendship when they're done using you.** If you are perceived as having little value to the narcissist, they will discard you.

Staying safe

Although the damage of having a narcissistic friend is usually not as devastating as having an intimate relationship with a narcissist, the friendship can cause pain. It's easy to fall under the spell of a narcissist, but more difficult to disengage. Often people who begin friendships with narcissists are confused by the treatment they receive. Those who befriend narcissists may give them multiple chances and gentle nudges that their behavior is unacceptable.

The easiest way to end a relationship with a narcissistic friend is to slowly disengage from them. Push out lunches, forget to return texts, hope that they get the message.

However, sometimes it's necessary to confront your narcissistic friend. Be direct. Tell them how much you value the friendship but that some parts of the relationship aren't working for you. Unfortunately, you can expect anger and possibly retribution. The former friend may gossip about you, lie about you, and even hold grudges forever.

WARNING

Narcissists don't like to be rejected. After you end a relationship with a narcissistic friend, that narcissist may use the same techniques that intimate partners use to reengage (see Chapter 9 for more info). They may apologize or offer flattery to entice you to reconnect. If you believe them and attempt to reconcile, they may cruelly reject you to retain their own sense of power and to extract revenge.

Working Alongside a Narcissist

When you start a new job, a narcissist may be the first one to greet you. In fact, they may be overly friendly and generous in order to secure your support. Their friendly manner may mask a desire to size you up and see if you might be useful to them. In the early weeks, you may have no idea that you are working with a narcissistic person.

However, as time goes on, you're likely to recognize the signs.

Watching for warning signs

Narcissists in the workplace typically

>> Seek attention and admiration

>> Exaggerate their own achievements

- » Think they're better than others
- » Believe that they deserve special treatment
- » Feel jealous when others succeed
- » Monopolize meetings and conversations
- » Bend the rules to get what they want
- » Lack empathy

Making it work at work

The best way to deal with a narcissist at work is benign neglect. Be polite. Look interested in what they have to say, give brief one- or two-word responses, and nod your head. Stay away when you can. Be very busy with your own work product, and don't openly reject a narcissistic worker if you can avoid it.

If you want a narcissist to do something at work, try to maneuver a way to ask questions so that they can come up with the idea themselves. Ask them for advice about something they believe they're an expert on, then praise them for their great minds. Narcissists want to succeed at work and get positive attention; take advantage of that.

Avoiding gaslighting and gossip

Gaslighting at work is a technique used by a narcissist to exert power and control by undermining the confidence of targeted coworkers. Gaslighting narcissists make people question their own sense of reality in the workplace.

The narcissistic coworker loves to get information that may be good fuel for gossip or to extract revenge. They may lie, manipulate others, exaggerate, or scapegoat. Typical examples of gaslighting at work include

- » Spreading false rumors about the incompetence of a colleague
- » Taking credit for other people's work products
- » Forming cliques that exclude some coworkers
- » Acting entitled, such as taking long lunches and then making lame excuses
- » Blaming others for their own bad performance

They may make negative remarks and then deny having said them, pretending to not recall what was said, saying someone else must have said that, or saying they were only joking.

REMEMBER

When dealing with a narcissistic coworker, never share personal details. Refrain from gossiping or complaining about your coworkers. The narcissist will use what you say to undermine you.

Dealing with any fallout

If you have had problems at work because your colleague is a narcissist, there are steps to take to decrease your risks. You may not need to use all of the following tips; feel free to pick and choose.

>> **Document any violations of company policy. Include dates, times, and details.** In addition, document any uncomfortable encounters such as insults, infringement of personal boundaries, or personally unethical behaviors. Even if you are unsure about the implications of a given incident, document it. Sometimes it's the pattern of events over time, as opposed to any specific incident, that gives significance to narcissistic misbehavior. Keep documentation private and secure.

>> **Try not to be in a position in which you have to criticize or overtly reject a narcissistic coworker.** If you do have to give negative feedback, try to give it gently by emphasizing their positive contributions to the project. However, remember they do not take even mildly given correction easily and may react with rage or revenge.

>> **Set clear boundaries and stick to them.** Stay assertive and calm. Walk away from verbal attacks and consider reporting abusive behavior to your boss or human resources, but don't expect counseling to create the changes you'd hope for. At the same time, you deserve to be respected at work.

>> **Don't take the narcissist's attempts to get under your skin personally.** This is all about them, not you. They are looking for validation, power, and control. If they don't get what they want from you, with any luck, they'll try someone else.

>> **If you can't find a way to negotiate a workable solution through mediation, working with your boss, or consulting human resources, strongly consider other job opportunities.** Long-term work stress is related to problems such as depression, anxiety, and/or substance abuse.

RECOGNIZING THE RAMIFICATIONS OF LETTING NARCISSISTS LEAD

There has been much interest in leadership roles in large companies. Many attempts have been made to determine whether these larger-than-life personalities, such as those seen in many of the big tech companies, lead to bigger profits for shareholders, as well as the impact on the work environment. Two studies are of interest.

One study looked at the relationship between employee stress, satisfaction, and job turnover. It found that narcissistic bosses had no effect on productivity. However, the employees expressed greater stress, less satisfaction, and were often thinking about leaving their workplaces and finding new employment. Turnover of employees is costly for businesses.

Another large study looked at the role of narcissistic CEOs on various outcomes such as stock price performance. It found that, overall, narcissistic CEOs performed more poorly than their humbler colleagues on stock performance. Relative to the S&P 500 (Standard and Poor index), they performed 12 percent lower than the index.

Reporting to a Narcissistic Boss

Narcissists are often found in the corner office. They have an ability to inspire and motivate others with their flair and inflated ideas. Narcissists communicate their visions and make positive impressions on others. They are born self-promoters.

REMEMBER

Research indeed indicates that a significant number of people with narcissistic traits end up in leadership roles. Remember, narcissists, especially in the beginning, present themselves as charming, charismatic, friendly, self-confident people.

If you find yourself working for someone who acts superior to others, feels entitled to special treatment, searches for admiration, brags about achievements, and blames others for losses, you may be working for a narcissistic boss. The warning signs are similar to those seen in narcissistic coworkers (see the preceding section). Remember, the trait of narcissism varies from slightly narcissistic to pathologically narcissistic.

Leaders with a few mild narcissistic traits may make excellent leaders. However, those with a wider variety of more intense traits are likely to create a toxic workplace. Depending on your boss's level of narcissism, you may or may not be able to emotionally survive the working environment.

Determining what type of narcissist you're working for

Chapter 2 describes four types of narcissists: grandiose, vulnerable, malignant, and mixed. When these types are applied to a boss, here's what you can expect to see:

>> **Grandiose:** This type of boss tends to be loud, demanding, and domineering. They want constant control and insist on getting attention and unwavering loyalty. When success happens, it's all attributed to their own hard work or brilliance; however, failure becomes someone else's fault. They lack empathy.

>> **Vulnerable:** This boss may at first present as demurring and insecure. At the same time, they show arrogance and conceit. Their self-esteem is quite fragile, and they overreact to criticism or failures. They also express their narcissism by acting holier than thou or morally superior.

>> **Malignant:** Beware of a boss with malignant narcissistic traits. Entitled and superior, they delight in cheating or abusing their staff. They see others as objects to use and discard. They also have fragile self-esteem and react to perceived slights or criticism with fury.

>> **Mixed:** A narcissistic boss with mixed symptoms needs to be at the center of attention. When things go badly, their egos are threatened and they become angry at staff, never assuming responsibility. Their behaviors are less predictable, and they may go from flattery and playing favorites to scorn and the silent treatment in a single day.

Remaining vigilant and minimizing the damage

If you find yourself working for a narcissist, here are some strategies you can implement to help protect yourself from abuse or harassment. Your boss can't be trusted to play fairly.

>> **Don't take your boss's behavior personally.** Narcissistic bosses only care about themselves. They want nothing from you except applause (and yes, you should humor them; see the following section, "Staying sane"). You may be unfairly blamed and on the receiving end of angry outbursts. And forget about being appreciated for your competence. It's not about you; this is the way of narcissism. Ignore and carry on when the behavior is not too toxic.

»» Document what you do every day. Keep a file on what you do every day. I know this sounds tedious, but you need a record of your worth if conflict occurs. Documenting should become a daily task that you do at the end of each day. Scribble notes throughout the day to help you remember. So, if or when your boss comes in and asks why it took you so long to complete something, you can pull out your file and respond.

»» Stay out of office politics. Who doesn't love a bit of office gossip or intrigue? Stay away from the water cooler. Don't post anything negative about your boss on internal or external message boards or social media. Remember, narcissists can be aggressive and vindictive. Gossip can be traded in a toxic work environment for power and control. Your narcissistic boss is gathering information for future confrontations. The boss may have a mole collecting potential dirt. Smile and walk away from those types of conversations.

»» Document boundary violations. Narcissistic bosses may expect that all staff work the long hours they work, take work home on weekends, or be available in an instant for text requests. Establish your boundaries and stick to them. In addition, document harassment, cruelty, ethical violations, or excessive expectations. What you do with this information depends on many factors, such as whether your boss has a boss and whether your workplace has a well-functioning human resources department. Nevertheless, you may use this document to help you make decisions about staying or ultimately leaving your situation.

»» Stay focused on work. Some work environments encourage cooperation and office friendships. If you have a narcissistic boss, I suggest you keep a low profile. Stay focused on your work and stay out of possibly damaging affiliations with others. Everything you say can and will be used against you. Try networking within the organization to get on a project with different leaders, so others, including the boss's boss, can judge your work. Find your friends outside of work.

»» Avoid conflict. Most narcissists crave excitement. Nothing is more fun than watching a fight. Don't engage in conflict, either with coworkers or especially your boss. In the end you will lose, even if your point of view is correct. This is not the place to win battles. Put your ego on the shelf and surrender.

»» Act with confidence. Know your value. You may not get validation from your boss, but you know that you're doing a great job. Don't let your narcissistic boss get under your skin. Stand proudly, assured that you provide a worthwhile contribution to the workplace.

WARNING

When faced with a situation in which your boss is acting unethically or illegally, decide how far you are willing to go. Narcissists can be seductively reassuring and extremely convincing that all will be well. Remember that if they get caught, they will blame others, including you. Know your moral limits and stick to them. Keep your résumé up to date and consider seeking employment elsewhere.

TIP

These actions and behaviors can be difficult to achieve, especially if you have problems with your own self-esteem or have suffered prior abuse. If you are in a work situation that is reigniting feelings of distress or memories of past abuse, you may want to consult a mental health professional.

Staying sane

Maybe this is your dream job. Or it's a great résumé builder. You want to make it work, despite the challenges of working for a narcissistic boss. You think you have the self-confidence and sturdiness to make it work. Being sane with a narcissist also takes a bit of manipulation. Okay, maybe you can survive. If that's your goal, consider the suggestions in this section.

TIP

Some of the following advice may seem like I'm recommending total capitulation, bordering on tearing down yourself. That's not the intent. These are temporary tips only meant for you to handle an unpleasant work environment. It's not sucking up; it's surviving. Appreciate that narcissists won't change. What works with non-narcissistic people does not work with a narcissist. If you find these suggestions too humiliating, it's time to look for another job.

>> **At every opportunity, praise and validate your boss.** Find any way you can to give your boss compliments. Say the meeting you just attended was great, even if your boss monopolized the conversation. Take every opportunity, including complimenting a new haircut or tie. If your boss makes a presentation and you want to add a small tweak, say "That was fabulous; just consider this and it will be absolutely perfect!"

>> **Don't expect praise for your accomplishments; instead, give it to your boss.** If, though unlikely, your boss gives you a compliment, turn it around. Reply, "Only under your leadership or with your support was I able to do this."

>> **Manipulate so that you can be seen agreeing with your boss.** Look for a small piece of your boss's idea that you can agree with and expand on it with your own ideas. Let your boss take credit for your ideas. Keep your ego out of it.

>> **Have other ways to get support.** Keep work/life balances. Get your support from meaningful relationships outside of work.

>> **Keep your personal goals in mind at all times.** Remember why you want to stay in this job, whether it's for the experience, the opportunity for advancement, or to gain new skills. Make sure you are getting what you want.

>> **Leave when you must.** If you are not getting what you want and need, make plans to leave. Don't advertise to others that you're looking for another job so that your boss doesn't attempt to retaliate. Consider other sources for references. Find another opportunity. Plan for a future in a different setting. And watch out for narcissists.

>> **Put it in perspective — it's work, not life.** Although there are times in your life when work seems all consuming, remember that family, friends, and taking care of yourself are greater priorities than work.

Chapter **8**

Exploring Vulnerabilities: Who Attracts a Narcissist

N arcissists naturally self-promote. They truly believe in their unique, attractive selves. And narcissists manage to create superb early impressions: They tend to be socially extroverted, entertaining, and charming. They make terrific first dates.

But however wonderfully a short-term relationship with a narcissist begins, over time, the narcissistic package begins to crumble. Studies have shown that narcissists are more likely to be unfaithful. They tend to exert power and control over their partners, cross boundaries, and be cold and distant. If their partners dare to end the relationship, narcissists are likely to spread nasty rumors through gossip or vicious social media posts.

Yet in spite of all the negative qualities of narcissistic relationships, they are quite common. So, it begs the question: Who gets involved with narcissists, and why? This chapter examines the various types of narcissistic victims and some of the reasons they are vulnerable to narcissists' charms.

Adult Children of Narcissists Make Easy Targets

Children of narcissists often acquire certain personality characteristics that make them more vulnerable as targets of narcissistic abuse (see Chapter 6 for more information). They find some comfort of sameness in the relationship that reminds them of their childhood experiences.

TIP

People tend to repeat emotional patterns that were established during childhood with their adult partners. They mistakenly believe that in this new relationship, they can get the love and nurturance they didn't receive as a child.

Feeling like you finally measure up

If you grew up in a narcissistic family, you may have deep feelings of shame. You may believe that you don't deserve happiness because you are a defective or damaged person. Overall, you believe that you can never face difficult challenges and are incapable of finding true happiness. That's the lesson you learned as the child of a narcissist.

When you meet a narcissist, you believe yourself lucky to find such a charismatic and (superficially) caring partner. You're thrilled by the initial flirtation and flattery. As those positive qualities begin to be replaced by entitlement, conceit, and lack of empathy, you revert back to feeling not good enough.

So, as the relationship continues, your feelings of inadequacy allow you to accept the narcissistic abuse of an adult partner. The following vignette displays this vulnerability.

Colton grew up with a pair of narcissistic parents. He was often the scapegoat in family feuds. He felt that he could never please his parents and that he was somehow unworthy of their love.

Today, although bright and relatively attractive, he avoids taking risks, under-achieves, and believes himself incapable of finding happiness or success. When he meets Emily, all of his feelings of inadequacy fade. She is interested in him; he can't believe his luck. She charms him with her flashy good looks, outgoing personality, attentiveness, and bright smile.

Colton thinks that he'll finally be happy. The couple quickly becomes intimate. Other than a few drunken one-night stands with women he picked up online, Emily is his first truly intimate relationship. Emily shows interest in him with frequent texts full of heart-shaped emojis. She makes it known that she wants to be around him as much as possible.

Emily senses Colton's vulnerability and willingness to do whatever she wants. She likes his devotion and responsiveness to her needs. Even during the early stages of the relationship, Emily insists on having private time with her old friends. She tells Colton that she is entitled to her privacy and reacts with irritation when Colton asks questions about what she is doing. Colton, feeling insecure, never really challenges her.

As their relationship matures, Colton notices that Emily slowly changes. Her enthusiasm for their relationship appears to fade. She seems distracted and distant. Colton tries to pump up his game, showing her more love and attention. When he discovers that she's been cheating on him, he's devastated. Falling back on childhood lessons, Colton tells himself that Emily was too good to be true and that he didn't deserve her. Colton returns to his quiet world of unworthiness.

The belief of these children of narcissists is that they don't deserve to be happy and treated fairly. They make great targets for narcissistic mates to seduce and discard.

Repeating themes from childhood

Adult children of narcissists may feel quite comfortable in a relationship with a narcissistic partner. They are used to being disappointed, discarded, and abused; it feels like home. Therefore, they have low expectations of what a good relationship should consist of. They may accept the narcissistic abuse as a familiar part of any relationship.

Another reason that adult children of narcissists remain in a narcissistic relationship is that they may be trying to fix or repair the original trauma experienced in childhood. They unwittingly believe that they can resolve early family conflict by having a successful partnership with someone who reminds them of one or both of their parents.

Unfortunately, this strategy hardly ever works, and these adults end up in unhappy, unsatisfying, and abusive partnerships that fail to heal their childhood wounds.

Adults Battling Low Self-Esteem

Adults who suffer unexpected failure, economic hardship, discrimination, trauma, or are cast aside in a relationship can experience drops in self-esteem along with subsequent vulnerability to the seductive ploys of narcissists.

Adults with low self-esteem are drawn to narcissistic partners to make up for their perceived deficits. For more information about the relationship of self-esteem and narcissism, take a look at Chapter 10.

Considering common causes of low self-esteem

Low self-esteem does not necessarily just come from early experiences with narcissists. The origins of low self-esteem can be found in many different areas of life. Low self-esteem usually takes hold during childhood. Common causes of low self-esteem that arise in childhood, but are not related to narcissistic parents, include the following:

>> **Not enough love, attention, or encouragement:** Children from those types of environments may not recall any specific abuse, but they feel somehow depleted and discouraged.

>> **Failure in school settings:** This failure may result from a of lack of parental encouragement, problems with attention, cultural or language differences, or learning disabilities. These children feel inferior and insecure when they do not measure up to the expectations of the classroom.

>> **Bullying in school:** Bullying can be brought on by the child's physique, discrimination, noticeable handicaps, or just by not fitting in with others.

>> **Growing up with disengaged parents as a result of substance abuse:** This scenario can cause the child to become discouraged and be ignored.

>> **Conflict among family members:** This may lead to unpredictable households that make a child feel fearful and inadequate.

>> **Growing up in a neighborhood rife with delinquency and crime:** These children may see no way out of their current circumstances and believe they are doomed to be defective.

>> **Exposure to one or more traumatic events:** This exposure may come from experiencing physical violence, psychological abuse, neglect, or tragic events such as gun violence, accidents, or natural disasters.

>> **Social media that reflects images of unrealistic standards of happiness or beauty:** These exposures appear to affect girls' self-esteem more than that of boys.

>> **Social media bullying:** Sometimes certain kids are targeted by a barrage of demeaning, negative posts. The effects of such an assault can be devastating to a teenager's or child's self-esteem.

>> **Economic instability:** Children who come from this type of environment may experience food or housing insecurity and receive inadequate nutrition or parental guidance. They feel like misfits at school, lacking adequate school supplies or acceptable clothing.

How feeling defective can make you more vulnerable

Low self-esteem leads to a sense of not deserving to be given what you need. Therefore, low self-esteem makes you a promising target for a narcissist. It's almost as if the narcissist can smell your weaknesses. Like adult children of narcissists, those with low self-esteem not caused by narcissistic abuse have insufficient defenses against possible entanglement with a narcissist.

The initial attractiveness, attention, and seduction of a narcissist is a welcome reprieve from pervasive feelings of inadequacy and defectiveness. When the inevitable crush of narcissistic abuse begins, those with low self-esteem feel that this is what life should be like for them. If this pattern describes you, it's important to shore up your defenses. One way to do this is to become more aware of red flags.

Ignoring red flags isn't the answer

A person with low self-esteem may be blind to the red flags that indicate possible narcissistic traits. Why? Those with low self-esteem are often gullible to the attraction of narcissists because they're so surprised and delighted to experience the early stages of seduction. Those early stages include excessive flattery, attention, and idealization. People who feel inferior may choose to ignore red flags so that they can maintain the hoped-for good relationship. The following red flags may be especially ignored by people who feel unworthy:

>> During the seduction phase, the narcissist wants to be with you every moment. That makes you feel special and desirable.

>> Narcissists attempt to make you dependent on them by helping you out with chores such as childcare or shopping. You can't believe someone is willing to pitch in and actually go out of their way to do something nice for you.

>> Narcissists may flatter you by telling you how much better you are than their former partner. You find this especially touching because you want to be seen as a better partner.

>> Narcissists may tell you a story about their past that includes overcoming some obstacle to gain sympathy and draw you in. You feel close because your potential partner seems to be expressing vulnerability.

These red flags are easily ignored because a person with low self-esteem desires being thought of as needed. That feeling gives them a sense that they are useful human beings after all. For more information about red flags, see Chapter 5.

Identifying Other Vulnerable People

Other situations can make adults feel powerless or helpless. Those qualities are attractive to a narcissist, who wants to feel superior in a relationship. Narcissists can present as knights in shining armor, ready to rescue the unsuspecting.

Suffering after a breakup or loss

People who have recently lost a loved one through divorce, death, or another event are particularly vulnerable to the manipulations of a narcissist. The narcissist, through careful questioning, can smoothly mirror the very characteristics that were missing in the past relationship.

For example, some people lose their partners to substance abuse. The narcissist may proclaim to be alcohol and drug free. Much more subtle manipulation is often at work, as illustrated by the following example:

> After a 14-year marriage, Alexander was ready to finally break up with his wife. He had a laundry list of complaints including her irresponsible spending habits, lack of care for the kids, being devoid of ambition, and habitually not showing up on time for appointments. Alexander basically ran the house while his soon-to-be-former wife sat endlessly scrolling through social media.
>
> He finally made the decision when she quit another job, saying it was just too boring. Alexander decided to talk to an attorney to see what he would face with a divorce. He was pleasantly surprised at how easy it was to separate and then divorce her. She seemed disinterested in the kids, now teenagers, and he kept primary custody.
>
> About a year later, Alexander meets Violet, an alluringly attractive, recently divorced woman. She appears to share his values, and Alexander feels comfortable with her. During the first few dates, they both talk about their former lives and what went wrong in their first marriages.
>
> The more they talk, the more Alexander believes he may have found an unexpectedly suitable match. Violet claims that she has a great career and is careful with her money. She states that she wants to grow in her occupation, hardly spends time on social media, and is always early for appointments.
>
> Despite not having children of her own, she tells Alexander that she loves kids, especially teenagers, and can't wait to meet his. It doesn't hurt that Violet is a very good and skillful lover and showers him with affection.

No need to describe the end to this story. The narcissist, Violet, takes in the information about what Alexander wants in a relationship and persuades him into believing that she is the perfect match. Clever. A typical narcissistic manipulation.

Lacking social support

Lonely people are also easy targets for narcissists. Isolated from others by distance or circumstance, narcissists are ready and able to fill the hole of loneliness with their big personalities and need for constant attention and admiration. The next example follows the path of Jasper, a recent college graduate who moves to a new city for a job.

Jasper, a software engineer, receives a fabulous job offer out of state. Despite being part of a large social circle and close family, he wants to experience being on his own, away from his comfort zone.

Although he likes his new job, he feels extremely lonely despite frequent texts and video calls with his friends and family. It just isn't the same. One day at lunch, Benjamin, a coworker, sits with Jasper. Jasper, glad to have someone to talk to in person, opens up to Benjamin about being lonely and new to the city.

Benjamin enthusiastically promises Jasper that he can take him to the best bars and restaurants. The two plan to meet after work. The following weeks are a blur of multiple bottles of wine, fine food, and visits to all the tourist spots. An obvious sexual attraction simmers in the background.

As their relationship develops, Benjamin becomes increasingly possessive of Jasper, demanding more and more of his time. He also starts constantly bragging about his own accomplishments and how much better he is than Jasper's old friends. He is jealous and tries to keep Jasper from communicating with his out-of-town friends and family.

Soon, Jasper finds himself exclusively in Benjamin's company. That is not what he wanted when he moved. He was looking for independence, and now he is once again immersed in an exclusive relationship. Jasper begins to cool down the relationship and make some effort to meet other people. Benjamin becomes excessively angry and viciously verbally attacks Jasper, accusing him of taking advantage of him and treating him like dirt.

Back at work, Benjamin refuses to talk to Jasper. Jasper starts to feel that others at work are avoiding him. One day, his boss calls him into his office. He tells Jasper that there's quite a bit of talk about Jasper having a quick temper and not being a good part of the team. Jasper is astonished by the feedback.

Jasper hardly ever gets irritable and is always happy to cooperate. He then realizes that Benjamin likely started that rumor to get revenge. Jasper feels more confused and isolated than ever. Maybe he should move back home.

Jasper has just encountered a narcissistic seduction, full of fun, flattery, and love bombing. When things didn't work out, Benjamin, the narcissist, took revenge by spreading false rumors at work. Jasper was vulnerable because he was socially isolated and lonely. Fortunately, he's likely to easily recover from this brief episode because he has love and support at home.

Healthy People Get Sucked In Too

Anyone can be initially attracted to a narcissist. The narcissist may be good looking, good sounding, and highly entertaining. They have engaging stories, witty repartee, and an easy, approachable presentation. They maintain positive attention tuned to themselves by practicing their multiple skills on all who surround them.

Narcissists tend to be overly confident and know how to work a room. What they crave is admiration, and their initial, socially skillful performances invite a large audience. Anyone could easily become one of their fans.

TIP

People with narcissistic traits can be interesting, engaging people to hang out with. They can make decent friends with normal, healthy people who know how to set good boundaries. Those with narcissistic traits often show drive, good social skills, and confidence that is admirable (see Chapter 14 for more about successful narcissists).

How being understanding and empathetic can backfire

People who understand and feel what others are feeling are called *empathetic*. One of the characteristics of narcissists is that they lack empathy. They do not understand (or care about) the feelings of others.

Those with high levels of empathy are often targets of narcissistic seduction. Narcissists want highly empathetic people to care for and understand them. They want continuous love and attention, even when they misbehave. An empathetic person cares deeply and will go to extreme lengths to help others. They may also be capable of understanding the pain from which narcissism often originates. A narcissist takes advantage of this quality and finds ways to manufacture an empathetic response.

WHAT IN THE WORLD IS AN EMPATH?

I have studied psychology for many years. As a matter of fact, my doctoral dissertation was about empathy. I was surprised in the preparation for this book to find another world, mostly online, all about empaths. So, I was curious and looked into the literature to see what I could find.

The wonderful world of technology puts millions of scientific journal articles within my reach in a matter of minutes. So, I poked around the scientific literature and found almost no references in peer-reviewed journal articles that contained the word *empath*.

Not finding what I wanted to know about empaths there, I decided to wade into the broader online community. Here's what I learned. First, the word seems to have come from science fiction literature. It was later used in a *Star Trek* episode that featured a woman who was able to take on the pain of others and cure them. In Marvel comic books, evil empaths use their abilities to manipulate others.

Empath was a word that likely came from telepathy, the ability to know what is in someone else's mind without speaking or some other nonverbal communication. An empath, shortened from empathy, is a highly sensitive person who feels what others feel, without effort. Okay, that works for me. Lots of people are empathetic. Apparently, it turned into a popular psychology concept during the 2000s. The struggles of empaths and their oversensitivity to other people's pain continued to expand online. Now there are huge networks, support groups, books, blogs, and classes. And people are making money hawking the concept.

I understand the burdens of being too empathetic. There is so much suffering that sometimes the vastness becomes overwhelming. And I know a little about empathy — I can tear up watching a commercial about a suffering animal. But I guess making empathy another psychological condition to be solved is another way of making something normal into a disorder. Empathy is a wonderful, although sometimes distressing, human power. Nonetheless, I have empathy for those who suffer from being an empath.

When caregiving comes naturally

Some people are natural caregivers. They become the go-to person when others are having trouble. Caregivers are good, understanding, compassionate listeners. They offer chicken soup to the sick, comfort to the injured, and love to the forlorn. Caregivers are usually eternal optimists believing there is good to be found in all people.

When a caregiver runs into a narcissist, they hope to help the narcissist become a better person. They gladly put aside their own needs to figure out how they can improve the life of a fellow human being. A narcissist takes advantage of that unrelenting hope and uses it to get the constant validation and attention they crave.

When narcissists snare a caregiver, they skillfully offer enough appreciation to keep the care and adoration coming. In the background, narcissists may view caregivers as pawns, easily duped, used, and when they become less appealing, discarded.

Enjoying the challenge of a fixer-upper

People buy fixer-upper homes or cars believing they will get them for bargain prices; put in some time, effort, and money; and come out ahead financially. For example, you could find a cute-looking bungalow in a trendy neighborhood that was neglected over the years. You think a good paint job, new roof, and some tender loving care are all the home needs to be brought up to current values. However, you neglect to see the mold and rot that infests the home and threatens its very foundation.

You meet someone. They're funny, bright, and engaging. A few dates later, you discover a history of broken relationships (never their fault), a lack of friends (we drifted apart), an unstable work history (haven't yet found the right niche), and some off-putting personality patterns (you must be imagining them).

Yet, you see promise. This person may just be worth fixing up. You can be a stable influence in this person's life. You can introduce them to your friends, help with career moves, and improve their slight personality faults with love, kindness, and just a little positive feedback.

When you begin your makeover, narcissists may welcome the attention. However, when narcissists realize that you are attempting to make them do something challenging, they resist your attempts to help. You work hard to smooth out rela-tionships, dive into deep discussions about career plans for the future, and gently point out personality traits that could be getting in their way of finding success and happiness.

Your fixer-upper person begins to show their deep personality flaws such as grandiosity, entitlement, and lack of empathy. Unfortunately, most people with narcissistic traits rarely change. Like a moldy or rotten house, narcissism runs deep into the foundation of a person.

IN THIS CHAPTER

» **Knowing when you're being abused**

» **Accepting help from others**

» **Watching out for attempts at reconciliation**

» **Making contact minimal**

» **Recovering from abuse**

Chapter 9

Surviving Narcissistic Abuse: A Tool Kit

This chapter is designed for partners, parents, colleagues, and adult children of narcissists who have suffered narcissistic abuse and are thinking about moving forward. Whether you need help setting appropriate boundaries, cutting off contact, or dealing with narcissistic rage, the answers are in the following pages.

Some tool kits overflow with screws and nails from projects long abandoned, multiple screwdrivers, duplicate pliers, and various other tools rarely used or needed. In contrast, I've pared down this tool kit to the essentials. Take these ideas and use them to get you through the tough moments. The tools will help you build a strong and sturdy foundation.

The following sections give you the necessary tools to build a new you, identify narcissistic abuse, get support, and avoid being traumatized again.

Giving Your Concern a Name: Cognitive Dissonance

Dissonance in music leads to disharmony. For example, a musical piece begins in a certain key and then suddenly switches, an unexpected note or screech is heard, or a pause seems to last a second too long. For a moment, the audience feels disturbed or uncomfortable, but then the harmony is reestablished. Composers uses dissonance to add a sense of emotion or urgency to their music.

Dissonance in writing usually involves odd word choices; unusual punctuation; or in poetry, strange rhyming. That out-of-synch feeling again alerts the reader or listener that something is jarringly discordant. Again, dissonance awakens the audience. Something is amiss; pay attention.

Cognitive refers to the process of thinking, remembering, and learning information. Although emotion certainly affects the way you think, recall, or interpret information, cognition is thought to be largely grounded in reality-based thinking skills.

Cognitive dissonance happens when there is disharmony in thinking. It's an unexpected reaction to holding two incompatible ideas. When you experience cognitive dissonance, you're uneasy. You feel uncomfortable and anxious. Yes, it's time to pay attention; something is amiss.

Common types of cognitive dissonance happen when you have a particular value, such as a strong belief in the preservation of forests, yet you proceed to cut down a Christmas tree. You feel a bit off, but somehow rationalize that Christmas trees are grown specifically for consumption.

Another example of cognitive dissonance occurs when you have a very good friend who confides in you about some fascinating gossip. Later, you're out with some other friends and you share that gossip with them. You feel guilty the minute it comes out of your mouth. Your desire to be entertaining has momentarily overwhelmed your warm feelings for your friend. Thus, cognitive dissonance is created. You can probably reduce that dissonance by rationalizing your gossiping as a common social weakness, something that everyone does.

Cognitive dissonance is a daily occurrence in relationships with narcissists. You have two thoughts, behaviors, or feelings that just don't seem to harmonize.

>> How can this person who declares devotion suddenly act like a stranger?

>> How can someone who wanted to spend every minute with me leave me behind?

>> Why does my best friend never show up when I have problems?

>> Why do I always feel like I'm walking on eggshells? My partner says I'm too sensitive.

>> Why does my partner claim that I am lying, exaggerating, or making things up?

>> Why does my partner blame me for this fight when I didn't start it?

>> How can my parents say they love me but treat me with such disrespect?

Recognizing Abuse in Your Relationship

Narcissistic abuse starts slowly and gradually increases over time. Like the story about a frog put in a pot of warm water, the temperature starts to rise, but the frog doesn't notice and eventually gets boiled to death. Narcissistic abuse is similar. It starts out small, but eventually the flame of narcissistic abuse is turned up to high. And it burns.

Like a frog in warming water, you may have feelings of unease early on in a relationship. You're not really sure that the water is getting hotter, but you know in your gut that something's just not right.

You may experience the discomfort of cognitive dissonance. You justify, rationalize, and excuse the abusive behavior. Because at the same time you hold the thought that your partner's treatment of you is not right, you hold onto the belief that you care deeply for this person and the hope that somehow, things will certainly get better.

TIP

When you find yourself in a state of cognitive dissonance, you are motivated to find harmony and balance between dissonant thoughts, behaviors, or emotions. For example, you might rationalize that your partner is overtired and that is why they treat you poorly. Rationalization is one main reason it can be hard to leave a narcissistic relationship.

TECHNICAL STUFF

I felt compelled to look up the frog metaphor. Just for your own information, the frog experiment really doesn't work. Researchers have found that if a live frog has a way out, it will jump out before being boiled to death. Keep that in mind.

Honing your lie detecting skills

Narcissists practice the art of lying. They are easygoing, comfortable liars, having little or no remorse or guilt. Their lies range from small white lies to giant whoppers. If you have a relationship with a narcissist, finding out how to spot a lie is a good first step to recognizing emotional abuse.

Although some people may be good lie detectors, most are not. There is no truth to the common myth that people who are lying almost always break eye contact and look to the left or right. Some people who lie purposely make direct eye contact. Others who are telling the truth sometimes break eye contact.

The best way to tell whether someone is lying is to detect and keep in mind their historical patterns. Know their speaking habits when they're not lying. Ask yourself the following questions when you're pretty sure your narcissist is lying:

>> Does what they are saying make logical sense?

>> Is there any concrete evidence to support what they are saying?

>> If a friend told you what your narcissistic partner did, what would you tell them?

>> Do they speak uninterrupted, without allowing for comments or questions?

>> Do they show any hint that they will listen to your perspective?

>> Do their details change over time with repetition?

>> Are they speaking loudly and repeating themselves incessantly?

>> Have they told you similar stories in the past that turned out not to be true?

>> Do they use exaggerated gestures when they talk?

>> Do you sense that they are lying? Listen to your gut.

TIP

Keep a log of your answers to these questions when you believe that the narcissist in your life is likely lying. It's the accumulation of patterns that provides the strongest evidence. If you are filling out many logs of answers to these questions, it should tell you something. Most narcissists lie repeatedly and frequently.

Changes in regular conversational styles are the best indicators of narcissistic lying. Narcissists who lie may make strong, direct eye contact. They may repeat details and gesture with their hands. They may get agitated and fidgety. Or they may become statue still and quiet. Listen to your instinct and use your best logic, but also know that people in general are bad at lie detecting and narcissists are expert liars.

TIP

When a narcissist is caught in a lie, do not expect them to admit their dishonesty. They are far more likely to repeat the lie — loudly and incessantly — hoping you will begin to question your own reality. (See Chapter 5 for more on this form of emotional abuse, known as *gaslighting*.)

Keeping a list of concerns and indiscretions

Narcissistic abuse takes on many obvious and subtle forms. It helps to know what you are up against. Somewhere, securely stored, begin a list of what you are concerned about. Don't count on your memory to recall instances of abuse. Your narcissistic abuser will use your uneasiness and confusion to distort your memory and make you distrust your own honest recollections. You need to document them.

TIP

You may want to open another calendar on your phone for this log. Spend a few minutes each day to see whether any of the following types of narcissistic abuse happened to you.

WARNING

If your narcissist has access to your phone, be careful. You don't want them to have more information to use as possible ammunition. You can keep the list in a more secure area such as with a trusted family member, friend, or at your therapist's office.

Start logging instances of the following:

» **Denial:** Doing something and then denying that it happened, making you confused about your own reality.

» **Verbal abuse:** Calling you names, questioning your ideas, putting down your abilities to manage your life.

» **Using envy or jealousy:** Parading other potential alliances in front of you or insinuating that you are cheating or flirting with others.

» **Narcissistic rage or blowups:** Getting excessively angry over small matters and frightening you with their intensity.

» **Gaslighting:** Deceiving you by lying, minimizing, or manipulating you into believing that what you are seeing or thinking is not actually happening.

» **Sullenness or the silent treatment:** Used to punish you by withholding all affection and shutting down open communication.

» **Blame shifting:** Blaming someone else for actions that they were responsible for. It can be as simple as saying that they asked you to take out the trash this week (they didn't) and asking how you could be so irresponsible.

» **Isolation:** Cutting you off from friends and family who may offer different perspectives, usually accompanied by considerable criticism of friends or family.

» **Exploitation:** Using you to complete tasks they don't want to be bothered with, making excessive demands on your time, or exploiting you financially with loads of justification.

PUTTING REINFORCEMENT THEORY INTO PRACTICE

Reinforcement theory has been studied over many decades. Basically, if you want a living thing (animal or human) to do something again, you reward them with a valued prize (treats for dogs, praise or cash for humans). If you repeatedly reward them, that behavior will increase. In other words, giving rewards increases the desired behavior. But what happens when you don't reward someone every time?

Intermittent reinforcement occurs when you reward sometimes, but not always. The science behind reinforcement theory indicates that when people are rewarded from time to time on an unknown schedule, they will continue to do the desired behavior. In fact, intermittent reinforcement is a stronger incentive than continuous reinforcement.

Narcissists are expert intermittent reinforcers. At times, they reward their prey excessively, then withdraw, and then at random intervals begin to reward again. That inconsistent but powerful reinforcement makes it very difficult for someone to leave a narcissistic relationship.

>> **Seesaw abuse:** Going from affectionate and loving to callous and abusive without a specific pattern or reason.

>> **Threats of physical or sexual abuse:** These threats may be direct or easily deniable yet subtle enough to have some other possible misinterpretation. Keep track of any hint of threatening behavior.

>> **Intimidation:** Throwing objects, punching walls, physically pushing people away, or other acts to intimidate.

>> **Chronic cheating:** Infidelity may be hidden or openly displayed, usually with at least mildly plausible deniability. Or justifying cheating because you don't satisfy them sexually.

TIP

Keep using this log over time. Write down your thoughts and feelings, even if you're not sure what is happening. If you are not yet ready to leave your narcissist, the log will help you stay grounded in reality. A log will also allow you to see if there are any patterns of abuse.

Seeing denial for what it is

Denial is a perfectly normal reaction to difficult feelings. You may deny a sense of abuse because to open up would expose you to raw and distressing emotions. You may deny a habitual problem, such as substance abuse, that you don't want to fight. You can deny that a relationship is troubling because you feel trapped.

Denial takes on many different forms:

» Simply ignoring that a problem exists

» Telling yourself that you will get to it later

» Blaming someone else for the problem

» Avoiding signs of the problem

» Pretending that everything will eventually turn out fine

REMEMBER

Denial decreases cognitive dissonance by justifying your decision to remain in an abusive relationship. Unfortunately, denial comes at a high cost. Denial, over time, slowly drains you of being yourself, or authentic. You lie or ignore feelings, and numbness creeps in. With denial, you can avoid facing problems or dealing with them directly.

The following example shows how denial of feelings leads to a long-standing pattern of abuse.

Melissa and David were married about 25 years ago. They were students together at a community college. Shortly after getting married, Melissa dropped out of school when she found herself pregnant. David continued his education and became a master electrician. The early years of their marriage flew by, and they had four more children within seven years.

David makes good money by working extra hours, and Melissa is a busy stay-at-home mom, chauffeur, cook, and homework manager to five growing children. It seems to her that she barely sees David, and their marriage suffers. Over the years, they become more and more distant, hardly speaking for days at a time. But neither complains, and they continue to function, superficially, as a family. As their children become less dependent on her, Melissa finds herself having more time to think. She realizes that David's extra work hours don't always show up in his paychecks. She also admits to herself that he doesn't treat her very well, often ignoring her requests for one-on-one time to hang out with his buddies again. She wants more from their marriage now that their children are leaving home to start their own lives. She stops denying the truth; she feels lonely and unloved by David.

When Melissa approaches David with her concerns, he reacts with surprising anger. He pounces on her, furious, bellowing that she doesn't appreciate the fact that he's been the breadwinner in the family and expects more respect. He grabs his keys and is gone for hours. When he returns, he does not speak to Melissa or acknowledge her presence.

Melissa used denial for years to ignore her problematic marriage. She was so busy with nurturing children that she had little time or energy to contemplate much else. When her situation changed and she had more time to reflect, she looked back on many instances of abuse, of his lengthy silent treatments, his sullen excuses for not being present at family gatherings, or his lack of affection, chalking them up to David's hard work. But she later realized that he had always put himself first while neglecting her and the children.

Placing blame with your abuser, not yourself

It is not your fault that you ended up in an abusive relationship with a narcissist. Whether you are the child of narcissists, a partner of a narcissist, or a colleague of a narcissist, you are not to blame.

REMEMBER

Narcissists make very good first impressions. They charm, entertain, and flatter. Most people are not good forecasters of the future. Whatever your relationship is, or began as, you didn't ask for abuse. No one trained you on how to detect a narcissist.

Nevertheless, many victims in abusive relationships blame themselves for their problems. There is frequently an "if only" stage when victims look back for ways they might have acted or behaved differently. Narcissistic abuse does not occur because the victim was somehow at fault. Stop blaming yourself. Blaming takes necessary energy away from your efforts to make rational decisions about what to do next.

Establishing a New Support Network

Once you become aware of your situation, it's time to start an action plan. The first step in stopping narcissistic abuse is to establish a support network. You need to find friends, family, and possibly a therapist who will give you their unbiased opinion, listen to you with undistorted hearing, and provide you with open-eyed help.

TIP

Some sharing is good. However, don't use your friends exclusively for personal confessionals. Your friends and family don't need to hear about all the sordid details of your history. Save those for your therapist.

Expanding your friend circle

A common tool of a narcissist is isolation. Narcissists may isolate you from former friends and family by falsely accusing them of controlling you or not having your best interests in mind. And, if narcissists believe that you may leave them, they pull out an arsenal of gossip or ambiguous lies to implicate your vices and deficits. They spread those lies to whoever will listen. And juicy gossip spreads like a wildfire in an arid western state. Here's what happens to Nick when he leaves Sandy:

> Nick has been married to Sandy for almost five years. He knew that the relationship was unlikely to last after discovering that Sandy was indeed a malignant narcissist. She has no trouble lying or cheating, has little to no empathy, and works to manipulate everyone in her life. She cruelly rejects and hurts those who get in her way.
>
> She fights with Nick viciously any time he doesn't do what she wants or give her what she demands. When he finally gets the courage to call it quits, Nick leaves without having a final argument, knowing it will only lead to horrible rage. He gives Sandy a generous settlement in the divorce, not wanting to engage in further conflict.
>
> After gathering himself together, he reaches out to former friends. His friends meet him with coldness. Nick is confused. He finally starts hearing rumors that he was a raging alcoholic prone to violent outbursts. This rumor spread not only among his friends, but also to family members and even colleagues. A couple of his family members offer to help him out, suggesting that he attend meetings to address his substance abuse. When Nick denies this substance abuse, his family members explain to him that denial is common among alcoholics.
>
> Although Nick did tend to drink too much beer from time to time, especially after fighting with Sandy, he was not an alcoholic. However, the damage was done. Sandy did a good job of getting revenge.

It's an unfortunate fact that because of the power of narcissistic persuasion, your former friends may believe the narcissist. They may reject any new overture of friendship, believing that you were at fault or deceitful. Furthermore, you may have attempted to cover up the behavior of your narcissistic partner, making your friends even less likely to believe you.

Sadly, you may need to find a new group of friends — not friends to dump your troubles on, but friends who can engage in the normal give and take of friendship. Find friends who don't know or don't dwell on your history of abuse at the hands of a narcissist.

Try to protect yourself by confiding in a trusted friend early on about your relationship. That friend may prove to be a valuable ally when things go sour with your narcissist. Be careful who you confide in, and make sure that the friendship is not tarnished by your complaints.

Seeking professional help

When you started your relationship with a narcissist, you may have considered yourself perfectly well adjusted. You weren't depressed or particularly anxious. Your moods were generally appropriate, you didn't over- or under-react. You had good relationships with family, friends, and coworkers. You handled your responsibilities in life, and when stressful events happened, you adapted as called for. In fact, you thought of yourself as reasonably resilient.

Narcissistic abuse or trauma changes that. You are no longer the same stable person you were before. You may never fully return to that comfortable base. You are less trusting, you've become more cynical, and you struggle to regain that innocent belief that things always work out eventually.

Psychotherapy is a sacred place to begin to reestablish your previous self. You will never be the same person after being abused, but maybe you'll be better. Therapy allows you to rehash what happened in a safe, nonjudgmental environment. You can bring your most private experiences to a session and expect that a good therapist will help you unravel what was imagined from what was real. You can begin to heal and grow from your experience and discover acceptance.

I strongly encourage you to seek psychotherapy from a licensed mental health provider when you experience narcissistic abuse. Even if you feel emotionally healthy, you need to explore clues to determine how you fell into the relationship and establish ways to protect yourself from future abuse. Unfortunately, returning to an abusive relationship with a narcissist is quite common. Without psychotherapy, you may even be seduced into becoming involved with another narcissist.

Strengthening Your Defenses: Don't Fall for a Hoovering Narcissist

A narcissist may have no love or affection for a former partner. However, they do not like to be discarded; it's a serious blow to their fragile egos. So, when a child, partner, or friend of a narcissist finally gives up and ends a relationship, the narcissistic ego implodes.

They want you back. Not because you mean anything to them, but because you left and that doesn't work well for a narcissist. They want to call the shots. Along with needing control, narcissists want to be admired, and being dumped causes them shame and humiliation. Narcissists don't mind discarding people, but they don't like being discarded.

Hoovering is a popular term in the online community of survivors of narcissist abuse that refers to the techniques a narcissist uses to attempt to suck you back into a relationship. Hoovering involves a return to love bombing, seduction, and promises of better behavior, all of which can be surprisingly compelling.

TECHNICAL STUFF

The Hoover vacuum was first invented in the early 1900s. Because of its popularity, the Hoover vacuum dominated the industry for decades. When you vacuum a rug, you suck up dirt and debris. Hoovering became a common verb meaning to vacuum in Great Britain because most of their vacuums were produced by the Hoover Company.

Talk is cheap: Words have little meaning

Most narcissists can talk. In fact, they are capable of delivering a lecture on a moment's notice. When you leave a narcissistic relationship, their impassioned sermons sound so convincing. They attribute their mistakes to too much pressure or too little time. They promise to change their ways and give you what you need. They propose a renewal of commitment to your relationship. They may say that they have changed by attending counseling or joining a religious organization.

Don't believe them. My guess is that you have gone down this road before of forgotten promises or unfulfilled vows. Your hopefulness has been destroyed, and your optimism has sunk. Don't listen to what they say; wait and evaluate what they do. But don't wait very long or expect too much. Your life is passing by.

Actions are short-lived

When you broach the subject that you are finished with being abused, a narcissist may try love bombing you showering you with gifts and attention. The abuse may completely disappear for a period of time. You are frankly thrilled at the change. Maybe they've finally gotten the message. You are serious. You won't put up with abuse.

However, over time, actions usually return to the baseline of abuse or neglect. Your narcissistic relationship slips back into a one-sided battle of wills. The narcissist wins, and you lose.

Surprise! The narcissist in your life hasn't changed

When a person has a long-term pattern of behavior, they are less likely to see themselves as needing fixing. Narcissism as a trait begins in childhood and blooms during adolescence. Over the long run, narcissistic traits may decrease slightly as people age.

In order to change, a person must be able to accept some responsibility for the problems they experience. A narcissist may experience some regret over struggles, but usually blames others for whatever problem they're facing. In fact, many narcissists feel victimized.

The narcissist in your life may promise to change. They may even agree to therapy (See Part 5 for information about treatment). Changing a narcissist with a personality disorder requires hard work by the client and a willingness to admit fault and responsibility. And that is a big problem. Narcissists believe that they have no significant faults. Although narcissists can learn new skills, improve their reaction to stress, and handle life with more understanding, the bottom line is that the core of narcissism rarely changes.

Regaining Control: Eliminating or Limiting Contact

Breaking up is hard to do, especially with a narcissist. You may believe that your relationship is so flawed that the narcissist won't be devastated and may even be relieved by a breakup. You're wrong. Whether you're dealing with a partner, family member, colleague, or friend, telling a narcissist that you want a clean break is likely to stir up powerful narcissistic rage.

They rage because you took control. And narcissists want control at all times. If anyone is going to do the breaking up, it has to be the narcissist. Therefore, if you decide to leave a narcissist, plan ahead.

See an attorney if you can afford one, even if there are no children involved. Don't tell the narcissist that you have seen a lawyer or that you plan to leave. Giving prior notice can lead to interference or increase the potential for escalation of conflict.

WARNING

Narcissists, especially vulnerable ones, feel shame about being left. They may turn that shame into rage or anger. If a narcissist has a history of aggression, be very careful about when and how you leave. It's best not to disclose any new relationship you have—a narcissist very well may seek revenge. Narcissists may attempt to sabotage your new relationship by spreading gossip or even making threats.

Expect to feel distress about giving up. You are probably a person with loads of empathy. At some level you feel sorry for the narcissist you are leaving. However, being abused is not good for you and does little to help the narcissist in your life. It's time to move forward without looking back.

TIP

Along with empathy, you may be experiencing sadness, defeat, and lack of initiative. You've been abused; don't expect to be able to accomplish this difficult task easily. I advise you to take one step at a time, make mental lists, set small goals. You can do this.

WARNING

I'm guessing that at this point, you've had multiple discussions with the narcissist in your life. You've tried everything. This is not the time for more worthless negotiation. If you want to leave, don't stay around to chat.

Blocking calls, texts, and online access

Of course, you'd prefer open communication. Never before have you been in a situation that can't be fixed by talking things over. Now you face one. Your narcissist may beg to reestablish the relationship. Narcissists feed on attention, and withdrawing attention saps them of their power. Feeling injured, they may cry and even threaten self-harm. You feel it's your obligation as a human being to reach out to help.

Although this may be hard, offer them the suicide hotline if they need help (dial 988, open 24/7) or 911 if they feel suicide is an imminent possibility. You can also call the suicide hotline for consultation or 911 if you believe that your narcissist is in danger. But that is where your help must end.

Block all calls and texts. Really. Otherwise, you will be bombarded with pleas and promises, or angry threats, which will lead to more pain. That time has passed.

WARNING

Resist making posts about your breakup. Stop following your ex. Stay as private as you can; this is not the time to broadcast your grievances. Maintaining a lack of contact over the long run can be extremely hard, but it's worth it.

When children are involved

Leaving a narcissistic relationship when there are co-parenting issues is extraordinarily difficult. The very best outcome is when both parents rise to the occasion to help their kids through the difficult adjustment of divorce or separation. That happens quite rarely for narcissists with custody issues.

If you are a coparent with minor children, the unhappy truth is that your former partner will be in your life until your children are adults. It is almost impossible, and incredibly expensive, to convince a judge that your ex is a narcissist. So, that fight is usually futile and unlikely to help.

To further muddy the waters, narcissists make excellent first impressions. They may charm attorneys or the judge with their fake sincerity that they are only concerned about what is best for the children. In custody cases, many narcissists simply seek revenge and use your children against you, even if it is detrimental to your kids.

Opting for mediation

Not everyone can afford an attorney experienced in working with personality disordered parents. If you can, good. Get an advocate to help you establish a parenting plan that includes safeguards for you and your children. If you can't afford an attorney, divorce mediators may be able to help.

Here's what you can do with mediation. A good, experienced mediator understands personality disorders and will likely sniff out narcissism. You need everything in writing about visitation, finances, and interactions. Some couples find that the only way to limit conflict is to drop off and pick up their children in neutral places.

Next, expect that your former partner will likely try to hurt you by stirring up the emotions of your children. They may form inappropriate bonds with their kids and encourage dependence. They may convince your children that you were the problem, and they were the victim.

Being empathetic to your kids' concerns

Be understanding when your kids come to you with complaints generated by your ex. Understand the impossible position your kids are in, loving both parents and confused by misinformation. Stay out of the fight and don't try to defend yourself by blaming your ex. Try to react to your kids' concerns with empathy and love rather than defensiveness.

If your ex blatantly lies to your children, simply tell the truth, but don't expect them to necessarily believe you. Remember, narcissists make great manipulators and liars. Refraining from justifying yourself is difficult, but it's the only way to stay out of the narcissistic cycle of abuse. Unfortunately, your children may not come to fully understand your reality until they are adults. Be patient and stay loving.

TIP

Keep a running document of the times your ex forgets to pick up your kids from school, runs out of money when a support payment is due, takes the kids during your time, or tells your children lies about you. Hopefully, you'll never need it, but it's better to be prepared than to face another round in child custody without documentation.

Try to maintain a stable home for your children. Kids can overcome adversity when they have a secure base from which they can explore the broader world. Be that base.

Giving Yourself Time to Refocus

When you break up with anyone, you stand in a particularly vulnerable place. Take care of yourself. Slow down. Don't attempt to figure out the who, what, when, where, and why of your loss. You don't need to solve anything right now. Make plans with people who support you. Watch a few good movies or go out to eat at a favorite restaurant. Practice self-compassion; you've been through a rough time.

Put off big decisions

Put off making other major life changes. You may have already had to change residences after the breakup. But now is not the time to quit your job and move to Uganda or Tahiti.

Even when a relationship was toxic, it was your emotional home for some time. Your task is to search for a new place for yourself in your new world, but that takes time. There is no rush.

Find self-forgiveness

It's easy for others to tell you to just move on after a breakup. That's easier said than done. Take some time to reflect on what happened. It's not really useful to just blame the narcissist for all of your problems. No matter how self-centered, entitled, and arrogant they were, somehow you got caught in their net.

So, now is a time of self-reflection. Try to look at your own strengths and weaknesses. How do you affect those around you? Listen to the way others react to you. Become more self-aware.

Now is not a time for self-loathing for the mistakes you made, but rather a time for growing self-awareness. From self-awareness you can learn to forgive. Forgive yourself for the sadness and disruption of your past relationship. Find the strength to take an honest view of what has happened.

Now, slowly, move on.

Grieve what could have been

Losing a toxic relationship is complicated. You will likely have feelings of not only relief but also grief. You grieve that you spent a part of your life hoping for something that was never possible.

Your sadness may make you want to isolate from others. You may feel irritable and wary of making another mistake. That is perfectly normal. Take it slowly. Try to participate in low-risk social situations such as taking up a hobby, joining a gym, or hanging out with friends.

You need time to heal.

Getting Hooked Again: Surviving a Relationship Relapse

Narcissists like to win. They may not care about the game or the person, but they like to control the rules. So, if you ended a relationship with a narcissist, prepare for a rematch. As discussed in the earlier section "Strengthening Your Defenses: Don't Fall for a Hoovering Narcissist," narcissists are likely to try to get you back into the game.

You may be able to resist, but unfortunately, the narcissist is a talented con and will often wait in the wings until you are at a vulnerable moment to re-enter your life. This pattern often occurs when the relationship was romantic, especially when there are children involved.

Don't put yourself down

So, you're back. You fell for the charm, promises, and excitement again. Your friends and family warned you, but there you were, hopeful and still thinking that *this time* will be different. And for a week, a month, even a year, you believed that things were better. They were. But gradually, ever so painfully, the reality of narcissism emerged.

You were fooled. You feel foolish. For some time, you try to cover up the obvious abuse. You make excuses and search for alternate explanations. Maybe you are being too sensitive or imagining things that aren't there. Much later, you admit the sad truth. Nothing has really changed.

Now is not the time to wallow in self-pity and blame. The pattern of multiple breakups is quite common with people involved with narcissists. You have the capacity to forgive; now forgive yourself. Again.

Keep trying until you break free

Never give up. You can become the authentic person you were before getting involved with a narcissist. You may have to make multiple attempts to disentangle yourself, but don't feel hopeless.

Others have struggled and lost. They've gotten caught up in the narcissistic love-bombing and been fooled again. But many eventually find the strength to finally live an independent life. So, have hope. Get up, dust yourself off, and go at it again. Be free.

REMEMBER

Narcissists are masters at charm and manipulation. Love bombing and hoovering are hard to resist. You are human and vulnerable but you're also resilient. Be strong.

Moving Forward: Taking Better Care of Yourself

You have broken ties as much as possible with the narcissist in your life. What now? Prioritize yourself. What do you need? Have you been spending too much time tending to others, and not enough time nurturing yourself? You are the only one responsible for the way you live the rest of your life. There is no one else to guide you. Take charge. Now is the time to think about how you can maximize your health and well-being.

Improving your health

You may have been overwhelmed by emotions through your time of abuse. And along the way, you may have taken up some lifestyle habits that may be impacting your physical and mental health. That's perfectly understandable. Moving forward, take stock of your habits. Are there ways that you can improve your health? Many health problems can be prevented by lifestyle changes. The following common chronic diseases can almost always be avoided:

» Heart disease

» High blood pressure

» Stroke

» Diabetes

» Certain cancers

Lifestyle changes that impact long-term health include the following:

» **Quit smoking or chewing tobacco.** Smoking causes lung cancer and increases your odds of heart disease, high blood pressure, and stroke. Get help quitting. There are medications that can greatly decrease your urges. Talk to your primary care provider. See *Quitting Smoking & Vaping For Dummies*, coauthored by Charles H. Elliot and myself and published by Wiley, for more information.

» **Maintain a healthy weight and eat healthy food.** Even being moderately overweight increases your likelihood of diabetes or high blood pressure. Obesity also increases the risk of certain cancers such as colon or breast cancer. Eat lots of fruits and vegetables, limit saturated fat, and consume heathy whole grains. Talk to your healthcare provider who can refer you to a dietician for help developing an appropriate diet. Medications and sometimes surgery are also used to help control weight.

» **Get exercise on most days.** Exercise helps maintain a healthy weight and also reduces the risk of heart disease, stroke, diabetes, arthritis, depression, and bone fractures. Find an exercise that you can enjoy so that you will be more likely to do it regularly.

Engaging in self-soothing activities

Negative emotions are likely to crop up from time to time. If you have experienced trauma or narcissistic abuse, learning to calm down and soothe yourself is important. Self-soothing activities can reduce feelings of anxiety, anger, trauma, and stress. Different strategies work for different people. Try some of the following to see what works for you:

» Do some deep breathing. Take in a deep breath, hold it, and exhale slowly. Repeat five to ten times.

» Try some stretching. Stand up and put your arms high over your head; then reach your arms behind your back. Stretch your back, roll your head, roll your shoulders, or do some leg circles while holding on to a counter. Move and breathe.

» Go outside and take a stroll. If it's sunny, sit in the sun.

» Take a warm bath. Add some bubbles or soothing oil.

» Do a ten-minute exercise or yoga routine.

» Give yourself a hug.

» Try writing about your feelings in a journal.

» Try meditation.

» Listen to soothing or well-loved music.

» Light a scented candle or burn incense.

» Drink a cup of hot tea.

» Think of five things you are grateful for.

» Engage in positive self-talk. You are strong; you have courage.

» Pet your cat or dog.

You get the idea. Stop what you are doing and change something in your environment to ease your stress. It only takes a few minutes. Put those self-soothing activities into your day.

3

Recognizing Narcissists' Emotions and Behaviors

Chapter **10**

Exploring the Nuances of Self-Esteem and Narcissism

Think about how you feel about yourself. Are you satisfied to be the person that you are today? Have you had periods of time in your life that you felt inferior or insecure? Have you had periods of optimism and security in the way you were managing your life?

Most people experience fluctuations in how they view themselves. They have some periods of discouragement mixed with periods of hopefulness. However, underneath those fluctuations, you probably have a sense of yourself, of the essence of who you are, that remains relatively stable.

REMEMBER

Self-esteem refers to how you see yourself, your worth, your values. It's your sense of how you add up in comparison to others and your own standards.

This chapter explains how self-esteem and narcissism are related and how they vary from each other throughout the lifespan, including how narcissistic self-esteem differs from adaptive high self-esteem. It further explains how fragile self-esteem, common with narcissists, can be easily challenged and deflated.

Focusing on Values: Self-Esteem Basics

Most people believe that it's extremely important to develop a high self-esteem. High self-esteem is related to school success, good relationships, and successful careers. High self-esteem is generally thought to increase overall emotional well-being and happiness.

Furthermore, they assume that low self-esteem accounts for a wide range of problems, including

>> Poor academic achievement

>> Violence and delinquency

>> Depression, anxiety, and other mental health problems

>> Interpersonal problems

>> Body image issues

>> Career underachievement

It's assumed that a major focus for parents, educators, and other important care-givers should be on helping children develop high self-esteem. The rest of this chapter challenges some of these assumptions and sheds light on the nuances of self-esteem and narcissism.

Factoring in three facets of self-esteem

I think of myself as a pretty good person. I have raised some great kids who enjoy rewarding work, good relationships, and satisfying lives. I've been honored to have careers in the fields of education and psychology that have given me consid-erable fulfilment. And I have a close, long relationship with my husband. These accomplishments have given me a reasonably high sense of self-esteem.

However, I am a horrible basketball player and a serial killer of tomato plants, I can hardly sew a button on a shirt, and I struggle to follow the directions for putting my grandson's toys together (if they have more than three parts).

I certainly possess those traits, so how am I able to hold onto a high sense of self-esteem with these considerable deficiencies? I can do so because I actually don't care about them — they don't shatter my sense of who I am or my worth as a human being.

Self-esteem has three features:

» The first aspect of self-esteem involves your perception of some quality or qualities about yourself. For example, I kill tomato plants on a regular basis.

» The second facet is your own judgment about those qualities. My judgment is that I lack skill in growing tomato plants.

» The third factor is how you respond emotionally to those qualities and how much you care about them. I have almost no response to this deficiency because I can get great tomatoes at the growers' market. Thus, my self-esteem is not affected by my horrible tomato-growing skills.

The bottom line is that self-esteem is not a global rating of your entire self. It is limited to those qualities about yourself that matter to you. High self-esteem doesn't mean you feel great about everything in your life. Nor does low self-esteem mean that you are a 100 percent total loser. Self-esteem is really about your values, how much you live by them, and your emotional buy-in to those values.

Developing self-esteem

A variety of factors are associated with the development of reasonably high self-esteem. Parental warmth and affection appear to be the most important ingredients in raising children who believe they are worthwhile and competent. In addition, allowing children to explore their environment with proper supervision and judicious use of praise for effort helps develop self-assured children.

Furthermore, while encouraging children to learn new skills through guidance and modeling, parents who raise children with high self-esteem avoid harsh criticism of the whole child when they fail. (See Chapter 6 for more information about parenting and high and low self-esteem.)

REMEMBER

When your child does well, don't say "good boy" or "good girl" (whole child); instead, focus on your child's effort or specific accomplishment (for example, "I like the picture you drew; you worked hard"). Also, when your child misbehaves, criticize the action, not the child. For example, don't say "bad girl" or "bad boy" when your toddler hits another child; instead, say, "I don't like it when you hit; that's not kind."

TECHNICAL STUFF

Psychologists like to come up with fancy names for explanations of everyday human behavior. Two theories, known as locus of control and attribution, look to explain the causes of behavior. Does behavior come from internal forces (dispositional or internal locus of control) or external forces (situational or external locus of control)? For caregivers or teachers, if something about a child's behavior is controlled internally, there is a chance to change or grow. If something is external, it's less likely to be able to be modified. The bottom line, it's really all about hope.

Looking at low self-esteem

For decades, psychologists believed that low self-esteem was responsible for all of society's ills. That is what motivated a movement designed to improve everybody's self-esteem to the highest level possible. This movement began in the early 1960s and continues to be practiced even today. The self-esteem movement is largely responsible for children getting trophies for participation, everyone being considered special, and parents and teachers having more trouble setting limits. Social media has also affected the way kids and teens feel about themselves. (See Chapter 16 for more on entitlement and culture.)

And yet, low self-esteem, though not desirable, has not proven nearly as detrimental to academic achievement, delinquency, or relationships as previously thought. In fact, narcissism and excessively positive self-esteem have been shown to be related to aggression and delinquency (see Chapter 11). However, some research links low self-esteem with interpersonal problems, education and work difficulties, and mental health issues such as anxiety and depression. Overall, the research has been inconsistent and at times contradictory. More needs to be done.

The problem is that raising self-esteem by pushing people to make positive self-affirmations or by giving unearned praise simply doesn't work. You can't take someone with low self-esteem and tell them that they are special and expect them to have high self-esteem. Self-esteem has to be grounded in acceptance, worth, and solid accomplishments consistent with a person's values.

Connecting Narcissism and Self-Esteem

Narcissists often score high on measures of self-esteem. Those measures consider whether or not a person feels worthy and satisfied. There is indeed a small positive correlation between high self-esteem and narcissism. The difference between high self-esteem and narcissism is, simply put, that narcissists believe they are superior to others.

Additionally, research indicates that some narcissists feel entitled, arrogant, and superior, but not worthy. Thus, sometimes the disconnect between thinking highly of themselves and feeling unworthy causes narcissists to have lower scores on measures of self-esteem. And many people who score high on measures of self-esteem do not necessarily score high on scales of narcissism.

Research on how people with high self-esteem or narcissism function indicates that both types of people seem to show assertiveness with others, seek out rewards, and have a sense of power or control over their actions. Furthermore, those with high self-esteem, but not narcissism, are generally very well-adjusted, conscientious, have the ability to persevere when challenged, and have good relations with others.

On the other hand, narcissists tend to be disagreeable, angry, uncaring, and entitled, as well as more prone to aggression. They are more impulsive and neurotic. Because of these stark differences, narcissism appears to be a totally different characteristic than overly positive self-esteem. The following sections discuss the relationship between self-esteem — both high and low — and narcissism.

REMEMBER

Narcissism can have different manifestations. *Grandiose* narcissists tend to be loud, entitled, and superior. *Vulnerable* narcissists may be less obvious or subtle in their expression of superiority. *Malignant* narcissists show all the grandiose characteristics along with a lack of morality and a willingness to be cruel. The *mixed* narcissist may have traits that vary over time and reflect the grandiose, vulnerable, and malignant types. (See Chapter 2 for more extensive explanations of the types of narcissism.)

Explaining explicit versus implicit self-esteem

The word *explicit* means clear and unambiguous. *Implicit* means that something is not out in the open; rather, it is implied. For example, say someone tells you that they feel superior to others, entitled to special treatment, and gladly use others to get what they need. I'd say that's an explicit statement of narcissism.

In contrast, imagine someone who never says they are superior or that they expect special treatment, and they don't admit that they use others. Rather, they covertly muscle their way to the front of the line because they secretly feel entitled. Such actions represent an implicit expression of narcissism.

Explicit self-esteem is based on a rational, thought-out, conscious process of consideration. In contrast, implicit self-esteem is more automatic, intuitive, and unconscious. Explicit and implicit self-esteem are not always the same.

In other words, someone can have high explicit self-esteem but still feel unworthy based on low implicit self-esteem. On the other hand, someone can have high implicit self-esteem but not believe that they are performing at that level; therefore, they have low explicit self-esteem.

How do these concepts relate to narcissism? Some researchers believe that narcissists have extremely high opinions of themselves, but underneath, they really feel inferior. This idea would suggest that tests should show that narcissists have a pattern of explicitly high self-esteem and implicitly low self-esteem.

If this is true, those narcissists with high explicit self-esteem and low implicit self-esteem are basically scamming. They tell the world how great they are, but underneath, they feel shame and unworthiness.

TECHNICAL STUFF

Scientists have identified two different ways the brain processes information. One path the brain uses is a quick path — it reacts immediately to what is in front of you. For example, when driving you may see a car's headlights coming straight toward you and have no time to think. Your brain instantaneously prompts you to pay close attention, be ready to turn the wheel quickly, or stomp your foot on the break. Then the slower path in your brain realizes that the car is turning onto another road and you are not in any danger. Consider the quick path implicit. You don't really think; you just behave. The slower path requires conscious thought; it is explicit.

To illustrate the concept of high explicit self-esteem accompanied by low implicit self-esteem, read the following example:

Rose grew up in a poor, single-parent family. Rose's mother worked at several low-paying jobs and was absent most of the time. There was little love expressed in the home. Rose had no relationship with her alcoholic father. Rose was never encouraged, and largely ignored. Education was not valued in the family, but Rose attended school because she got free meals. Her mother bought beer and unhealthy snacks, but rarely had decent food in the house.

In middle school, Rose befriended a classmate who was a high achiever. They became inseparable. Rose was a good listener and provided her friend with emotional support. With her friend serving as a role model, Rose became more interested in academics and found that she easily mastered the material. This was Rose's first taste of success.

Rose continued to do well in high school, and a counselor took her under her wing. The counselor encouraged Rose to apply for college scholarships. She attended the local state university on a full scholarship. Her mother was quite angry that Rose chose to go to school instead of work to contribute to the household expenses.

Eventually, Rose moved out and, after graduation, was recruited by a large financial firm. Rose's intelligence and diligence led to rapid advancement in the company. However, she became less considerate of others, felt superior, and took on an arrogant demeanor. She believed that since she was able to overcome adversity, everyone else should be able to as well. She regularly demeaned and abused her colleagues. She became especially disdainful of the poor.

You might assume that Rose would be very proud of her accomplishments and have a high self-esteem. In reality, her self-esteem blossomed into narcissism. She did *explicitly* feel good about herself, but *implicitly* she still felt like the wounded, neglected child she had started out as. In other words, her explicit self-esteem was high, but underneath, her implicit self-esteem reflected her early childhood experiences and was quite low.

Although several studies have indeed found this discordant relationship between explicit and implicit self-esteem, research findings have been somewhat inconsistent. The research doesn't really tell us that narcissists have low self-esteem on the inside and high self-esteem on the outside. Instead, conclusions suggest that something else, such as early childhood experiences, may be going on that explains the different presentations of narcissism. More research is needed in this area.

Assessing authentic versus arrogant pride

How narcissists express pride may contribute to differentiating between narcissism and high self-esteem.

>> *Authentic* pride occurs when someone has accomplished something through hard work, effort, and perseverance. Authentic pride is a pleasurable feeling that comes after doing something that resulted in achieving a specific goal.

>> *Arrogant* pride occurs when someone refers to themself as a special, unique, and superior human being. When a goal is accomplished, those with arrogant pride take advantage and assume total responsibility, attributing the success solely to themselves, even when others contributed.

Authentic pride appears to be related to high self-esteem and leads to successful relationships and stable, well-adjusted people. Arrogant pride is more highly associated with anger, aggression, and antisocial activities. Narcissists are more likely to express arrogant pride than authentic pride.

Here's an example:

Isaac is the first-born son of highly successful parents. His upbringing was difficult. His parents expected him to be perfect and rejected him when he did not measure up. At the same time, they treated him as if he had to become someone special or grand in order to be accepted and loved by them. He felt like a misfit at school and really didn't excel at anything.

Isaac graduates from college mainly because his family contributed large sums of money to an endowment fund. After graduation, he reluctantly joins his father's demolition business. He is given his own office and a personal secretary. He does very little, basically tagging along with his father on bids and meetings. Although a bit reserved at first, he quickly learns that he can intimidate staff at work because of his relation to his father. He becomes rude and entitled, expecting special treatment from the employees.

Isaac is paid an amazing salary, buys a new car, and gets a great apartment. He starts to feel pretty grand about himself. He easily finds dates who are impressed by his seeming success. He grows into an entitled narcissist, bullying others, becoming nasty and angry when thwarted, and bragging constantly about his business prowess. He shows considerable arrogant pride.

TECHNICAL STUFF

Arrogant pride is called *hubristic pride* in the scientific literature. Hubris is a cocky, vain, pompous arrogance not based on real accomplishments. Hubristic people overestimate their achievements and blame others when they fail.

BLOWING UP A BALLOON OF SELF-ESTEEM

Instead of seeing low self-esteem as bad and high self-esteem as good, a more nuanced approach can explain how narcissism fits into the self-esteem picture. One way to look at self-esteem can be found in the balloon model.

Think about a balloon representing self-esteem. Low self-esteem is like a balloon with too little air. It's pretty useless, incapable of providing amusement. Basically, it lingers on the ground, deflated. Indeed, those with low self-esteem often lack motivation to get things done.

When a balloon is properly filled, it can float and bounce. You can play with a balloon that has just the right amount of air. The balloon is fairly resilient. That resilience can be compared to high self-esteem. Those with high self-esteem feel worthy, accomplished, and as good as others. They tend to be resilient, successful, and accomplish their goals.

Now, blow that balloon to the max. An overfilled balloon can float through the air. But be careful, it's almost ready to burst. Don't handle it roughly, and watch out for sharp objects because it might be punctured. Too much air makes the balloon fragile. Here, the overfilled balloon is just like narcissism. Narcissists have too much superiority, grandiosity, and entitlement, but are easily punctured.

Considering fragile self-esteem

A significant number of people with high self-esteem are able to remain fairly stable in their view of themselves despite the ups and downs of life. Stable, secure self-esteem leads to psychological resilience. People with stable high self-esteem can experience failure and still feel worthwhile. They may be disappointed at the failure, but they don't view it as an overall condemnation of their whole self-view.

Additionally, people with balanced, stable high self-esteem view success in realistic terms. They have no problem feeling proud but are glad to share their achievements with others who may have helped or participated.

By contrast, fragile self-esteem fluctuates up or down depending on current circumstances. Those with fragile self-esteem are constantly surveying their environments for possible threats. Like an over-inflated balloon (see the nearby sidebar, "Blowing up a balloon of self-esteem"), their sense of self-esteem is easily punctured.

Three factors appear to increase the likelihood of fragile self-esteem:

>> **Contingent or conditional self-esteem:** Contingent self-esteem is based on whether or not a person meets certain standards. It fluctuates depending on that particular value. For example, a teenage girl may base her self-esteem only on the way she looks. So if she doesn't meet particular standards (such as those on social media), her self-esteem plummets.

>> **Unstable self-esteem:** People with unstable self-esteem change their opinions of themselves frequently. Their self-esteem changes depending on the environment they are in. For example, a person with unstable high self-esteem may feel worthless because of an unexpected mistake or overconfident in other situations. Even moods can alter unstable self-esteem. Those with unstable self-esteem tend to be defensive and self-aggrandizing.

>> **Low implicit self-esteem:** See the section "Explaining explicit versus implicit self-esteem," earlier in this chapter. Implicit self-esteem refers mainly to unconscious feelings about self-worth. Those with low implicit self-esteem also show fragile self-esteem.

Narcissism is related to self-esteem and seems to fit well with the idea of fragile self-esteem. Narcissists also survey their environments for threats to their self-views. However, they tend to overlook negative evaluations and their grandiose view of themselves is relatively stable.

Narcissists with some aspects of fragile self-esteem, such as low implicit self-esteem, are likely to show aggression when threatened. See Chapter 11 for more information about the relationship between narcissism and aggression.

TIP

When dealing with someone who appears to have fragile self-esteem, watch out and try not to engage. They are likely to overreact to any threat to their egos. They, like many narcissists, tend to blame others when things go wrong.

Chapter **11**

Assessing Narcissistic Aggression

A s Chapter 2 explains, there are many degrees of narcissism. Some people have minor traits of narcissism that don't have a great impact on their day-to-day functioning. As the narcissistic traits become more prominent, their lives get caught up in a battle to maintain superior status, obtain much-needed admiration, and demand special treatment. And narcissistic people often turn to *aggression* (harming, injuring, or intimidating someone else) to get their way.

Interestingly, aggression is linked to mildly narcissistic, moderately narcissistic, and severely narcissistic individuals. In other words, even a little bit of narcissism increases the odds of antagonistic, hostile, and sometimes violent behavior.

This chapter explains why narcissists get aggressive. All four types of narcissists (grandiose, vulnerable, malignant, and mixed) are more likely to become aggressive than non-narcissists. The chapter discusses the types of aggression that narcissists engage in and ends with strategies for coping with narcissistic aggression.

Threatened Egos: When Narcissists Get Aggressive

Many narcissists appear to have fragile or unstable egos. Specifically, they have very thin skin, easily punctured by negative feedback. They react with aggression when ridiculed, humiliated, or embarrassed. And sometimes, the people who are supposedly humiliating them have no idea what they did to anger a narcissist. That's because narcissists are on continuous lookout for even the slightest insult or challenge to their sense of superiority.

GO BLUE: NARCISSISM BETWEEN RIVALS UNIVERSITY OF MICHIGAN AND OHIO STATE

Quite a few studies of narcissism and aggression are carried out on college campuses. They often involve giving all the participants tests of narcissism, and then putting them in situations in which they are given negative feedback that constitutes a threat to their egos. Participants are then given the opportunity to respond aggressively to those who gave them negative evaluations.

The aggressive responses often include subjecting their alleged opponents to loud, unpleasant noises, sham administration of electric shocks, or giving their opponents sauce of varying heat levels (hotter sauce is considered more aggressive than mild).

Unknown to the research participant, none of these aggressive responses actually get delivered to another person. Results then compare those with low levels of narcissism to those with high levels of narcissism. Analysis consistently shows that the more narcissistic the participant scores on the test of narcissism, the more aggressively they respond.

For example, one study was conducted near Ann Arbor, Michigan, home of the University of Michigan (UM). Students were given a task and told that the task was very easy. In fact, they were told they should do very well on the task and beat their opponent. They were then pitted against an opponent who was supposedly not very good on the task (there really wasn't an opponent).

There were two situations. During the first, students were told that they lost to an opponent from Columbus, Ohio, home to Ohio State University, UM's top rival. They were then allowed to give a loud blast of noise to their opponent. Choosing to administer loud, noxious noises was considered a measure of aggression. As predicted, narcissists gave louder blasts. However, when the opponent was not identified as being from Columbus, Ohio, there was not as much difference between narcissists and non-narcissists. These results suggest that the shame of losing to a rival was humiliating and pushed them into an even more aggressive response.

Reactive aggression

The most common reason for narcissistic aggression is the feeling of being provoked. The provocation is usually perceived as a threat to the narcissist's inflated ego. However, those provocations can seem very mild and would rarely call for aggression from those who are not narcissistic. This act of aggression after being provoked is called *reactive aggression*.

Narcissists excuse their behavior because of a real or imagined threat. They must react or lose, and losing is intolerable to a narcissist. Their reactions are impulsive and include high emotional arousal, usually accompanied by anger.

This belief that they are being attacked immediately puts the narcissist in the position of being a victim, so they can implicate someone other than themselves for the aggressive response. Here are a few examples of narcissists' excuses:

>> He cut me off in traffic. He needed to learn a lesson, so I gave him the finger, cut him off, and slammed on my brakes.

>> He broke up with me, so I told all of my online friends to start sending him insulting and mean messages. I even posted his cell number so they could leave dirty texts.

>> He never even told me I looked beautiful before the party, so I refused to speak to him for the next two weeks.

>> I should have won; the other guy was probably cheating. The game was rigged, but I'll get them back.

>> I deserved a bigger raise, and when I told my boss, he basically threatened me by saying that I might get fired. He needed to be taught a lesson, so I took a gun to the office to intimidate him.

>> Those kids think they're so dope. When I got suspended, I just wanted to show them exactly how dope *I* am.

>> She was asking for it, dressing like a slut and flirting with me, and she really meant yes, even when she said no.

>> Those people are moving into our neighborhoods and stealing our jobs; they need to be taken out.

Narcissists respond to provocation with hot-tempered reactions. Those reactions are aggressive and over the top. Narcissists engage in verbal aggression, physical aggression, passive aggression, and intimidation. They retaliate in order to maintain their superior status or their affiliation with a particular group.

Proactive aggression

Unlike reactive aggression, *proactive aggression* is deliberate. Proactive aggression is planned in advance and particularly cold-blooded. It is used to get something that the narcissist wants. Although the reactive type of aggression is more common, proactive aggression is often more cruel and violent.

Examples of proactive aggression include:

>> Robbery to obtain money or goods

>> Among children, pushing someone down to get a desired object

>> Some rapes, although most rapes are not planned in advance

>> A few murders, though again, most murders are impulsive

>> Planned cyberbullying to get revenge

>> Bullying behaviors to obtain higher status

>> Planned mass shootings

Proactive aggression is associated with a lack of empathy and a belief in the inferiority of others. Proactive aggression among teens predicts antisocial behavior in adulthood.

Identifying Forms of Narcissistic Aggression

Aggression takes various forms such as verbal abuse, physical abuse, passive aggression, or bullying. Aggression is directed toward a specific individual target or a particular group. It can also harm innocent individuals who just happen to be in the wrong place at the wrong time, for example, at work, a movie theater, a mall, a grocery store, a parade, a night club, a park, a community event, a school, or a house of worship.

Narcissists deeply crave attention and want to maintain their perceived superior status. Therefore, any threat to their overinflated egos can result in an aggressive response. Those responses can be impulsively reactive or proactive, involving plotting and planning.

Bullying

Bullying is a strategy that narcissists use to maintain their superiority over others. Bullying may occur at home, at work, online, or in the schoolyard.

Narcissists make great bullies; they believe themselves to be superior and lack empathy. Bullies ambush their victims through not only physical abuse but also words by spreading rumors to others. Cyberbullying has become a frequent form of bullying for cowardly narcissists who anonymously cause untold pain to their vulnerable victims.

Verbal

Some bullies stick to verbal abuse. They may tease, taunt, threaten, or intimidate. They adopt aggressive postures accompanied by loud and threatening voices. These bullies tend to operate under the radar of authority figures and are unlikely to be caught. If caught, they deny their abusive behavior and blame the victim for lying. Because the behavior is verbal, it's pretty hard to prove.

Social

Social aggression involves making someone feel bad by telling other people in the group lies about them, spreading rumors, hurting their reputations, or blatantly humiliating them in front of a group. Children who are social bullies cause serious harm by excluding their victims from a group or telling others to stop being friends with the victim.

Social bullying exists among different groups, including some religious-based organizations. In-group members may shun out-group members or individuals who have somehow broken the norms of the religion. For example, a person who gets married after a divorce may not be allowed to participate in some religious rites. Shunning has been found to be particularly emotionally harmful to those who experience it.

Physical

Physical bullying ranges from mild to serious. A bully may push someone aside, such as when a narcissist who wants to be in the front of a photo opportunity literally shoves another person away. This feeds their narcissistic ego. Physical aggression can escalate into domestic violence, assault, and even murder. When a narcissist is threatened, the outcome can be unpredictable.

Cyberbullying

Narcissists spend considerable time online. Online platforms allow narcissists to promote and enhance their overly inflated view of themselves. The more clicks and likes they get, the better they feel.

In addition, the internet provides narcissistic individuals a sense of anonymity; they perceive themselves as invisible to others. Feeling invisible in this way gives the narcissist, especially vulnerable narcissists, a greater sense of power. Therefore, they tend to be disinhibited and openly display their hostility and lack of empathy.

TIP

The impact of cyberbullying in teenagers is likely more acute because the entire school body is often linked through social media. Thus, the humiliation is often comprehensive, and the narcissists/bullies get their recognition the very next day in person. It's a tight feedback loop with more dire consequences than cyberbullying strangers.

There is some evidence that narcissists frequently engage in cyberbullying. It's made easier by the fact that they can conduct their bullying behavior without suffering consequences. Malicious online behavior or online harassment can involve a spectrum of abusive activities. The following are some of many examples:

>> **Trolling:** The purposeful act of making provocative or disturbing comments online to cause emotional arguments. Trolling doesn't usually target any particular individual but can cause damage by inflaming others. Trolls ignore evidence, dismiss others, and make off-topic remarks.

>> **Revenge porn:** A form of abuse in which sexually explicit pictures or videos are shared online without a person's consent. It often involves former or current partners and can be used as blackmail or simply for revenge. Sometimes victims are photographed or videotaped without their knowledge. These pictures can then be used to threaten or control the victim.

>> **Cyberstalking:** A form of stalking that involves invading someone else's online information. Cyber-stalkers gather personal information, spread rumors, and sometimes use personal information to send unwanted

deliveries to their victim. Many of the victims are former partners of the stalker. However, some victims do not know the identity of the person stalking them.

>> **Swatting:** A dangerous form of cyberbullying. The abuser makes a prank call to the police and makes up a story involving a potentially violent situation at someone else's home. The SWAT team arrives at the unsuspecting victim's address. Swatting can also be directed at public places, such as when someone calls in a fake bomb threat. Swatting has resulted in injury and even death.

>> **Mobbing:** Mob harassment occurs when someone recruits a group to send someone hateful or frightening messages.

>> **Doxing:** This type of cyberbullying occurs when someone releases personal or private information online. For example, people have engaged in doxing by giving out private telephone numbers, email addresses, or physical addresses, inciting more harassment or threats of violence.

>> **Exclusion:** Uninviting or blocking someone from a group.

Other forms of cyberbullying include spreading rumors or lies to others and sending threats or vulgar content. All of these activities can cause considerable distress and suffering to those who are victims.

TECHNICAL STUFF

LULZ (or LOLZ, a plural derivation of the online shorthand for "laugh out loud," LOL) refers to the amusement or laughter derived from someone else's suffering, embarrassment, or pain. It is commonly used online and in texting and refers to offensive behavior intended to amuse the perpetrator and disturb the victim. LULZ is similar to the word *schadenfreude*, which means to get pleasure from someone else's failure or suffering.

Passive aggression

Passive-aggressive behavior is indirect rather than obvious aggression. It is often used by a narcissist because the intent can easily be denied. The following are examples of passive-aggressive responses:

>> Deliberate procrastination

>> Silent treatment

>> Sarcasm

>> Denial of feelings

>> Pretending to forget something

THE CORRELATION BETWEEN SELF-ESTEEM AND AGGRESSION

Prior to the 1990s, most people, including parents, teachers, and psychologists, blamed low self-esteem for aggressive behavior. Common sense would predict that people who feel bad about themselves might be inclined to be aggressive. There was actually little to no research that supported this theory; it just seemed to make sense.

In the mid-'90s, researchers started taking a closer look at the relationship between self-esteem and aggression. They found overwhelming evidence that excessively high self-esteem, especially accompanied by narcissism, predicted aggression.

This result was exactly the opposite of what had previously been predicted. Early studies led to more interest and more studies about aggression and its relationship to narcissism. Since the '90s many of the original studies have been replicated, supporting the idea that aggression is linked to overly high self-views.

>> Pouting

>> Performing poorly or making intentional mistakes

>> Constantly being late

>> Belittling behavior

>> Behavior such as loud sighs, eyerolls, or slamming doors

Emotional abuse

The purpose of emotional abuse is usually to control the victim. It wears down a person's confidence, self-esteem, and emotional resiliency. As victims become less secure, they may become more emotionally dependent on the abuser.

Emotional abuse may be completely obvious or quite subtle and difficult to detect. The following are some of the red flags of emotional abuse:

>> Attempts to isolate the victim from family and friends

>> Over-the-top jealousy

>> Constant criticism

>> Close monitoring and checking on the target's location

>> Accusations of cheating (when there is no evidence)

>> Withdrawal of affection

>> Silent treatment

>> Name calling

>> Blaming the victim

>> Constant threats of leaving

>> Invasions of privacy, such as checking texts or social media

>> Maintaining complete authority over the victim's activities

If you are in a relationship with a narcissist, you may find many of these red flags familiar. Research into abuse finds that emotional abuse may be as psychologically damaging as physical abuse.

Note that many of the ways narcissists express passive-aggressive and emotional abuse overlap somewhat. Abuse takes many forms and is often a combination of more than one type.

PETS AND DOMESTIC VIOLENCE

Domestic violence occurs throughout the world. Shelters offer victims safe havens and help them get through their immediate crisis and plan a safe future. These shelters take parents and their children, and now more than ever, they are also including a safe haven for family pets.

Pets are a loved part of many families. It should come as no surprise that victims of domestic violence fear for the safety of their pets. Pets are often a target of abusers who realize the emotional importance of pets to their victims.

The Urban Resource Institute, an organization developed to help people stay safe and secure, paired up with The National Domestic Hotline, a support system for victims of abuse, to look at the impact of pets on those who suffer from domestic abuse. After surveying almost 2,500 people who reached out to the domestic hotline, they found the following:

- Almost 30 percent of pets are harmed in homes that report domestic abuse.

- Over 35 percent reported that threats were made by the abuser to harm the family pet.

(continued)

(continued)

- About half of the victims worried that their pet might be killed or hurt by the abuser.

- About half of the victims said that they would not leave the abusive situation unless they could take their pet with them.

- A third of the children in the abusive household had witnessed abuse or threats of abuse to their family pets.

- More than three fourths of the respondents indicated that their pets had changed behavior because of abuse.

- Over 90 percent revealed that keeping pets safe would help them recover and that pet ownership was an important factor in choosing to stay in or leave an abusive situation.

A few domestic violence shelters are able to take in pets. However, this report suggests that many more are needed. Pets are an important part of a family and need to be considered when addressing domestic abuse and recovery.

Physical violence

Narcissism increases the tendency to become violent. Violence is defined as intentionally harming someone physically. In fact, studies among prison populations find that prisoners convicted of rape, assault, and murder all have higher levels of narcissism than a similar sample of people who were not incarcerated.

Narcissists who feel entitled, lack empathy, and act impulsively may be more prone to violent aggression. Perceived threats to their status and ego are often significant reasons why narcissists become violent.

Although the connection between narcissism and violence has been firmly established, more studies that directly measure types of narcissism, circumstances of violent behavior, and consequences of violent behavior are needed.

Most homicides are unplanned crimes of passion, often involving substance abuse. Murderers generally lack sufficient self-control and act impulsively following a threat to their overinflated beliefs about themselves. Sometimes murderers are engaged in another felony crime, such as a robbery, that involves guns and turns deadly.

However, some murders are carefully planned in advance. In fact, some research supports the premise that serial murderers may exhibit a vulnerable form of narcissism. Underlying feelings of inadequacy along with a sense of superiority and lack of empathy may form an important part of the personalities of serial killers.

Mass shootings and narcissistic rage

While some people call for gun control and others call for more funding for mental health, so far little has been done to stop the common tragedy of life in America, mass shootings.

Much of the public assumes that mass shooters have low self-esteem and are suffering from mental illness. However, many of those characteristics are identified after the shooting and may be subject to bias. Some other personality characteristics, such as narcissism, may be in play.

TECHNICAL STUFF

Brad Bushman, a well-known researcher on aggression and narcissism, wrote a fascinating article titled "Narcissism, Fame Seeking, and Mass Shootings" in the journal *American Behavioral Scientist* (2018). In this article he argues that mass shooters likely have significantly higher levels of narcissism than other violent offenders. Bushman writes that mass shootings frequently involve threats to the ego, such as being fired, suspended from school, or otherwise rejected.

Furthermore, the Federal Bureau of Investigation (FBI), in a paper titled, "The School Shooter: A Threat Assessment Perspective" suggests that the personality of a student should be considered when assessing a threat. Among the characteristics determined to be important are

>> A student's ability to bounce back after humiliation or other negative feedback

>> A need for control, attention, respect, and admiration from others

>> Determining if the student views others as inferior

>> Failing to demonstrate empathy

Do these characteristics sound familiar to you? Is it possible that mass shooters suffer from violent narcissistic rage after a negative evaluation or threat to their egos? More research is needed, especially longitudinal research that looks at normal samples of students over time.

But meanwhile, because of the thinking of both scholars and law enforcement that a narcissistic desire for fame and attention may be involved, there is now a call to not give press attention to those who commit mass shootings. This new stance of not giving attention to the shooter may help to show other potential copycat shooters that they cannot achieve fame from killing innocent others.

Suicide and the aging narcissist

Narcissists rarely seek mental health treatment. Suicide is an infrequent but obviously serious act of violence. Do narcissists commit suicide? Yes, but relatively infrequently.

Among most people, depression increases the risk of suicide. However, depression does not appear to increase the risk of suicide among narcissists. Because narcissism appears not to be associated with depression in the middle adult years, it may actually protect against suicide.

However, the risk of suicide may change as narcissists grow older. In one study, older psychiatric patients were followed over a 15-year period. Those who had previously been diagnosed with narcissism were more likely to have committed suicide than other patients. Their suicide attempts were highly lethal and planned. Some suggest that as narcissistic individuals get older, they don't continue to get the attention and adoration that they believe they deserve. So suicide is thought to be a way out of their distress with the aging process.

The relationship between narcissism and suicide is complex. Much more research is needed to answer these questions.

Malignant Narcissists Know No Limits

Malignant narcissists have symptoms of all the types of narcissism, such as grandiosity, feelings of uniqueness, power seeking, demanding attention, expecting special treatment, jealousy, lacking empathy, and a tendency to exploit others. Combine that with impulsivity, irresponsibility, no remorse, and a lack of regard for others, along with willingness to become aggressive or even violent to get their needs met, and you have a very dangerous person, a malignant narcissist.

Even with these negative characteristics, a malignant narcissist, like all narcissists, can initially be quite charming and interesting. They use superficial charms to manipulate others in order to get what they want. People with malignant narcissism can lie, cheat, and hurt others without feeling bad. They have little regard for the impact of the hurt that their behavior inflicts on others. They even revel in it, while remaining aloof and arrogant.

Although there has been some thought that, like the vulnerable narcissist, malignant narcissists hide a fragile, unstable ego, there is little empirical data about the core of their personalities. Malignant narcissism is a term that has gotten considerable attention from self-help online groups as well as law enforcement. But, like other narcissists, malignant narcissists rarely reach out for mental health services and are unlikely to sign up for a research study. Thus, more research is needed.

Overlapping symptoms with antisocial personality disorder

Malignant narcissists have many similarities to people with antisocial personality disorder. Symptoms of antisocial personality disorder include

>> Disregarding laws or social expectations

>> Lying easily

>> Conning others for pleasure or profit

>> Displaying irritability and aggression

>> Taking risks without worrying about consequences

>> Being irresponsible

>> Feeling indifference to hurting others

MALIGNANT NARCISSISTS SHARE TRAITS WITH PSYCHOPATHS AND SOCIOPATHS

Malignant narcissists share some characteristics with *psychopaths* and *sociopaths*. Although both terms are commonly found in popular literature, courtrooms, and movies, professionals do not consider them to be mental health disorders.

Psychopaths act charming when manipulating others. They have no empathy and are cold and calculating. They may have families and jobs but are never able to form real attachments to others. Psychopaths may be CEOs of major companies or violent criminals. They have no problem with breaking laws or hurting others.

Sociopaths also break laws and hurt others. However, they make good gang members because unlike psychopaths, they can form some loyalty to a group or an individual. Sociopaths are less likely to be CEOs and more likely to be undereducated people who live on the periphery of society. They tend to be disorganized and impulsive rather than cold and calculating.

The dark triad of personality traits

The *dark triad*, a cluster of personality traits first described in the early 2000s, is a combination of three sinister personality characteristics:

>> Narcissism: People who believe in their own superiority and entitlement

>> Machiavellianism: People who are cunning, manipulative, and skillful at obtaining what they want

>> Psychopathy: People who lack empathy and willingly hurt others for their own gain

People with these traits show typical narcissistic entitlement along with callousness, an absence of morality, a gift for manipulation, and a total lack of empathy. The combination is often accompanied by smooth talking and charismatic charm. They can make great salespeople.

People with these traits take advantage of their own family, friends, or coworkers without remorse. They may be expert liars, self-promoters, and con artists. Like the malignant narcissist, those exhibiting the dark triad are often hard to spot.

WARNING

The dark triad can be a lethal combination. Those who have these characteristics can become dangerously aggressive. Think of the malignant narcissist as a narcissist on steroids. Once again, they can come across as smooth manipulators, but they will hurt you without giving it a second thought.

TECHNICAL STUFF

The term Machiavellianism comes from Niccolò Machiavelli, who was a 16th century philosopher and nobleman from Italy. He was known to be a master at manipulation. His writings influenced many in the past and continue to be considered by those in power. One of his better-known points was that it was better to be feared than loved. He believed that fear was a more reliable way to manipulate people than love. Sounds a bit dark, right?

Coping with Narcissistic Aggression

When narcissists become aggressive, they hurt those around them. Unfortunately, they may hurt those who care about them or complete strangers when in an aggressive state of mind. From domestic violence to road rage, narcissists can be dangerous.

If you are a person who has suffered narcissistic abuse, consider your long-term options carefully. Look at Chapter 9 for ideas on protecting yourself if you choose to leave the harmful relationship.

Sometimes, there is little you can do to proactively prevent aggression in a relationship with a narcissist. The following tips help you manage in the moment and avoid escalating the situation.

>> Physical distance is the best first response to narcissistic rage. When the aggression becomes apparent, move away slowly and deliberately if you can. Do not try to physically confront the aggressor.

>> If physical distancing is impossible, stay calm. Try to keep your body relaxed and your hands at your sides.

>> Avoid overreacting. Keep your voice low and speak slowly.

>> If you are in a public place, try to move closer to others.

>> Even if you are frightened, try to keep your face relaxed and neutral.

>> If possible, acknowledge their feelings, such as saying "I see that you are upset."

>> Listen without arguing to give them an opportunity to vent and possibly calm down.

>> If you are alone and feel that the situation may become violent, call 911 as discreetly as possible and leave the phone on so the dispatcher can hear what's happening.

REMEMBER

There is no reasoning or productive discussion with a rageful narcissist. And there is certainly no way to win an argument. Don't even try.

Chapter **12**

Feeling Entitled to Everything

ntitlement is a core feature of narcissism. Narcissists believe that they are worthy of extra privileges, special treatment, attention, prestige, and a constant stream of admiration. Narcissists also believe that these special privileges should occur whether or not they deserve or earn them.

When narcissists don't get what they want, they may exhibit anger or rage, seek revenge, or attempt to reestablish their privileged status by showing off. This chapter takes a deeper look into narcissistic entitlement and how it shows up under various circumstances. It furthermore highlights the different reactions to threats of entitlement by grandiose versus vulnerable narcissists. Finally, the chapter also offers up some tips on how to react to and handle narcissistic entitlement.

Exploring Narcissistic Entitlement

Everyone feels entitled from time to time. For example, you might use your airline miles and splurge for business class on a trip. If the flight attendant asks you to trade with someone in coach, you might resist doing it. After all, you saved up all of those miles and you usually sit in coach. This is a privilege that you earned, and you feel entitled to keep your seat. And it's not a completely unreasonable assumption on your part.

However, for a narcissist, entitlement is not a "once in a blue moon" characteristic. Narcissists feel entitled most of the time. They think nothing of demanding special treatment, for no particular reason, just because they believe that they deserve it. Narcissists express their entitlement in various ways depending on the setting.

At school

Narcissists in high school and college feel academically entitled to excellent grades. If they don't get a good grade, they often blame the teacher. They believe that they should be able to negotiate a higher grade by asking for special accommodations, even if they have no reason to need extra help. They feel free to argue with the teacher, and some send their parents to argue on their behalf.

If a student has something better to do, they will ask the teacher to change the date of an important test. They have no trouble lying about needing to be home with a sick relative or traveling out of state to say one last goodbye to their elderly grandparent. Anything necessary to get what they want is possible and completely permissible to a narcissist.

Narcissistic students also believe that the teacher works for them. Therefore, teachers are expected to please the students by giving easy assignments, being flexible about make-up work, allowing for extra credit, and negotiating deadlines as well as grades. They also think that cheating to get a better grade is perfectly acceptable, as long as they don't get caught. And if they do get caught, they have plenty of excuses ready to cover up their misdeeds. Remember, narcissists are skilled liars.

Narcissistic students go to school to get good grades or meet the requirements for a certificate that leads to a job. They are less concerned about learning the material than achieving the result they are entitled to.

At work

Entitlement can also be observed in the workplace. In fact, it may start with the application for a job. Studies show that narcissists are more likely to inflate, exaggerate, and distort their résumés. They claim that they have education, experience, and skills that they don't.

ENTITLED OR MISTREATED?

Organic chemistry is a difficult class. Some call it a weed-out class, referring to the requirement to pass organic chemistry to get into medical school. If you can't pass organic chemistry, your pathways to becoming a doctor are limited. Many believe that this is a totally legitimate gate to keep out those students who do not have the academic rigor to pursue more challenging and advanced classes. Narcissistic students who feel entitled to special treatment might find the rigor of organic chemistry frustrating. The following example may be a reflection of that frustration.

Maitland Jones Jr., a professor teaching organic chemistry, was fired by New York University (NYU) in 2022 after about 80 students filed a petition with the administration complaining about the difficulty of the class, their poor grades, as well as a lack of help and resources. The other approximately 280 students in the lecture class did not sign the petition. Although the petition did not ask for his firing, Dr. Jones was terminated from the university.

Dr. Jones previously was a tenured professor at Princeton University who retired and then taught part-time at NYU. He was an acclaimed professor known for authoring a text on organic chemistry, as well as receiving awards for his teaching.

This petition happened after two years of the pandemic, which greatly impacted student learning. Because of that, Dr. Jones made videotapes of his lectures for students who were quarantined and weren't allowed to attend class, and those videos are still used as learning tools at NYU. He also noted that students were misreading exam questions, so he made his exams easier.

Other professors noted cheating on online exams. And Dr. Jones received considerable support and sympathy from his fellow faculty members. Even still, his best efforts and intentions, as well as his colleagues' support, didn't save Dr. Jones's NYU teaching job.

Considerable research supports the view that students are becoming more narcissistic and therefore entitled. Although no research was conducted on the particular students who complained about Dr. Jones, one has to wonder about their motivations. After all, narcissists expect to get high grades and may not be as concerned about mastering difficult material.

Narcissistic tendencies may also impact the evaluations given to review college professors. Student evaluations of their professors are frequently used to make decisions

(continued)

(continued)

about employment or tenure. It's quite possible that teachers with low expectations who are also prone to give high grades may get better evaluations than the teachers with high expectations and fair grading receive. This can lead to lower expectations, less learning, and grade inflation.

There continues to be much debate over lowering academic standards to please students and their parents. These complaints by parents and students are heard from kindergarten through graduate school. Many different solutions have been called for, but none have been able to entice entitled students to work harder. See Chapter 16 for more information about grade inflation.

Entitled employees may

>> Expect to be treated favorably by bosses

>> Flaunt time guidelines by coming in late or leaving early

>> Take advantage of paid time off

>> Expect raises or bonuses even when they don't work very hard

>> Resent authority figures

>> Be less likely to cooperate when working as a team member

>> Expect to be named as the leader of a project or team

>> Feel like they are more gifted than other employees

>> Make claims about their accomplishments that are grossly exaggerated

>> Take credit for colleagues' work products

Counterproductive work behaviors (CWBs) are behaviors that hurt the organization or employees of the organization. CWBs include such things as petty (like stealing paper clips) or major theft (embezzlement or other white-collar crime), gossiping and rumor spreading, deliberate work slow-downs, and aggression.

When entitled narcissists' egos are threatened at work, or they become frustrated by a difficult task, they react with anger or aggression. Because of their rage, they seek revenge by engaging in CWBs. These actions are retaliations aimed at the organization.

In addition, narcissists have low levels of integrity, are less ethical, and feel free to exploit others to obtain self-gain. Many don't hesitate to lie, cheat, and claim others' work as their own.

In everyday life

Entitled people believe that they deserve special treatment for no other reason than that they are somehow special. The world owes narcissists favors because, well, because they deserve to be treated better than others. Entitlement makes very little sense to a person without narcissism. Of course, it's nice to be treated as special, but why would anyone expect it unless they have somehow earned it?

Narcissists don't care if their entitlement causes distress to someone else. For example, a narcissist may demand that their partner stop doing what they are doing to tend to their needs. When their entitlement is rewarded with goodness or special service, they are not thankful because they feel that what was done for them was expected.

Entitled narcissists believe that they deserve more than they or others have. They blame others for not meeting their every expectation and put their own needs ahead of anyone else in the household. They lack empathy or understanding of their impact on other members of the household.

If you live with an entitled narcissist, watch out for land mines. You never know what may set off the narcissist's rage when things are not exactly right. Something as simple as not hanging clothes the right way, not getting a chore done immediately, or forgetting to put the dishes in the dishwasher on time can set off a barrage of abuse.

Seeking Status: Why Narcissists Feel They Deserve the Latest and Greatest

Similar to feeling entitled, narcissists revel in status. They use their possessions to impress others and are easily convinced that they need the latest and greatest gadget. Being superior and entitled, they must look good and feel good. This desire can lead to trouble.

You're so vain: Looking good at any cost

Narcissists are vain. They want to look good. That is reflected in studies that show narcissists tend to wear clothes that lead others to notice them. Women with narcissistic traits wear more makeup and dress in especially provocative clothes, with the intention of being the center of attention. Men with narcissistic traits are also more likely to dress to get attention and take more time with grooming than those without narcissistic traits.

Narcissists may not be objectively more attractive than non-narcissists, but their appearance seems to draw the attention of others. They have a talent in using accessories to make themselves seem more attractive.

When the natural aging process begins to be noticeable, the narcissist quickly makes an appointment. Narcissists want to keep their perfect young bodies and faces. Research has shown that people with a narcissistic personality are more frequently found in the plastic surgeon's office than those without that characteristic. In addition, narcissists are more likely to have injections and use cosmetics to keep aging at bay. There is no such thing as graceful aging to the narcissist.

IDENTIFYING NARCISSISTS BY THEIR EYEBROWS

A study published in the *Journal of Personality* noted that previous research had found that people are sometimes able to identify grandiose narcissists simply by their looks. Since narcissists often present themselves as friendly, engaging, and extroverted, the study hoped to help people identify narcissists early, so that they can avoid getting entangled with them.

Therefore, the purpose of this study was to determine what aspect of a narcissist's face was most important in identifying them. The surprising result was that eyebrows, especially their thickness, density, and grooming, were the primary distinguishing characteristics of a narcissistic face.

The study was able to come to this conclusion through a series of experiments. Participants took the Narcissistic Personality Inventory to determine their levels of narcissism. Then they were asked to maintain neutral expressions while being photographed. Through a series of experiments, which included photo manipulation and switching eyebrows from person to person, the researchers found that eyebrows were the single most accurate way to discern a narcissist. This result was found to be true among both men and women.

So, calling all narcissists. If you want to maintain secrecy, stop plucking those eyebrows!

Since reading this article, I have been obsessed with looking at other people's eyebrows. First, I noticed that everyone on television has nice-looking eyebrows. Many of my friends also have nice-looking eyebrows. Does that mean that all people on television are narcissists? Maybe. But I know that some of my friends are not narcissists. So, the bottom line is that research studies only capture some of the trends and there are many exceptions to the rule.

Bragging about brands

The products that you use and buy may help support your own view of yourself. If you tend to view yourself as practical, you may evaluate purchases on their relative cost and utility. However, if you have narcissistic tendencies, you are more likely to choose prestigious brand-name goods even when they are more expensive but not necessarily better quality than other brands. Narcissists' decisions to buy brand-named goods stem from viewing themselves as entitled, special, and better than others.

Narcissists buy products to show their affluence and distinguish them from others. Their egos may be fragile or vulnerable; therefore, they become materialistic to strengthen their self-worth and show the world how superior they really are. Narcissists buy flashy and fashionable goods that pump up their overly inflated but unstable egos. The brands they choose become status symbols that convey their wealth and superiority while also reaping recognition and admiration.

Focusing on flash over functionality

When given a choice, narcissists choose bling over utility. An interesting experiment gave participants two choices of products. One was more attractive but less practical. Four products were featured. Results suggested that people with narcissistic traits were more likely to choose the attractive product even if it was less reliable or practical.

The choice of fancy versus sensible is another way that narcissists can show off. They also like to be able to choose unique and customized goods. For example, most people choose standard colors for their cars, such as white, gray, or black. Narcissists are more likely to choose unique colors and customized features when buying a car. Consider the case of Ethan:

Ethan is moving from New York, where he used public transportation, to Los Angeles, where he certainly needs a car to get to and from work. He begins to search online for used cars. He narrows the search to two cars, which I call brand X and brand Y. Here are the features of each car.

Brand X:

- Well known for its reliability
- Good gas mileage
- Low mileage to date

- No accidents reported

- Outstanding, clean condition, painted gray

Brand Y:

- Has a prestigious name

- Bright blue metallic paint

- Ranked low for reliability

- Has custom wheels

- Has worse gas mileage but more power

If Ethan has a high level of narcissistic traits, which car do you think he will choose? On the other hand, if Ethan does not show narcissistic traits, which car will he choose? I'm guessing you're correct. The narcissist goes for bling over practicality and chooses brand Y.

Narcissists also buy to be competitive with their friends and neighbors. They don't just want to keep up with the Joneses, they want to exceed them. In order to accomplish this, narcissists will gladly go into debt, thinking about their short-term goal of showing up their neighbors rather than practical long-term financial goals.

Scoring exclusive items

When items are rare, their value typically increases. For example, during the holiday season, popular toys that are hard to get usually become more desirable. Rare coins, paintings, or books command a much higher price than more common ones.

In other words, scarcity increases the perceived value of a product, independent of quality. Advertisers use this concept rather than quality to increase sales. In fact, the products may be deliberately underproduced for a time to increase the impact of scarcity.

Narcissists desire uniqueness and exclusivity. They believe that by obtaining scarce products, they will be envied and admired. Narcissists are more likely than non-narcissists to buy scarce products without considering the purpose or quality of the product. This suggests that narcissists are relatively easy targets for advertisers that use the scarcity message.

Materialism refers to the value consumers attach to goods. Among non-narcissistic people, materialism is associated with a decreased sense of well-being, as well as higher rates of anxiety and depression. However, among narcissists, materialism does not lead to a higher rate of anxiety, depression, or a lower sense of well-being. Some suggest that because narcissists desire status and engage in conspicuous consumption, materialism is consistent with their belief system. Therefore, materialism and the assumed status it provides to them is welcomed by narcissists.

Consuming goods conspicuously

Narcissists' purchases of material goods to boost status, enhance self-worth, and draw attention to themselves is *conspicuous consumption*. They enjoy high-status, impressive brands in order to make themselves look unique, show economic power, and potentially be a desirable romantic partner. Narcissists acquire goods to boost their self-esteem, especially when that self-esteem is unstable or fragile.

Both grandiose and vulnerable narcissists engage in conspicuous consumption, but their goals appear to be slightly different:

» **Grandiose narcissists:** Grandiose narcissists buy luxury brands simply to puff up their already overly positive self-view. They want to distinguish themselves as *unique* and special, entitled to copious amounts of envy. There are no other deeper needs or desires for the grandiose narcissist. They feel good about themselves and just want to establish their superiority by acquiring luxury goods.

» **Vulnerable narcissists:** Vulnerable narcissists buy luxury brands to get more attention and *approval* from others. This helps them build up their self-esteem, which is likely to be fragile and unstable. To a vulnerable narcissist, conspicuous consumption validates their worth. They hope that high-status material goods will help them avoid negative evaluations from others.

The Charitable Narcissist: Doing Good Only to Gain Recognition

Some narcissists show off their grandiose selves by doing supposedly selfless charitable work. These do-gooder narcissists, referred to as *communal narcissists*, get their dose of grandiosity and power through their important roles in a community charity or nonprofit organization.

Communal narcissists gain their entitled self-esteem by controlling or directing aspects of the organization. They feel a deep calling to serve the organization, thus serving their own interest in self-promotion. They believe that they possess unique and special skills.

When involved in their work, they may neglect other responsibilities they presume to be less important, such as their children or partner, because these routine activities don't bring the same public recognition or status. Their particular charity becomes a major focus in their lives and conversations. They harshly criticize others who do not share their excessive dedication.

When engaged in charitable work or giving, they make sure that they are recognized as special. That recognition is best when it is well publicized. Research supports the idea that when donation information is made public, narcissists are more likely to donate than when there is no public acknowledgment of their donation. This is especially true for grandiose narcissists.

Communal narcissists can cause quite an uproar in a charitable or nonprofit organization. They like drama and status and may act in a way that produces infighting among other members of the community. Communal narcissists may put down other members who don't meet their own standards, and they demand to be in leadership positions rather than work with a team.

They promise to be better than those who went before them and fix all the organization's problems. They expect to get plenty of praise and recognition for their efforts. They believe themselves to be the best volunteer or the most understanding person in the organization. Other volunteers may disagree. The following example shows the grandiosity of a communal narcissist:

> Bethany is new to the community. She and her husband move frequently because of his job. Bethany knows the quickest way to make friends is to find an organization and volunteer. Although she's had lots of experience doing charitable work, she often leaves after the members don't show adequate appreciation of her efforts and work.
>
> An article in the local paper features the historical society and its need for board members. Bethany immediately calls and offers her services. She describes all the previous organizations she has worked for and her incredible successes.
>
> The board of directors meet and discuss Bethany's application. Because they are always short of willing volunteers, they decide to invite her to participate in a meeting prior to voting on her to join. When the president of the board asks Bethany to describe her interest, her answers indicate that she has researched the purpose of the historical society and some of its recent events.

Somehow, her enthusiasm causes the board to vote that very day to make her a member. She volunteers to lead a walk through the old cemetery the very next week. Impressed, board members are thrilled to get some help. Almost immediately, more than a dozen people sign up for the walk.

Without consulting other members, on the day of the walk, Bethany shows up with bottles of water, name tags, and baggies of trail mix for all the participants. She also hands out a detailed map of the various historical graves.

The board member who was previously in charge of hikes and walks is a bit put out that Bethany did all of this without first checking with him. He explains to Bethany that the organization already has permanent name tags, and that food is not allowed in the cemetery.

Bethany ignores him and passes out her name tags, maps, water, and trail mix. The other board member tries to stop her, and she becomes enraged. This behavior continues for about a month with Bethany taking on projects and not following the customary rules. Finally, after six weeks she announces to the board that she is being sabotaged at every step and quits without notice.

Communal narcissists do good in order to gain the recognition and glory that they think they're entitled to. When they don't get sufficient praise, they quickly disappear. Bethany is a serial volunteer, moving from one nonprofit or charity to another.

Handling Entitlement in a Relationship: Setting Firm Boundaries

If you are in a relationship with an entitled narcissist, it's important to set firm boundaries. Just because they want special privileges and favors from you doesn't mean you have to provide them. Following are some tips to help you establish those boundaries:

>> Don't take the entitlement personally. Their insatiable needs are impossible to fill. This is not about your willingness or ability to indulge or placate the narcissist.

>> Guard your own financial resources. Be careful not to allow a narcissist's desire for status to influence your financial decisions. If you are in a partnership with a narcissist, watch out for overspending on unnecessary material

goods and services. Try to discuss the benefits of practicality over glitz. Separate your finances if possible, or at least keep a portion of your resources separate. You may need to talk to a lawyer to find ways to protect yourself financially.

» Get feedback from trusted friends, family members, or a therapist. Remember, narcissists are great manipulators and can cause you to question your own sense of what is right or wrong or even what is appropriate or affordable.

» Curb your willingness to put in time. You probably have other obligations. Don't let a narcissist make unrealistic demands on your time. They may ask you to run errands that they are quite capable of doing themselves. Try stating specific times you are available to help. Don't try to explain why you can't do what they want when they want it. Also, make sure you save time for yourself and your own needs. Narcissists don't care about your life or responsibilities.

» Evaluate your willingness to give undeserved praise or attention. A narcissist wants to get approval even when unearned. Are you sure you want to participate in this charade?

» Realize that a narcissist really isn't getting what they want. There is never enough attention, admiration, praise, or special treatment to satisfy a narcissist's craving. They are attempting to fill a bucket that has holes in the bottom. Impossible. You cannot supply enough to satisfy their never-ending demands. You are not responsible for a narcissist's happiness.

» Stop trying to satisfy a narcissist's entitlement. It will likely cause you to have negative emotions about your relationship. You will become resentful if the rewards are always going in one direction, from you to the narcissist. Over time, you may become cynical and dissatisfied. Keep that in mind when you think you can successfully manage a relationship with a narcissist.

Chapter 13

The Struggling Narcissist: Coping with Co-Occurring Disorders

Comorbidity is the term used to describe the presence of two or more distinct illnesses at the same time. Comorbidity may happen because the diseases have similar risk factors or because one disease leads to another. Or they may simply be the result of bad luck. Comorbidities often make treatment more difficult. For example, people with diabetes and high blood pressure are more likely to have heart diseases and chronic pain.

This chapter describes the comorbidities that frequently occur with narcissism. In the field of mental health, comorbidities usually aren't as easy to diagnose as they are in medicine, and one illness can be difficult to differentiate from another. For example, the symptoms of anxiety and depression can be very similar.

With narcissism in particular, the symptoms of two different personality disorders — histrionic and antisocial — often overlap. In addition, other conditions such as mood disorders, eating disorders, substance abuse disorders, and even suicidal ideation may be present.

Almost any kind of mental health disorder can theoretically co-occur with narcissism. This chapter details the most common combinations and a few that are not as common but when they occur along with narcissism can increase suffering.

Looking at Histrionic and Antisocial Personality Disorders and More

Personality traits are long-standing, relatively consistent, habitual responses to the environment. Personality consists of your values, your self-concept, your identity, and your enduring ways of coping with the world around you. Personality involves your range of normal emotions, your way of relating to others, your ability to control your impulses, and the way you think.

A *personality disorder* also represents long-standing, enduring patterns of behavior. However, these patterns are different from what is usually expected in the culture at large. These habitual responses cause distress or impairment in many areas of functioning, including relating to others, reasoning, expressing emotions, and controlling impulses.

THINKING ABOUT THE WEATHER

Today there are clouds in the sky where I live in New Mexico, there is a 40 percent chance of snow flurries, and the wind speed is approximately 10 miles an hour with gusts up to 15. I just described the current weather.

In comparison, the general *climate* in New Mexico is mild and arid, with less than 15 inches of rain annually. Sunny days are common. More than 300 days of sunshine are typical in New Mexico over the course of a year. This describes some aspects of the climate in New Mexico.

Think of your personality as your climate or your general weather pattern over time, and think of your current weather as short-term variations in that pattern.

For instance, you may be a laid-back person, not easily upset or rattled. That is part of your general personality. However, if you were attacked by a bear, you might get loud (screaming), upset, and frightened. You'd probably do a lot of yelling. That behavior, unlike your normal easygoing self, would be your weather for the day.

Someone with narcissistic personality disorder (NPD) experiences high levels of narcissism that cause impairment and distress in functioning long term. NPD co-occurs most frequently with two other enduring personality disorders, antisocial and histrionic.

Leading with hysterics: Histrionic personality disorder

People with histrionic personality disorder are quite emotional; they can cry, wail, scream, and carry on about the smallest upset. They easily switch from one emotion to another in an instant and appear to others as superficial and quite shallow. They're drama queens (or kings) who exaggerate and flaunt their emotions in a theatrical manner.

They crave attention of any kind and try to get whoever is in the room to look at them. Those with this disorder act in a seductive, flirtatious manner, often wearing clothes that emphasize their sexuality. They tend to believe that their relationships are more intimate than they really are. People with histrionic personalities are easily influenced by others.

Both narcissists and histrionics crave attention and admiration. However, a narcissist wants to be admired for uniqueness and success. A histrionic person will take any kind of attention and at times acts dependent and fragile to get that notice.

So, what would a narcissistic personality disordered person who also has histrionic personality disorder look and act like? As you may imagine, their need for attention and admiration is the primary characteristic. In addition, the narcissistic demand for special attention would be accompanied by wild, demanding emotional outbursts. Both personalities tend to look good in order to get attention. You're likely to see sexy, dramatic outfits that both flatter and seduce.

Common to both disorders is the way they consider relationships with others as more intimate than they really are. They can be initially quite appealing to others, but both tend to drive people away in the long run. Take a look at the fictional Naomi:

> Naomi makes sure that she stays at the center of attention. She does that by dressing seductively, flirting with all she has contact with, and getting emotional over the smallest incident. She gets others in her circle to comfort her when she is sad and party with her when she's happy. She often shifts from giddy to despairing in a matter of hours — no one knows what kind of mood she is going to be in. And she makes her moods known to everyone around her.

Naomi is a loan officer in a mortgage company. She's already had brief affairs with most of the attractive real estate agents she's worked with. She's known in the office as a drama queen, constantly waiting until the last moment to get her loan papers completed and getting frantic. She then demands that others help her. These behaviors would likely qualify her as having a histrionic personality disorder.

In addition, Naomi thinks she is superior and special. She believes that she is entitled to extra compensation because she thinks she is the most unique and popular loan officer. She takes advantage of others in her office whenever the opportunity presents itself.

She demands recognition for her efforts not only from her boss, but from others in the office as well. She is arrogant, haughty, and self-aggrandizing. At this point, you probably recognize the symptoms of a narcissistic personality disorder.

Would you enjoy working with Naomi? Not likely. She would be a high-maintenance coworker.

TIP

People with personality disorders usually show traits of more than one personality disorder diagnosis. For example, someone may have some symptoms of narcissism and some traits of histrionic personality. They may even have a few traits of other personality disorders, such as borderline personality disorder (see the section "Other personality disorders that co-occur with narcissism") or antisocial personality disorder (see the next section).

Rules are meant to be broken: Antisocial personality disorder

Someone with an antisocial personality disorder disregards rules and regulations. They think nothing of breaking the law; lying; or conning strangers, friends, or family. They tend to be irritable and aggressive. They display their anger impulsively and don't mind getting into physical fights.

People with antisocial personality disorder are irresponsible and have difficulty finding steady jobs. They don't plan for the future. They also don't care about hurting others or risking their own safety in the pursuit of a goal. If someone gets hurt, they're indifferent, and they often blame the victim.

When narcissism is combined with antisocial personality disorder, be careful. These are not the kind of people you want to interact with. This combination takes narcissism and adds evil to the mix. Think of a narcissist who can charm and make good first impressions, but who then victimizes those who fall for the initial appeal.

The combination of entitlement, exploitation, and lack of empathy in a person who easily breaks laws, hurts others, and doesn't care makes for a very scary picture. The following vignette illustrates the chilling combination of narcissism and antisocial personality disorder.

Jack believes he's the best money manager on Wall Street (the fact that the market is continuing to climb doesn't hurt). He believes that others are in awe of his performance and likes the attention he garners wherever he goes. He fantasizes that most people know him by sight, because his name and picture are often found in the financial sections of the newspaper.

Jack uses his resources to rent a luxurious apartment, buy expensive suits, go to the best restaurants, and attend the latest shows. He always demands the best seat in the house and feels entitled to ask for special treatment. Jack is superficially friendly and has a circle of acquaintances who have given him the praise and adoration he thinks he deserves.

Unfortunately, the market turns downward, and Jack's investments begin to lose money. He decides to turn his customers into his personal bank account by starting up a Ponzi scheme. He's sure that his past performance will make people jump at the chance to invest with him.

In fact, Jack has no problem getting people to invest in a fake fund. He gives the initial investors good returns by using money from more recent investors. He has no moral compunction about taking money from people on social security hoping to increase their retirement savings, his friends, and even family members. His lifestyle improves, and he moves to a larger and more prestigious apartment, buys more expensive suits, and goes to even more exclusive restaurants.

Eventually, his source of investors dries up. Jack has a problem. With little new money coming in, he can't pay his investors their fake returns. He decides to abandon the whole scheme and starts slowly moving his assets to Montenegro, a country that doesn't have an extradition treaty with the United States.

About six months after his fake investment fund starts to collapse, Jack moves to Montenegro where he is able to flaunt his success with the millions of dollars he stole from others. He has no regrets, although he misses the restaurants of New York City.

Jack has both narcissistic personality disorder and antisocial personality disorder. He's grandiose, entitled, craves attention, and doesn't mind breaking the law. He leaves thousands of victims impoverished, and it doesn't matter a whit to him; in fact, part of him enjoys inflicting pain. At least he wasn't violent.

Other personality disorders that co-occur with narcissism

People with narcissistic personality disorder are much more likely to have comorbid antisocial personality or histrionic personality, but they may also have symptoms or diagnoses of other disorders that are also thought to be part of a long-standing, enduring personality disorder. The following brief descriptions give you a flavor of additional co-occurring personality disorders and their key symptoms.

>> **Paranoid personality disorder:** People with this personality have an extreme distrust of other people, don't believe people, and think others are out to get them. They tend to interpret the world around them as threatening. Paranoid people are so focused on themselves that they believe others are also focused on them, looking at them, or talking about them.

>> **Schizoid personality disorder:** These people are strange, detached loners; they lack friends, and they have little interest in sex. They don't enjoy regular activities and are indifferent to feedback from others.

>> **Schizotypal personality disorder:** These people are not only detached from others, but they also have very strange beliefs and are susceptible to magical thinking. They often have odd thinking and speech patterns.

>> **Borderline personality disorder (BPD):** The most remarkable characteristic of those with BPD is that they are frantic about the possibility of abandonment. They also have highly unstable relationships and moods.

>> **Avoidant personality disorder:** Avoidant people also are detached from others, but it is because they fear criticism, have low self-esteem, and lack confidence. They think of themselves as lacking the skills to socially interact with others.

>> **Dependent personality disorder:** These folks have an extreme need to be taken care of, they seek help from others, and they believe they are incapable of living independently. They have a hard time making decisions and ask for input from others.

>> **Obsessive-compulsive personality disorder (OCPD):** Those with OCPD are driven to seek perfection, order, and symmetry. They believe that they know everything. In other words, they consider themselves experts in all subjects. Those with OCPD dwell on rules, organization, and schedules. They are often excessively devoted to their careers.

Chapter 2 describes the symptoms of narcissistic personality disorder as opposed to traits of narcissism. The other two main personality disorders, histrionic and antisocial personality, are covered in the two preceding sections.

Considering How Other Mental Health Disorders May Relate to Narcissism

Narcissistic personality disorder can sometimes co-occur with disorders that are not thought to be part of a long-standing, enduring personality such as histrionic or borderline personality disorder. In other words, the disorders included in this section, such as depression, may be apparent at times, but sometimes go away either on their own or through professional treatment. As you consider this group of comorbidities, be aware that research related to the relationship of narcissism to other mental health issues has limitations.

Recognizing research's limitations

Interestingly, grandiose narcissists usually report high satisfaction with life and rarely admit to other problems such as anxiety and depression. Grandiose narcissists think of themselves as superior, unique, and entitled, and they lack empathy. Most research studies on comorbidity only include people with narcissistic traits of the grandiose type.

On the other hand, vulnerable narcissists are rarely captured in the research literature. This may be because of the way researchers define narcissism, focusing mostly on grandiosity, or because vulnerable narcissists decline to participate in research as it may uncover their vulnerability.

Vulnerable narcissists also think of themselves as superior but are more introverted and fragile. Thin-skinned, they constantly scan their world for any hint of criticism. What little is known about comorbidity suggests that the vulnerable narcissist is more likely to suffer a mood disorder such as depression or bipolar than the grandiose type.

REMEMBER

Mental health research usually involves giving participants surveys and interviews. These studies largely rely on self-report. So, it's quite possible that someone, especially someone with grandiose narcissism, would not admit to any kind of emotional problem. That makes research findings somewhat difficult to interpret. Therefore, the literature most likely underreports the comorbid disorders of narcissism.

WARNING

The next sections describe various mental health disorders that sometimes co-occur with narcissistic personality. These are simply *brief descriptions and are not complete*. Do not use them to diagnose yourself or someone else. If you have concerns that either you or someone close to you suffers from one or more mental health problems, please see a professional mental health provider to obtain a diagnosis and develop a treatment plan.

Depressive disorders

Depressive disorders involve feelings of deep sadness over a period of time. They also include a lack of interest in activities that were once pleasurable. For example, someone who loves to dance would find dancing uninteresting when depressed. Depressive disorders significantly diminish the quality of life. They also interfere with regular sleep, appetite, and levels of energy.

The subtypes of depressive disorder are quite similar to each other. They include:

>> **Major depressive disorder:** Severe depression

>> **Persistent depressive disorder:** Also known as *dysthymia,* less severe but chronic

There are other depressive disorders, but these are the most common and more likely to be associated with narcissistic personality disorder than other types of depression. For more information about depression and its treatment, see *Depression For Dummies* (coauthored by Charles H. Elliott and myself and published by Wiley).

A narcissist may become depressed when they can't live up to their overly idealized self-image.

And the data support the fact that many narcissists experience enough stressors, such as being shamed or humiliated or rejected for their obnoxious behavior, that they may become overwhelmed with depression. Depression is a frequent complaint when narcissists seek mental health treatment. See Part 5 for more information on treatment for narcissism.

Bipolar disorders

Bipolar disorders are distinguished by a combination of manic episodes and periods of depression. Manic episodes involve a period of unusually persistent and elevated or irritable moods.

People in the manic phase often make very poor decisions, have lots of energy, talk too much, have grand and irresponsible plans, and exhibit elevated or grandiose self-esteem. They act impulsively and may go on wild shopping sprees. They often use drugs or alcohol to manage their mania. Unlike narcissists, their grandiosity is confined to the length of the manic episode and is often followed by a crash in moods and self-esteem.

Logically, narcissists with fragile or unstable self-esteem may be particularly vulnerable to bipolar disorder. However, very few research studies have linked narcissism to bipolar disorder.

There are various subtypes of bipolar disorder based on the intensity and length of both manic and depressive episodes. Bipolar disorders require treatment by a trained mental health provider. Most often, that treatment includes medication. For more information about bipolar disorder, see *Bipolar Disorder For Dummies* (coauthored by me and Charles H. Elliott and published by Wiley).

Anxiety disorders

Anxiety disorders all involve avoidance of feared situations. These fears are excessive and often debilitating. People with anxiety disorders often retreat out of fear and miss out on living a full life. The good news is that anxiety is highly treatable.

UNDER THE UMBRELLA OF ANXIETY DISORDERS

Some of the major types of anxiety disorders include the following:

- **Specific phobia:** Unreasonable amounts of fear in response to specific situations, objects, or events. Common examples include fear of spiders, snakes, heights, elevators, or blood.

- **Social phobia:** Fear that arises when a person confronts evaluations or scrutiny by others. A particularly common example is giving a speech in front of others.

- **Panic disorder:** An intense flood of fear often accompanied by a variety of physical symptoms such as shortness of breath, tightness in the chest, shaking, sweating, and rapid heart rate.

- **Agoraphobia:** Intense fear of two or more situations such as being in open spaces, enclosed places like shops or theaters, or having to leave the home.

- **Generalized anxiety disorder (GAD):** Unusually apprehensive and worried most days. This worry can be about just about anything, including work, school, children, or other situations. The anxiety seems difficult to control. A person with GAD can be tense, irritable, have trouble sleeping, and feel on edge all the time. For more information about anxiety disorders and their treatment, see *Anxiety For Dummies* (by Charles H. Elliott and myself, published by Wiley).

One might think that narcissists could develop an anxiety disorder, especially vulnerable narcissists because of their constant attempt to maintain their elevated sense of self. However, studies suggest that anxiety disorders rarely occur in people with narcissistic personality or traits. These studies may once again reflect the narcissistic tendency to deny that there is anything wrong with them. Common sense suggests that narcissists may have considerable worry about always presenting themselves as the most superior human in the world. That seems to be quite a bit of stress!

Obsessive-compulsive disorder (OCD)

People with OCD have intrusive, uncomfortable, distressing thoughts, images, or urges. They try to stop them, but they can't. These thoughts, called *obsessions*, can cause considerable discomfort.

They attempt to decrease their discomfort through specific repeated behaviors, called *compulsions*, such as repeating words, washing, cleaning, rechecking to see that something is turned off or locked, or other rituals. OCD consumes considerable amounts of time.

People with OCD find themselves consumed with fear, worry, and spend long periods of time dealing with their obsessions and compulsions. For more information about OCD and its treatment, see *Obsessive-Compulsive Disorder For Dummies* (also by Charles H. Elliott and myself and published by Wiley).

Like anxiety, narcissists rarely admit to having comorbid obsessive-compulsive disorder.

TECHNICAL STUFF

Obsessive-compulsive personality disorder (OCPD) and obsessive-compulsive disorder (OCD) sound very much alike. However, there is a key difference. Those with OCPD believe that they are living life the correct way and have no desire to change their rigid, inflexible, rule-bound behaviors. Those with OCD are mired in the misery of horrible obsessions and compulsive behaviors such as being fearful of germs and washing their hands until they are bleeding and painful.

Substance abuse disorders

Drug and alcohol abuse disorders are fairly common among people with narcissistic traits. Those with grandiose narcissism may be drawn to feeling good through the use of substances. After all, they feel entitled to feel good all the time.

Those with vulnerable narcissism turn to substances to rid themselves of unpleasant feelings of insecurity. They find relief from their negative feelings by getting high on the substance of their choice. As is the case with all people who abuse alcohol or drugs, these good feelings tend to be short-lived. And a repetitive pattern of abuse goes on and on.

Eating and body dysmorphic disorders

Eating disorders vary from ingesting too little food (*anorexia*) to binge eating copious quantities of food followed by an attempt to purge the excess calories through laxatives, exercise, or vomiting (*bulimia nervosa*). Another type of eating disorder is binge eating without attempting to eliminate the excess intake.

Body dysmorphic disorder represents an overconcern or obsession with a small imperfection in one's appearance. The person spends considerable time either looking at themselves in the mirror or camouflaging the minor flaw. People with body dysmorphic disorders are often found in the offices of plastic surgeons.

Although narcissists focus on their appearance, there is little evidence that narcissism is more likely to be found in the population of people with eating disorders or body dysmorphic disorder than any other personality characteristic. However, narcissists are likely to deny having trouble with their eating behaviors, so the true overlap is unknown.

Suicide and Narcissism

A well-researched theory of why people commit suicide includes a couple of possible reasons why narcissists might commit suicide. First, people who attempt or commit suicide often believe that they no longer have purpose in life. They feel that their lives are worthless and have no value, that the world would be better off if they didn't exist. Since narcissists think of themselves as extremely important and unique, when those strong beliefs are threatened, they may succumb to thoughts of lacking purpose.

Second, they may also have what is known as *thwarted belongingness*, which refers to the belief that they lack meaningful connections to others. They feel unwanted and unappreciated. Perhaps, because narcissists tend to have superficial and troubling relationships, they eventually may feel alienated from others, especially following the breakup of a relationship. These beliefs may increase their risk of suicide.

However, very little research has been done on suicide and narcissism. One study looked at Israeli men in the military who committed suicide. By looking at their records, the study concluded that almost a quarter of these service members had narcissistic personality disorder.

There is speculation that narcissists are attracted to specialized military groups that require rigorous training and education. While they serve, they are rewarded with high esteem and respect. However, when they leave the service, the reinforcement of being in a special unit stops, which may be part of the reason for the high rates of suicide among former military personnel. However, the effects of trauma and post-traumatic stress is a more likely explanation.

Inpatient psychiatric patients, especially older geriatric patients with narcissism, also appear to have a slightly higher risk of suicide. As they age, they may be looking for an escape from the pain of losing their narcissistic sense of superiority. Specifically, they may lose their looks, energy, or health.

TIP

Although there are some reasons that narcissists may become suicidal after experiencing a string of rejections or failures, data regarding this notion are quite limited. Again, the problem of getting narcissists to agree to be research subjects makes these studies very hard to do.

Narcissists, Self-Absorption, and Emotional Disorders

There is one aspect of narcissism that is shared by most psychopathologies, and that is self-absorption. *Self-absorption* refers to an intense focus on the self. That obsessional self-focus leads to all sorts of emotional problems, including narcissism.

Whether self-focus is overly positive or overly negative, it leads to emotional dysfunction and interpersonal disruptions. When people are self-absorbed, their attention is stuck on everything that is happening to them. They don't take in information from the outside and lose focus on their current circumstances.

Thus, someone with self-absorption and depression only processes the negative information available to them and disregards any positive information. Those with self-focused anxiety concentrate on what makes them fearful, and not what is safe and secure.

Too much or too little of any mood, characteristic, or trait usually causes problems. For example, the self-focused narcissist only pays attention to those messages that confirm their superiority, entitlement, and grandiosity. In the process, they overlook information that might help them adapt and relate to others more successfully.

Chapter **14**

Success Is in the Eye of the (Narcissistic) Beholder

B eing successful means that you have achieved goals that are meaningful to you. For example, some people would view success as having a meaningful career, friends, and a loving family. Achieving that, those people live successful lives consistent with their values.

For a narcissist, success likely involves gaining power, admiration, attention, money, and feeling superior. Their values tend to be self-centered and grandiose.

Narcissists who assume leadership roles or celebrity status believe themselves to be highly successful. And in the sense that their prominence is consistent with their values, they are successful.

In fact, narcissists often find themselves in positions of leadership. Their outgoing, self-confident nature along with an arrogant, entitled, and manipulative manner allow narcissists to promote themselves successfully. When you put narcissists in with a group of strangers, they are the first to introduce themselves. They are rarely socially anxious and readily charm those around them.

Narcissistic leaders, celebrities, and social media influencers are sometimes very effective. They can be creative, take risks, and make big changes. However, their success is often short-lived.

This chapter helps you identify the seemingly successful narcissist in business and politics, in music and film, and on social media. Knowledge is power, and understanding narcissistic behavior protects you from being victimized or seduced by the narcissist in your life.

Enjoying Short-Term Success as Business Leaders and Entrepreneurs

Narcissists often assume leadership positions in business. In these positions, like other realms of their lives, they demand attention and admiration. Narcissists display a self-confident, competitive, driven personality. They are noticed by others. And they have no hesitation about promoting themselves.

Narcissists believe they are more talented than other employees and communicate with braggadocio to anyone willing to listen. They assume all credit for success and always blame someone else when they encounter failure. Narcissists use and manipulate others to get ahead.

Narcissistic business leaders tend to be independent, innovative, and focused on success. Their magnetic personalities convince others to believe in them. However, they may not be good managers of people because of the same traits that put them in leadership positions in the first place. Their sense of superiority, willingness to use others, and arrogance do not always lead to good team building or sensible management strategies.

TIP

Not all people with narcissistic traits fail at business. In fact, a modest proportion of narcissistic traits likely contributes to success. Numerous highly successful narcissists lead major companies. Their charismatic personalities energize and inspire their employees.

Struggling to relate to others

Research on narcissistic leaders back the tendency for narcissists to emerge as leaders early on, but many eventually fail at long-term effectiveness. Narcissistic leaders are often unpredictable, make unreasonable demands on staff, and fail to nurture good working relationships. They lack empathy and don't like to listen to the opinions of their staff, especially if those opinions differ from their own.

They exhibit arrogance and insensitivity, which leads to frequent staff turnover. Those staff changes cause the business to become less efficient and waste money on hiring and retraining new employees. In addition, the typical narcissist is on the lookout for threats to their overly inflated self-esteem. They often become suspicious, seeing threat or danger in the success of other members of the organization.

They may pump themselves up by putting others down. When criticized, they lash out and at times appear to be abusive. Studies show that narcissistic leaders are perceived to be more sadistic by staff members who have low self-esteem than those with high self-esteem.

Workers with low self-esteem are easy targets for a narcissistic supervisor. When criticized, those with low self-esteem become less efficient and productive as well as experience greater amounts of burnout. Those with high self-esteem may be protected from narcissistic abuse because they understand the source, don't personalize the message, and are more secure in their belief of their inner worth.

Practicing risky business

Bold, confident, risk takers, narcissists often make good entrepreneurs. They imagine the unimaginable and are great at vision statements and strategic thinking. They seek out opportunities and make inspiring pitches. In fact, they are often quite good at attracting early funding opportunities. They're decisive, self-confident, and charming, which encourages and excites investors. They look for businesses that will provide them with lots of admiration and attention.

However, over time, some lose their enthusiasm for fundraising and fail to develop long-term relationships with funding sources. They become less interested in the day-to-day functioning of the company. Unfortunately, although some narcissistic entrepreneurs are successful, they generally don't reach out or allow others to give them valuable feedback.

Thus, they limit their opportunity to learn from their own mistakes. Furthermore, narcissists usually surround themselves with people who don't dare to criticize them. Since they don't acknowledge problems, they can't solve them. Therefore, they engage in drama as an alternative. Because they lack knowledge about their flaws, they may be seduced into a more grandiose form of narcissism along with growing paranoia and distrust of others. That growing narcissism increases their risk of failure.

TIP

A little narcissism may be what it takes to have the confidence to dream big, but too much narcissism can overpower the dream and turn it into a nightmare.

REMEMBER

Some narcissistic leaders are wildly successful in business either as CEOs or entrepreneurs. However, the trait of overly positive self-view, along with excessive entitlement, usually leads to risky business and underwhelming productivity, sometimes even shocking failures, over the long run.

Looking to Win: Narcissists as Politicians and Dictators

In today's political climate, who would ever consider putting themselves out there to run for public office? Well, considerable research has been done about the personality traits of people who seek to win elections.

The most frequently reported personality trait of people who run for office is extroversion. Politicians are naturally socially outgoing. They can talk to just about anyone. They also tend to think highly of themselves and are willing to promote their ideas in a campaign. Politicians also show fearless boldness, declaring themselves to be better than their rival candidate.

TECHNICAL STUFF

Interesting research conducted in both the United States and Denmark suggests that narcissistic people engage with politics and become politicians more frequently than non-narcissists. Those with narcissistic tendencies want power and status. Like all narcissists, they are grandiose, believing in their own superiority. This pattern has the potential to negatively affect the policies of a government full of narcissists. If narcissists control the government, you can expect legislation benefiting those who lack empathy, desire control, and feel entitled to become the norm.

Making more extreme politicians

There has been some speculation that certain political candidates also have traits that are consistent with the dark triad of personality (see Chapter 11 for more about the dark triad). Briefly, the dark triad features traits of narcissism mixed with psychopathy and Machiavellianism. Psychopaths are impulsive, lawless, reckless, and lack empathy. Machiavellian traits include an uncanny ability to manipulate others with trickery or flattery for personal gain.

These traits, especially narcissistic extroversion, are understandably beneficial to winning office. Politicians sometimes have to step on toes to get ahead, so lacking empathy can be an advantage. They make empty promises, offering platitudes that have no real meaning. While providing no details on how they will actually achieve their stated goals, they manipulate others to support them.

Just like narcissists in general, narcissistic politicians are often charismatic and appealing. It's easy to be swayed by a narcissistic politician. Who wouldn't vote for someone who, with seeming sincerity, pledges to make their lives better and the world a better place? Watch what they do, not what they say.

TIP

All political parties inevitably select a certain percentage of candidates who exhibit narcissistic traits, including grandiosity, entitlement, and exploitiveness. Unfortunately, solid, reliable data concerning precisely which parties choose a greater proportion of such candidates are lacking. Thus, I advise readers to review what they have gleaned about narcissism from this book and make their own judgments about whether to factor in each candidate's narcissistic tendencies when deciding who to vote for in any particular election.

Controlling personality traits of dictators

Dictators and autocrats assume total control of a population. They attempt to suppress any opposition, disregard laws, suspend or discredit elections, and ignore previously held civil liberties. These leaders recruit followers who seem to act as if they were members of a cult. The personality of a dictator is often charismatically seductive to those who want to believe and take part in the spoils of victory.

Dictators display many characteristics of the dark triad (narcissism, psychopathy, and Machiavellianism). They lack empathy as well as guilt. Their grandiosity allows them to discount input from their staff or followers. They can be vindictive, revengeful, and violent. Their cruelty does not cause them anxiety or distress.

DEMOCRACY, SELF-ESTEEM, AND NARCISSISM

How does self-esteem relate to support for democratic values such as having fair elections, peaceful transfer of power, or an independent judiciary? A recent study published in the *British Journal of Social Psychology* took a closer look at how people evaluated themselves and whether or not they were supporters of democracy.

Earlier studies suggested that those with high self-esteem were more likely to support democracy than those with low self-esteem. What these researchers wanted to find out was what role narcissists played: Were they supporters of democratic values (like those with high self-esteem), or more likely to distrust democracies?

(continued)

(continued)

The scientists surveyed groups in the United States as well as Poland. They chose these two countries because the United States has a long-standing democracy, and Poland has a newer, less-established democracy. Results were consistent in both countries. Those with high levels of self-esteem but without narcissism supported democracy. Those with narcissism or low self-esteem did not.

People with high levels of self-esteem are secure in their feelings and have more tolerance for diversity of opinion. The authors suspect that because narcissistic self-evaluation usually includes defensiveness, those with narcissism are less likely to trust others. Thus, they become threatened when others disagree with their "superior" point of view. They tend to believe others are out to get them and have little tolerance for opinions that clash with theirs. Therefore, they do not share the democratic values that everyone has the right to express themselves and that other opinions possibly have merit.

The authors ponder what effect the possible increase in narcissism will have on democracy. Will a voting block filled with puffed-up narcissists threaten democracy? We'll have to see.

Basking in the Public Eye: Celebrities

Public interest in celebrities has been evident for as long as people have been able to communicate. Many of the earliest celebrities were probably people born into royalty. Celebrity interest was less apparent or intense before mass communication allowed adoring fans to have easy access to information about celebrities' adventures, love affairs, breakups, opinions on recipes, makeup, hairstyles, and fashion.

Research suggests what common sense would tell you: Celebrities are typically more narcissistic than the general public. Interestingly, female celebrities showed more narcissism than males, unlike the findings in the general population in which males are more likely to be narcissistic than females. Female celebrities felt superior, vain, and enjoyed showing off their bodies, indicating more emphasis on their physical presentation.

The Narcissistic Personality Inventory (NPI) is commonly used in research to determine levels of narcissism. This instrument mainly captures the overly positive grandiose narcissistic traits. There are seven aspects of narcissism that the NPI purportedly measures. They are

>> **Authority:** This concept reflects the need to be in a leadership or successful position.

>> **Exhibitionism:** A person with this trait desires to be the center of attention, whether through showing off, being charming, or being the life of the party.

>> **Superiority:** The essence of narcissism is thinking of oneself as better than others.

>> **Entitlement:** This narcissistic trait captures the demand for special privileges and attention.

>> **Exploitation:** An exploitive person is willing to use others to get what they want regardless of the cost to others.

>> **Self-sufficiency:** This is the belief that a narcissist doesn't need others and is the best at getting things done.

>> **Vanity:** A narcissist with this trait is like the original narcissist in ancient mythology. They are riveted by looking at their own reflections.

The NPI has been used to assess celebrities' views of themselves. The results show that various categories of fame show different patterns of narcissism. In addition, other studies have looked at the various personality characteristics of an assortment of types of celebrities.

Celebrities probably need a bit of narcissism to give them the confidence necessary to open themselves to an audience and perform. However, too much narcissism also leads to problematic behaviors, such as manipulation, cruelty, willingness to cheat, and a tendency to degrade others.

The next sections detail some of the most prominent tendencies.

Reality TV stars

Of all the celebrities, reality TV stars tend to be the most narcissistic. They crave attention and power, are grandiose and vain, and willingly exploit others. They present as arrogant and are quite happy to put themselves and their personal issues in front of their audiences. In addition, reality TV stars relish conflict and drama.

Comedians

In order to become a comedian, comics are required to make a name for themselves. Many try, but few are successful. Comics write and perform their own material. It takes considerable persistence and drive.

Like most celebrities, they exhibit narcissism. Comedians want to be successful, at the top of their game, and generally feel superior to others. They are entitled and disposed to use people to get what they want. In addition, they're open to new experiences and enjoy being the center of attention.

Actors

Actors are often vain and extroverted. They demand attention, want to be center stage, and long for success. Despite these narcissistic tendencies, actors are quite good at being able to empathize with others. They're usually agreeable and able to get along well with others. They understand perspectives different from their own. These abilities make them better able to assume multiple roles during their work. Thus, actors often have some toxic narcissistic traits along with socially desirable attributes.

Musicians

Of all the celebrities, for the most part, musicians appear to be the least narcissistic. Although there are notable exceptions, musicians are open to new experiences, stable, and get along fairly well. They work hard to achieve their fame. Generally, musicians do like the spotlight, and they show independence, creativity, and curiosity.

Sports figures

Successful sports figures must have grit, determination, motivation, focus, and work especially hard to achieve fame. They may also have higher rates of narcissism than the general public. Sports offer players with narcissistic tendencies opportunities to be the center of attention; to feel special and grandiose. Highly successful players are often given certain privileged status, which often leads to excessive entitlement.

Like Moths to a Flame: Narcissists and Social Media Fame

Most Americans have access to a smartphone. And about 80 percent of Americans use social media. The rate is even higher among teenagers, many of whom spend hours daily on social media. Although social media platforms change over time, most offer chances to connect with other people, share information, and get feedback.

For a narcissist, posting on social media is a no-brainer. In fact, multiple studies have linked grandiose narcissism to greater use of social networking. Narcissists post more frequently, have more followers or friends, and are more likely to post pictures of themselves than people who don't exhibit narcissistic traits.

Narcissists use photo manipulation software in posts of themselves to suggest that their lives are magical and happy, and they always look good. They easily establish social media personas that enhance their grandiosity. Social media use operates as a two-way street. Narcissists are naturally drawn to social media, and social media increases their narcissism. Busy road.

Everyone can be famous (for 15 minutes or so)

About four-and-a-half billion people use social media. World figures suggest that the average time spent on social media is about two-and-a-half hours every day. Around half of American teens report that they use the internet almost constantly.

With those kinds of numbers, it's easy to see how someone can achieve internet fame with a viral post. A viral post is one that is liked, commented on, or shared and viewed by millions. With a viral post, a narcissist can get instant admiration, attention, and sometimes surprising financial reward.

Monetizing social media fame

Narcissists spend more time on social media than others. Since narcissists love power, control, fame, and fortune, it's understandable that they attempt to make money off of their internet use.

Video blogging or *vlogging*, involves making videos and posting them on social media. It's the perfect sport for a narcissist, who enjoys attention. Successful vloggers can get funded by the platform; for example, TikTok has a creator fund that rewards vloggers with over 100,000 followers and views. Other vloggers receive money for online courses, advertisements, or direct sales.

In addition to satisfying narcissists' need for attention, vlogging can also be a place where the unempathetic narcissist can stir up trouble. To gain power over others, a narcissist can post content that results in controversy, anger, or revenge. See Chapter 11 for more info on cyberbullying.

Interacting with the Successful Narcissist

Interacting with someone who is a successful narcissist takes a bit of finesse. However, in general, the same strategies suggested for dealing with any narcissist are also applicable to a successful narcissist. See Chapters 5 and 7 for more information.

REMEMBER

People are successful when they lead lives that are consistent with their goals and values. The successful narcissist is one that has achieved power, attention, and admiration.

In the long run, those narcissists who maintain lasting success are less likely to be malignant or severely narcissistic. So, interactions should be less fraught with toxicity. You may be able to successfully navigate your relationship with a successful narcissist with mild to moderate symptoms.

WARNING

You're not likely to be able to get your need for intimacy and connection met, even with a mildly narcissistic individual. Take time to find a source of connection through other relationships such as friends, family, or spiritual pursuits.

4

How Culture Cultivates Narcissism

See the relationship between digital media and narcissism.

Find out what really happens when everyone wins.

See the damage that narcissism has created in a civil society.

Chapter **15**

Staying Connected but Alone: Narcissism and the Social Media Effect

As the use of social media has increased, so has narcissism. I was excited about writing this section when I first began looking at research for this book and found that research supports this conclusion.

Various research studies described the steep rise in narcissism across the globe. Studies looked into data collected over several decades beginning in the late 1980s. And some of this literature tied narcissism to a stunning rise in the use of social media. Although the research was mainly correlational and can't definitively establish causation, the graphs of narcissism and social media use rose in tandem.

For the purposes of this chapter, social media is defined as web-based networking sites that allow sharing of information, ideas, personal messages, or content. Examples include such platforms as Facebook, Instagram, and TikTok.

However, as I spent more time with the research, another disturbing trend came to light. It appears that as time has gone on, young adults and teens are reporting more anxiety, depression, and higher rates of suicide. Some think that the isolation that resulted from the pandemic caused this increase of negative emotionality. Yet, these trends predated the pandemic, starting in the last ten years, and have steadily increased over time. Therefore, the rise in emotional problems among teens may, in fact, be related to social media consumption along with a rise in narcissism.

This chapter looks at the likely link between narcissism and social media consumption. It further explores how time spent on social media leads to *self-absorption*, and how the self-focused social media user is susceptible to developing fragile, vulnerable narcissism along with an increased risk of experiencing negative emotions such as anxiety and depression. See Chapter 2 for information about vulnerable narcissism.

Considering Social Media Consumption

No doubt about it, social media has changed the world. Social media was first introduced in the 1990s but blossomed in the 2000s. Some of the early platforms no longer exist, but others have grown from small attempts at communication to huge networks with billions of users. Most people use social media as a source for current events, a way to communicate with others, a place to show off, a means to share information, and for entertainment.

Identifying trends

Globally, about 4.7 billion people use social media (2021). That represents a steady increase of about 10 per cent each year. Many of those users access social media on their mobile devices. Considering that mobile devices were fairly primitive through the 1990s, it seems amazing that smartphones, introduced in the 2000s, have overtaken the world. It is estimated that 99 percent of the 4.7 billion global users access apps, social media, and websites through their mobile devices. Today's trends in social media are reflected in the following statistics:

>> About 75 percent of the U.S. population regularly uses social media.

>> U.S. citizens typically use social media about 3 hours and 30 minutes a day.

>> Worldwide, the average length of engagement on social media is about 2 hours and 30 minutes daily.

   The rate of social media usage is growing rapidly in developing countries, especially in Asia and Africa.

>> Young adults and teens use social media at least eight hours a day.

They're the most active demographic. Older Americans tend to use it less.

>> U.S. women use social media slightly more than men.

Seeing the implications

Increasingly, people get their news from social media instead of more traditional sources such as newspapers or television. Research has shown that people getting news online generally receive less accurate and sometimes even blatantly false information.

Social media allows people in marginalized groups to connect and establish online communities. These communities may be able to exert some political muscle and change policies. However, "liking" a certain cause does not substitute for meaningful political activism.

Social media has also changed business and commerce. Considerable advertising occurs online, and job applications are primarily completed via online platforms. Consumers rely on online reviews of products, services, businesses, entertainment, and travel options. One downside to social media for commerce is that a few negative reviews can ruin a business's reputation.

Although social media was promoted to increase connections, it all too often leads to isolation and despair. Those who lack face-to-face communication in their lives are more likely to experience the negative emotional effects of social media.

Why Social Media Appeals to Narcissists

The vast increase in the use of social media over the last decade as well as the surging rates of narcissism seem to suggest a link.

Research shows that narcissists use social media more frequently than those without narcissistic traits. Did social media use germinate narcissism or did narcissists simply become entranced with social media? It's the old "which came first, the chicken or the egg" question. And it's almost impossible to determine the answer.

SEEING ALL THAT NARCISSISM RESEARCH ENTAILS

Imagine a randomized controlled study of narcissism and social media. Here's an example of a possible study or experiment.

1. Gather a group of 99 people willing to participate.

2. Measure the current level of narcissism in each participant.

3. Randomly assign participants to one of three groups.

4. The first group agrees to avoid using social media during the experiment.

5. The second group is asked to use social media for 3.5 hours per day (about the amount the average U.S. adult spends on social media).

6. The third group agrees to spend 8.5 hours on social media (about the amount the average U.S. teen spends on social media).

7. After two months, have each participant retake the measure of narcissism.

8. Results indicate whether or not social media usage increased narcissism. They also show whether more usage increased narcissism.

Good luck doing that study. There are several obvious problems. First, how many people would agree to limiting, or for that matter, increasing the amount of time they spend on social media? Second, how would you monitor compliance? Would you check their usage on their phones? How about their computers? How about devices they might access outside of their homes such as public computers or work devices? These are the types of issues researchers face.

The best way to examine relationships between two variables, such as social media and narcissism, is to run an experiment that includes random assignment to different groups and measures of the outcomes that may be expected. The nearby sidebar provides an example of such an experiment.

As the sidebar "Seeing all that narcissism research entails" shows, research into narcissism and social media can be daunting to conduct. So, the question remains, which causes which: Does social media increase narcissism, or does narcissism increase social media usage? There is no easy answer.

Self-promotion

Never before has it been possible for just about anyone with access to a smartphone or other digital device to promote themselves to an almost unlimited audience. Online businesses have blossomed, from the small entrepreneur selling handmade gifts to mammoth e-commerce sites.

Self-promotion usually involves making yourself known on various platforms, starting a blog, or developing a website. People who are already well-known may self-promote by frequently posting on social media. Unfortunately, there are few censors on social media posts, blogs, or websites, and they can be either truthful or deceptive.

For example, it's unlikely that you can turn back time and wipe away decades in two days by applying a simple cream, or lose a significant amount of weight by popping a few vitamins. Yet promises such as these are heavily promoted on the internet.

Narcissists love to promote themselves. They take selfies for all to see and present their flawless lives to show off. They really don't care to follow others, but are quite aware of their likes, comments, and shares. Social media gives narcissists platforms to display their superiority, without the sometimes-uncomfortable feedback from real people. But, just as false advertising for products exists, so do false presentations about people, especially narcissists.

Although social media has brought many opportunities to legitimate online websites, information, and e-commerce, buyers beware. That's because narcissists and other people lie all the time on social media. They may exaggerate, mislead, and yes, spread fake news.

Manipulation

Narcissists are masters of manipulation. No wonder they use social media to push their cause or line their pockets. Social media customizes what users see. When users like, share, or comment on a particular post, the algorithm behind the source increases the flow of similar content to that user. In addition, algorithms enable popular or viral posts to proliferate. Popularity, however, may be manipulated on social media. Common means of manipulation include:

>> **Social bots:** Automated programs designed to mimic human engagement. Some report that there may be more bots than humans on social media. Bots manipulate opinions and can be misleading, manipulative, and dishonest.

>> **Fake accounts:** Accounts opened to increase the illusion of popularity.

>> **Trolls:** People who post comments in order to instigate conflict or increase suffering. Narcissists enjoy manipulating others; thus, they make excellent trollers.

>> **Clickbait:** Attention-grabbing headlines that are either totally fake or exaggerated that entice or influence users to click on them to find out more.

>> **Astroturfing:** An illusion that an individual or cause has significant support designed to help sway users to believe in a false narrative. Often conducted using social bots, fake accounts, and clickbait.

The bottom line is this: Don't believe everything you read online. Realize that, like narcissists, social media is designed to sell, convince, and manipulate you. Slow down; don't automatically like, share, or respond to social media. You may be fooled by a social bot or a narcissist.

TIP

Social media can be thought of as a playground for narcissists. Take care and beware. You may be seduced into becoming a victim of narcissistic manipulation.

Anonymity

Another aspect of social media that appeals to narcissists is the relative cloak of secrecy allowed. Narcissists are free to bully, brag, and betray. Anonymity allows users to become their most uninhibited selves. That can lead to aggression such as cyberbullying and manipulation, as well as inciting others to misbehave. See Chapter 11 for more information about narcissists and online aggression.

Anonymity also allows narcissists to behave without the benefit of a critical audience. Although narcissists imagine themselves as grand and superior to others, on social media, they lie and boast to their heart's content. Any negative feedback can be quickly erased and discounted.

Social Media's Impact on Youth and Young Adults

Common Sense Media is a leading nonprofit organization that relies on research for their reviews of the appropriateness of media for children and teens. They recently published staggering statistics. Teens (ages 13 to 18) spend an alarming 8 hours and 39 minutes on their screens. Tweens (ages 8 to 12) spend about five and a half hours. Much of that time is spent on social media. Young adults also spend considerable time on social media — studies indicate that many are spending over three hours a day.

Does social media consumption also increase narcissism among youth? The research is unclear. Like adults, teens with narcissistic traits tend to post more, have more online friends, and accumulate more likes. However, there is no definitive causal relationship between time spent online and narcissism. Nonetheless, common sense suggests a causal relationship between time spent online and narcissism.

Although popular platforms come and go, teens are particularly drawn to posts that disappear and short videos shot by people all over the world. Although the benefits of communication, entertainment, and expression are significant, long-term, excessive social media exposure has many negative consequences.

Lacking maturity, teens are more likely to be vulnerable to narcissistic manipulation. Kids who access social media may be exposed to troubling material, including films that are sexually explicit, violence, scams, examples of self-harm, and cyberbullying. In addition, teens can be victims of sexual exploitation, identity theft, and a multitude of misinformation. Furthermore, while teens are accessing social media, they miss out on interactions with people, sleep, exercise, and homework.

Encouraging self-absorption

Filters and editing result in glamourous pictures with plumped-up lips; intense makeup; and no hint of flaws, spots, or wrinkles. These pictures are produced and displayed on social media. Teens often add bunny or cat ears or other special effects. The perfect faces displayed in the photos on social media lead to an inflated representation of beauty.

Furthermore, young people post photos depicting a parade of happy, fun times with friends and sometimes family. Teens most often post the very best times, often through a lens of enhanced distortion. They rarely show the struggles, challenges, or day-to-day, boring reality of life.

Teens may also overshare and post content that is inappropriately personal or highly sexualized. The posts are usually accompanied by boastful commentary. Of course, narcissists enjoy showing revealing pictures accompanied by bragging. Distortions of reality, in both filtered pictures and overly positive descriptions of activities, paint warped pictures of reality. These overly positive depictions lead to distress for teens who try in vain to obtain the impossible standards depicted on social media.

Social media encourages self-absorption. Like narcissists, teens who frequent social media become obsessed with appearance, positive feedback, or numbers of followers.

Fueling fear of missing out (FOMO)

For centuries people probably worried that they weren't invited to the best parties or gatherings. However, social media has significantly inflated that fear. With people posting their fun times, get-togethers, and parties in vivid color, those who see them and weren't invited can get more than a bit jealous. People look at these glamorous, exciting depictions and believe that others are having more fun, are more attractive, and have better lives than they do. Teens and young adults are especially vulnerable to this worry, or fear of missing out.

Today, fear of missing out, or FOMO, leads to frequent checking of social media. Those with FOMO are apprehensive that others are having more fun and want to stay connected to those experiences. Thus, young people with FOMO may use their phones to obsessively check social media during class or while driving, leading to lost opportunities to learn and inattentive, dangerous driving. In addition, research showed that FOMO leads to:

>> Problematic smartphone use

>> Reduced life satisfaction

>> Difficulties completing daily responsibilities

>> Greater materialism

Interestingly, a couple of studies have linked narcissism with FOMO. It has already been established that narcissists are known to use social media more frequently than others. Furthermore, they believe themselves to be superior and entitled. They also believe that they should experience all of the best experiences in life. Therefore, it makes sense that they experience FOMO, leading to more problematic use of social media. It's a vicious cycle.

Leading to loneliness

Loneliness suggests a lack of connection. It is a state of being that involves feelings of isolation and a desire to connect with others in a meaningful way. People can feel lonely even when surrounded by others. If interactions with others are superficial, then loneliness can occur.

Loneliness, as well as narcissism, has swollen among teenagers over the past few decades. Increases in loneliness and narcissism have been linked to the increase of time spent on smartphones and social media. This increase, like the increase in anxiety and depression, predates the pandemic. During and after the pandemic, loneliness has continued to increase.

Narcissists collect many online friends and followers. But these friends do not involve close, face-to-face, personal interactions. In other words, their interactions are superficial. However, do narcissists feel lonely? Hard to say; narcissists rarely admit to anything that might seem to be weak.

Increasing risk for anxiety, depression, and suicide

Anxiety and depression rates among teens have climbed significantly in recent years. These increases predate the pandemic by at least five years and continue to rise. In addition, suicide rates show an even greater jump. More teens than ever are seen in emergency rooms with suicidal thoughts or attempts. Sadly, completed suicides are also on the rise.

Some believe that time spent on social media increases mental health issues. When kids are on their phones, they are missing out on the in-person connections so important to happiness. They also get less sleep and fewer opportunities to exercise, both also necessary for good mental health. In addition, social media can sling hurtful insults, abuse, and slights, potentially increasing anxiety and depression.

TECHNICAL STUFF

Duck syndrome is the term, first defined at Stanford University, that describes a troubled teen or young adult. Like a duck, on social media, life looks good. All the posts are positive and depict a smooth path; the student seemingly glides through life. However, underneath the water, the duck paddles frantically, like a very troubled teen. The term was used to describe students who presented an amazing life on social media, but ultimately committed suicide. Family and friends were often stunned by the act because there were few clues of struggle.

TIP

Grandiose narcissists appear to have some immunity to anxiety and depression. However, vulnerable narcissists, with their thin skins, are more likely to experience those negative emotions. Perhaps social media use promotes vulnerable narcissism in teens.

Those young people who look for their self-esteem through interactions on social media typically have a fragile, easily punctured sense of who they are. They may be vulnerable to negative feedback that dominates social media. More research is, of course, needed.

Chapter 16

Everyone Is Just So Special: How Culture Fans the Narcissist's Flame

N arcissists believe themselves to be special and better than others. Thus, they are entitled to win all contests, receive the biggest prize, and be cheered on by adoring audiences, full of fans, friends, and followers. These friends or followers of narcissists are necessary to prop up their ravenous self-esteem. The narcissistic culture, reflected in reality television, social media, and the status of celebrity, provides more than ample support for such narcissistic needs.

A culture of narcissism rewards success, beauty, youth, power, money, and status. It is essentially *self* rather than *other* focused. Once thought to be a culture found primarily in industrialized western countries, the culture of narcissism is spreading throughout the world largely because of ease of communication through social media.

In fact, culture provides most people, narcissists or not, opportunities to be seen and celebrated by others. These opportunities occur regardless of the talent or celebrity status of the individuals. Reality television and social media showcase the mediocre as well as average, even without any notable skill or talent.

This chapter takes a look at how a narcissistic culture provides rewards and attention for anyone who seeks it. In addition, culture casts off aspirations such as curiosity, hard work, moderation, and excellence. Instead, it embraces looking good and young, and staying thin as worthy goals to strive for. Those superficial ambitions often lead to devastating behaviors for those who struggle to achieve them. The chapter also examines those behaviors and their consequences.

Rewarding One and All: Downsides to the Self-Esteem Movement

The self-esteem movement began in the 1960s, around the time of civil rights and Vietnam War protests, the assassinations of John F. Kennedy and Martin Luther King, Jr., and the first space walks. The movement, seeded by protest, tragedy, and hope, blossomed like a perennial flower, enduring and persisting to the present day. The movement established sturdy roots in psychology, education, business, advertising, and the popular press. The crusade promised that increasing and preserving high self-esteem would result in happiness, high academic achievement, good mental health, stable relationships, improved physical health, financial success, and socially responsible citizens.

Decades of research have utterly failed to support the promises of the self-esteem movement. In fact, research has demonstrated that despite efforts to improve self-esteem, most of the benefits promised have not been realized. Despite the facts, the self-esteem movement continues to flourish like a tenacious weed.

One tenet of the self-esteem movement is that it's critical to keep negative feedback to a minimum. That idea holds especially true for children. This perspective has shown up in sports and most markedly throughout the educational system.

The self-esteem movement ties in nicely with narcissism. Narcissists believe themselves to be wonderful and hate negative feedback. Even when they fail, they either deny their failure or blame others. Overly positive self-esteem fits hand in glove with narcissism. (For more on how self-esteem relates to narcissism, check out Chapter 10.)

Empty accolades: The rise of the participation trophy

I recently looked at a friend's post on social media that illustrated the problem with participation trophies. The family had attended a school program, including a pizza lunch, celebrating their child's award for "respect." Pictures of the proud parents accompanied by the beaming child who held up a certificate bordered in gold were displayed for all to see.

I couldn't help but wonder what particular act of respect was noteworthy enough to merit a reward, let alone a pizza party. Shouldn't respect just be a normal expectation in school? Apparently not. When children receive rewards for what should be considered ordinary, normal behavior, what is the message? Perhaps it diminishes the expectation that children should respect those around them because it is the right thing to do, not because they'll get a gilt-bordered reward.

Participation trophies have embedded themselves in sports and schools. It's an attempt to eliminate bad feelings, failure, and disappointment as well as pump up baseless, unsupportable self-esteem. Children receive trophies simply for being on a team, participating in a science fair, or as previously noted, for being respectful.

Whether they win or lose, have worked hard or sloughed off, everyone takes home a trophy. Over the years, many children have accumulated piles of meaningless, insignificant ribbons, certificates, and trophies, usually stashed and forgotten on dusty shelves.

I am aware of the argument that rewarding behavior is usually good for children and, to a degree, it is. But rewards should convey a meaningful message based on actual achievement. And it's not just about winning. For example, if a child on a team works hard and improves throughout the season, it's perfectly fine to acknowledge their effort with a certificate indicating "most improved."

But when all children receive trophies for merely showing up, it rewards all participants, even those who were scrolling through social media during practice and treating teammates and the coach with dismissive disrespect. That behavior is not exactly commendable, but it is rewarded, with participation trophies, nevertheless.

On the other hand, parents, teachers, and coaches should note that participation trophies have some place in sports. When very young children, who haven't yet acquired the concept of winning or losing, work hard on a team, it's perfectly fine to reward their efforts. However, over time, winning and losing take on much more meaning and significance. And participation trophies should be faded out.

Tell kids what a great effort they are making or pat them on the back for good, clean, fair play. Hand out certificates for special accomplishments. And give all kids a pizza party at the end of the season whether they win or lose; just save the trophies for the top finishers.

Empty rewards give people the message that they deserve attention and acclaim whether or not their effort justified it. Unearned trophies plant the seeds for narcissism. And narcissists don't mind a bit accepting those meaningless trophies.

Inflated grades and the ill-prepared student

Not that long ago, a letter grade of C referred to an average performance and an A reflected excellence. If that is true, how can it be that almost half of graduating high school students today have a grade point average reflecting an A+, A, or A–? Are half of all recent graduating seniors considerably above average — in fact, excellent — students?

Grade inflation has been a problem in American education for years. Many educators report being hounded by students and their parents to raise grades. Some educators worry about revenge or consequences for not bending to their wishes. Administrators also face angry students and parents demanding grade changes despite poor performance.

Yet as grades have risen, standardized tests have declined. Both the SAT and the ACT report decreasing test scores. However, these test scores hold less value because colleges across the United States are abandoning them as conditions for enrollment.

So, what does it matter? Kids with high grades feel better about themselves and still get into college without taking those annoying tests. What could go wrong? Kids can feel special without working too hard. In reality, plenty goes wrong.

When students are ill prepared for college, they are more likely to drop out. In fact, 40 percent of college freshmen drop out before graduating. Thirty percent of those dropouts leave during their first year. Students who drop out of college often incur expenses that don't vanish when they leave school. They remain mired in debt, more often defaulting on it, but have none of the benefits that a college education delivers.

Some would argue that grade inflation is a result of our narcissistic culture, in which everyone gets prizes whether they deserve them or not.

GRADING THE TEACHER

College administrators rely on many factors when deciding on pay raises, class schedules, and tenure. One measure that is commonly used is student evaluations of classes taught by their teachers. Research has shown that there are big problems with that approach.

The first glitch is that students may not care as much about what they learn as the grade they receive. It makes sense then that students rate instructors better if they are easy graders. They give positive feedback when the course is easy and the grades are good. Students also look at prior feedback and choose classes that seem undemanding and have instructors who give good grades.

The second problem is that teachers want good feedback in order to obtain raises and achieve tenure. This desire may influence teachers to inflate grades in order to get good evaluations. The data support this pattern. Grades in colleges and universities have gradually risen over the course of several decades.

Research has also shown that student evaluations are not reliable indicators of good teaching. Perhaps college administrators need to look at other ways to determine the merits of their teaching staff.

Considering the results: Degraded education systems and low literacy rates

Has grade inflation and lessening of standards impacted the literacy rate in the United States? A study published in 2020 found that over half of the adult population, 54 percent, reads below a sixth-grade level. Newspapers are generally written at least at a ninth-grade level. That means many citizens are unable to access information about current events. Uninformed citizens make poor decisions in everyday life, especially in the voting booth.

During the same year (2020), slightly over 90 percent of U.S. citizens graduated from high school. How many of those graduates are literate? The Nation's Report Card, an assessment mandated by Congress, indicates that 63 percent of 12th-grade students are below the proficient level in reading. In other words, they cannot read competently at their grade level.

I wonder, if graduation rates have reached 90 percent and 63 percent of those graduates are presumably not proficient in reading, is the problem with illiteracy a result of grade inflation? Perhaps.

Narcissists will gladly take their diplomas and feel delighted that they got off easy. As long as they have the paper, they can use that to gain status, obtain jobs, and move on to college. Once in college, they can sweet-talk professors into giving them more inflated grades.

Mirror, Mirror on the Wall: Obsessing about Appearance

A prominent component of self-esteem relates to beauty and attractiveness. This aspect of self-view has been exacerbated by the media. Consider tracking the percentage of ads that feature weight loss, cosmetics, and ways to look younger. Furthermore, commercials and social media posts display perfect faces, bodies, and lives.

Today, people are always on display. Our culture reflects an obsession with appearance. Narcissists are very aware of their appearance and are known to dress with flair. They also tend to be rated as better looking than others. Their flashy appearance gives them attention, something which they constantly crave.

Reflecting on mirrors: Benefiting from being considered attractive

Narcissists' focus on looking good may have some additional benefits. Multiple studies have looked at the probable pluses of looking good. Results indicate that attractive people are

>> Judged as more honest

>> More likely to get hired for a job

>> Given more compensation

>> Less likely to be found guilty in court cases

>> Able to get more help from others

>> More likely to get away with bad behavior in school

>> Especially adept at finding mates

>> Perceived as more intelligent

>> Likely to receive better grades in school

» Able to obtain better grades on tests

» More likely to win an election

» More attractive to babies

» Perceived as more trustworthy

» Thought of as more competent

There appear to be many reasons to present oneself as an attractive person. Certainly, the culture that reinforces narcissism pushes looking good. However, that doesn't mean that attractive people deserve better treatment or are more worthy, intelligent, or competent than others.

Looking good

Narcissists are exquisitely aware of the benefits of looking good. They are much more concerned about maintaining a pleasing exterior than a pleasing interior. The narcissistic culture pushes this perspective.

Evolutionary theory contends that reproduction motivates a considerable amount of human behavior. In other words, humans survive by passing along their genes. People who are seen as attractive are more likely to secure mates in order to reproduce.

Attractiveness has been associated with a variety of characteristics. Studies suggest that what is seen as attractive is consistent across a wide variety of cultures. Some of the characteristics of attractiveness that have been identified include

» **Youth:** Younger people are considered more attractive than older people.

» **Symmetry:** Both body and facial proportional balance are seen as particularly appealing.

» **Whites of eyes (sclera):** Get those eye drops out; the whiter the better.

» **Body shape:** The ratio of the waist to hips in both men and women. A small waisted, curvier shape is considered more desirable in women; for men, a muscular, large chest is seen as more attractive.

» **Health:** People who look healthy are more attractive to others than those who look sickly.

Narcissists are consumed by a desire to look attractive to others. They're also driven to find attractive mates that increase their own status. When narcissists do not meet standards of attractiveness, they turn to deception such as cosmetics, plastic surgery, and hair dyes or implants.

You can't be too fit

Multiple studies have been conducted about narcissism and its relation to excessive exercise. Narcissists want a perfect body, and many believe that exercise is one way to achieve that. Narcissists are at risk for developing an addiction to exercise.

In addition, some research links narcissism to *orthorexia nervosa*, an eating disorder that involves radical diets in which a person obsesses about the purity of food. This obsession leads to issues with relationships, excessive spending on special diets, and sometimes malnutrition.

Narcissism is also particularly common among bodybuilders. Again, the focus is on striving for a perfect body. Interestingly, one study looked at steroid use among bodybuilders. After bodybuilders started using steroids, their levels of narcissism tended to increase.

Fading reflections: Ageism

In some cultures, people who achieve old age enjoy many benefits. They are revered, and their opinions are highly valued because of the vast experience they are based on. In narcissistic cultures, old age is thought of as the deterioration of attractiveness, strength, and mental sharpness.

The fight against the perception of old age begins during the middle years. Procedures that promise a more youthful look include wrinkle creams, Botox, plastic surgery, and cosmetics. Unproven supplements promise sharper minds. And surgery pumps up and tightens sagging bodies.

REMEMBER

Narcissists long for lasting attractiveness. Therefore, they obsessively look for the fountain of youth and seek cures for what they perceive as the ravages of old age.

Chapter **17**

Incivility and Narcissism: A Growing Concern

I n 2009, the United States was shocked when a presidential State of the Union speech was interrupted by the opposing party's heckling. Never before was such disrespect displayed in the halls of Congress. The congressman who insulted the chamber almost immediately offered an apology.

Now, more than a decade later, hecklers have become a regular part of the State of the Union show. Many would argue that incivility runs unrestrained throughout society, not just in politics, but in crowds, on the highways, between coworkers, and among family members.

This chapter explores the rise of incivility in today's world and how narcissism is feeding the rise of rudeness. As the number of narcissists grow, self-centered entitlement also increases. The chapter highlights common settings of misbehavior and the underlying problem that causes incivility to proliferate. Lack of give and take of friendly relations and a disregard for the rights of others lie behind this descent into a world full of hostility, disrespect, and vulgarity.

Civility in a Nutshell

The word *civility* originates from the notion of citizenship. A good citizen is expected to act with concern, respect, knowledge, and empathy for others. When there are disagreements between citizens, discussions can be passionate, but should remain respectful, without open hostility. Discourse should remain focused on the common good and seek to find answers that can benefit as many of the populus as possible. Different views are both tolerated and welcomed. Diversity adds nuance and greater understanding about current issues or problems.

TIP

Think of civility as the act of living by the golden rule. Treat others with the same respect and kindness that you desire and deserve.

In contrast, incivility involves rudeness and a disregard for others, often accompanied by impulsiveness, entitlement, and aggressiveness. And incivility often spreads like a wildfire. When sparked by one outburst, if the flames of incivility are not immediately drowned out, others quickly join in. Today, incivility is often modeled by politicians, celebrities, and sports stars, but especially narcissists as the following sections explain.

Investigating Narcissistic Incivility

Narcissists feel special and entitled; therefore, they're often consumed by getting what they want when they want it. They disregard the needs of others and don't really consider their own impact on those who interact with them. Enter narcissistic incivility. Narcissists believe that they have the right to criticize others, ridicule them, or push them aside when it suits their needs. No wonder most narcissists fail to show basic respect, politeness, and civility in their interactions with others.

WARNING

Every rule has exceptions. Narcissists can be extremely civil and respectful when they want something from someone else. This is especially true at the beginning of a relationship. Be wary of their excellent, award-winning performances.

TIP

Incivility and narcissism run rampant throughout social media. Anonymity allows even the meek, vulnerable narcissist to become a raging bully. See Chapters 11 and 15 for more about narcissistic aggression and incivility online.

Today, a culture of narcissistic expectations permeates what was once considered civil society. These expectations lead to more rudeness, selfishness, and lack of empathy. The question of origin is unanswerable. Does narcissism fuel incivility or does incivility fuel narcissism? It's more like a two-way street. The following sections take a closer look at how incivility interacts with narcissism.

Entitlement on display

Entitlement is almost always a symptom of narcissism. Entitlement has worked its way into the fabric of our times. When narcissists become frustrated, they almost always find a way to blame someone else. This sense of entitlement finds root in almost any setting, especially one that involves evaluation.

For example, when narcissistic students do poorly in school, they tend to blame the teacher for ineffective teaching. The fact that they neglected to read the material, regularly attend class, or spend adequate time studying for an exam does not enter into their harsh criticism of the instruction.

Similarly, a less than glowing evaluation in a work situation is usually dismissed as unfair by an employee, especially if the employee is also narcissistic. There are, of course, a few people who take negative feedback and use it to improve future performance, but many are defensive and deny its accuracy.

Entitlement also abounds in public. Have you ever been in a theater when someone feels free to answer their phone? That's despite deliberate warnings to silence phones prior to the beginning of the show. Are all the people who answer their phones narcissists or simply entitled? Probably both.

Rudeness in the friendly skies

In recent years, air travel has been full of frustrations. From long lines to get through security, to canceled or delayed flights, and overcrowded, stuffy planes, most people find travel irritating to say the least. Adding to the already aggravating mess, there has been a recent uptick in anger and violence among passengers, and between passengers and the crew. What once remained at an annoying level, today quickly escalates into a terrifying drama.

Gone are the days of eagerly anticipating a well-deserved vacation or a trip to see family. Now, passengers dread the possibility of long waits in overcrowded airports or, worse yet, an overnight delay trying to get some sleep on, at best, an uncomfortable chair, or worse, on a filthy airport floor while attempting to guard luggage. Reactions to these frustrations often lead to conflict and gross incivility.

If lucky enough to get on a plane, travelers must then be worried about potential outbursts from unruly passengers. From physical fights brought about because a seat was tilted back too far, to assaults on flight attendants, to passengers threatening to bail out through a back door, violent outbursts are not uncommon occurrences.

Mask mandates during the pandemic and too much alcohol have both been blamed for the increase in violence. However, the incidents continued to occur even when masks became no longer required. In addition, many airlines temporarily stopped serving alcohol, but incivility continues unabated.

A recent example of narcissistic air-rage was filmed by several passengers. A man was standing in the aisle screaming obscenities at a passenger with a crying infant. The flight attendant calmly asked the man to stop screaming. He replied that the baby was screaming, why couldn't he? Talk about a lack of empathy mixed with entitlement.

Do these rude, disruptive, and violent episodes on airplanes stem from an increase in narcissism among the flying public? Of course, it's one of those questions that isn't easy to study.

For example, imagine your job was to study the relationship between air-rage and narcissism. Would you interrupt a person that is screaming or punching the flight attendant and ask if they'd be willing to participate in a study about narcissism? Probably not a great idea.

There has been some speculation that passengers with narcissistic features make up a disproportionate share of unruly passengers. They do not like being told what to do, especially by a flight attendant. Narcissists likely believe that attendants should be subservient to them. Furthermore, narcissists in general want what they want immediately. They are not known to possess patience.

Road rage

Aggressive drivers kill. In fact, about a third of all fatal accidents involve some sort of aggressive driving. Narcissists believe that they should have special treatment, and that includes on the road. Therefore, if a fellow driver is not going as fast as the narcissist believes they should, a narcissist may react with anger in the form of tailgating, blinking high-beamed lights, honking, yelling, making aggressive gestures, or even illegal passing.

Aggressive thinking leads to more aggressive driving. Those who drive aggressively speed, rapidly switch lanes, and run red lights. They openly express their impatience and anger at other drivers. Basically, narcissists think that other drivers should move out of their way so that they can get where they want to go unimpeded.

IT'S ALL ABOUT ME AND MY CAR: NARCISSISM AND AGGRESSIVE DRIVING

Dr. Brad Bushman and colleagues looked at the relationship between narcissism and aggressive driving. They conducted three studies, two in Luxembourg and one in the United States. They found that high levels of narcissism, youth, and being male were all related to more aggressive driving.

These studies were conducted on those with grandiose narcissism, not those with predominately vulnerable narcissism. The findings were consistent with earlier research about the relationship between narcissism and aggressive driving. However, this study included groups of people who were not primarily college students, which made their results more robust than those of earlier studies.

About 1.35 million people are killed annually around the world on roadways. Much of the carnage is due to speeding, driving while impaired, and road rage. People with road rage think that other drivers are somehow intentionally out to infuriate them. They may believe that the driver who forgets to signal a turn is doing it deliberately to make them mad. Or a driver who slows down to make a turn is deliberately trying to make them angry. In other words, they *personalize* the intentions of other drivers.

Exploring Why Incivility Is on the Rise

Civility in America is an annual poll that looks at how people perceive their current culture. Referring to 2019 data, this poll recently found that about two thirds of Americans believe that incivility is a problem. Most people report encountering about ten incidents of incivility each week. More of these confrontations occur online than in person.

People have different views about who and what are contributing to the increase in incivility. These include

>> Social media

>> Politicians

>> News media

>> Celebrities

- » Sports figures
- » Racial and cultural animosity
- » Young people

The increase in incivility also increases the risk of bullying, harassment, rule breaking, hate crimes, and intolerance. Narcissism and incivility are closely intertwined. They both assume a superior right to disregard or denigrate others.

Narcissists believe that it's perfectly fine if they infringe upon the rights of others. They feel free to humiliate and harass. Their lack of respect for others is displayed by their rude and disrespectful behavior. Uncivil behaviors may be a source of amusement or a way to gain power for a narcissist. Their lack of empathy allows them to act aggressively without guilt or remorse.

A Two-Way Street: The Role of Reciprocity

Reciprocity involves an exchange between people that is designed to be mutually beneficial. Reciprocity is a foundational skill that helps build good relationships. It allows people to get things done that they couldn't manage by themselves. You scratch my back and I'll scratch yours.

The expectation of reciprocity flows through many relationships. For example, a worker expects to perform tasks and be compensated with a certain amount of pay. Teachers teach and expect their students to pay attention, participate, and learn.

Friends enjoy the benefits of reciprocity in multiple ways. For example, they may be good listeners when one of the pair needs to talk, or they may offer help on a task that requires two people.

Friendships and other relationships require a balance of reciprocal acts. When giving takes place on one side of a relationship and not the other, the connection may suffer. A good relationship flourishes when each partner receives somewhat close to equal care, support, and love.

There are some relationships that do not require reciprocity. Parents dote on their children without expecting an equal return. Caregivers help out their loved ones without receiving compensation. For these types of relationships, the payoff is, hopefully, love.

WARNING

Beware the marketer that uses the principles of reciprocity to sell you something. Some send small gifts in the mail with appeals to contribute to a charity. Others ask for something small and easy first, and then ask for something much more difficult (the foot-in-the-door technique). Still others ask for a big contribution and then back off, and when refused, ask for something smaller (the door-in-the-face technique).

Narcissism and reciprocity

Narcissists fail miserably at the art of reciprocity. Since they are special and entitled, they believe that they deserve extraordinary treatment. They perceive themselves to be better than they actually are and have an overinflated view of their worth. The needs of others are rarely on their mind. Their initial demand when asked for a favor is, "What's in it for me?"

How does lack of reciprocity work out for narcissists? Not very well. Their relationships tend to be superficial and filled with conflict. They may have many acquaintances but few true friends. Over time, lots of people in a relationship with a narcissist get tired of the one-way nature of the connection and walk away or gradually disappear.

If culture is taking a narcissistic turn, what are the implications? One might venture to guess that relationships would become less intense, more one-sided, and shallow. Incivility would become the expected norm. Instead of having real friends, people would relate online to their followers. Road rage would explode, bad manners would proliferate, and entitlement would replace kindness.

It's not a happy, peaceful-looking future. One can only hope that's not where we're headed, but it's reasonable to fear that the lack of reciprocity will lead to an avalanche of incivility.

Civility and balanced reciprocity

When people perceive that there is a balance of give and take, they are more likely to act in a civil manner toward others. Civility can be encouraged by some easy-to-implement strategies. Here are a few:

>> **Practice gratitude.** Every day write down three things that have pleased you or given you contentment.

>> **Be kind.** Take a minute out of each day and do something nice for someone. It doesn't have to be terrific; hold open a door, give a compliment, or tell someone how much they mean to you. Let another driver into your lane.

>> **Teach children the importance of civility.** If you are a parent, teacher, or have contact with children, take every opportunity to notice and practice civility.

>> **Stay away from shaming on social media.** Don't participate in negative postings, and if possible, reach out to those who are being bullied.

>> **Carefully call out incivility when you observe it.** Be safe and gentle. Sometimes people just need to be reminded to mind their manners.

>> **Enforce civility in schools and the workplace.** Leadership has the responsibility to set standards of appropriate behavior and enforce those rules.

TIP

You may think that as an individual, you don't have the power to influence civility. But think of civility as being infectious — one act can quickly grow. Do your part.

5

Treating Narcissism

IN THIS PART . . .

Discover what motivates narcissists to seek help.

Explore how childhood plays into narcissism.

See how cognitive behavior therapy (CBT) helps narcissists.

Look at skill training for narcissists through dialectical behavior therapy (DBT).

Chapter 18

Seeking Help

S ince most narcissists believe in their own superiority, it's hard to imagine why they might want psychological help. After all, not only are they better than other people (or so they think), but they are uniquely able to defend themselves when their perceived magnificence is attacked. So, they deflect criticism, deny fault, and haughtily push aside demands.

They also have an uncanny ability to stave off negative feedback, discredit their opponents, and seem blithely unscathed after conflict. Of course, narcissists sincerely believe that they win all fights and that they are always in the right. They enjoy seeing themselves victorious, even if the victory is one-sided and only in their minds.

However, sometimes narcissists face significant consequences for their obnoxious behavior. Whether due to trouble with relationships, with the law, or because of unrelenting episodes involving a loss of face, narcissists occasionally find themselves in the offices of therapists.

This chapter explores the types of situations that push some people with narcissistic traits to seek help. It also addresses the typical reactions narcissists have to the help they receive, including common responses to *psychotherapy* (or, simply put, talking about your problems and looking for solutions with a mental health professional). Spoiler alert: Those reactions are not usually conducive to receiving help.

This chapter ends with a tool to decide whether or not to seek help. You can use it to possibly convince a loved one to try working through issues with a therapist. That work might help them develop skills for improved mental and interpersonal functioning. Or you can use it for yourself if you think you might need some help in clarifying your relationship, becoming more immune to narcissistic manipulations, or managing your own emotions.

REMEMBER

You may have seen movies or shows that depict a patient lying on a couch, talking, while the therapist sits behind the patient, passively taking notes. Although a few therapists still do that, most psychotherapy today takes place in an office with comfortable chairs facing each other. The therapist and the client are both active members of the therapy team.

Trouble in Paradise: Why Narcissists May Agree to Therapy

Despite their steadfast belief that they are superior, flawless human beings, the world eventually catches up to most narcissists. Those with narcissistic traits can become entangled in conflict in many arenas such as

>> With their partners or family members

>> In other close relationships

>> At work

>> Within the legal system

In addition, narcissists can undergo multiple disappointments in life. They may lose opportunities or relationships over time that result in their feeling overwhelmed. Multiple threats to their ego injure them and can lead them to despair. As such, they may reach out to a mental health professional, often to validate their grievances with others.

Relationship disruptions

Many narcissists find it difficult to maintain long-term, stable relationships. They may have multiple partners and a history of broken friendships. They have struggles and quarrels with their parents, relatives, and their children. Within those relationships, narcissists usually deny, dismiss, or blame conflicts on other factors, never themselves.

However, at some point, a loved one may demand that the narcissist attempt therapy or risk the friend, partner, or spouse leaving the relationship. A narcissist, not pleased with the threat of abandonment, may reluctantly agree. In the back of their minds, they usually assume they can win over the therapist to support their view that they have been wrongfully accused.

Narcissists and/or their partners may seek couples therapy or individual therapy to deal with the emotional upheaval of their relationship or conflicts within the family. See the section, "Preparing for Pushback: Common Responses to Therapy" for more on how therapy with narcissistic people turns out.

Work-related problems

Not surprisingly, narcissists often engage in and create conflicts at work. These clashes may result in discipline or dismissal. Infrequently, work issues may cause narcissists to reflect on how their behaviors contributed to the problem, to the point of independently seeking solutions.

A referral to a mental health provider may come from their own initiative or after a series of problems at work that leads to undesired consequences such as loss of bonuses or lackluster pay raises. Some large companies have employee assistance programs that offer counseling services. An employer may suggest that an employee seek counseling but cannot require an employee to agree.

TECHNICAL STUFF

Employers may not demand that an employee seek counseling because of the Americans with Disabilities Act (ADA). If a narcissistic employee claims that they have a mental health problem, the ADA forbids discrimination or mandated treatment. For example, in an actual legal case, an employee was asked to get counseling after a work-related incident. Following the request, the employee sued their employer declaring that in effect, the employer was ordering a medical evaluation. The court agreed and that request was determined to be illegal based on the ADA. The act protects people who have or may have a disability, including a mental health disorder.

Court mandates

A person with narcissistic tendencies can become involved in court-mandated therapy as a result of another problem that accompanies or is exacerbated by their self-focused traits. For example, therapy is sometimes required during a child custody dispute. Other situations or troubling behavior that can lead to legally required therapy include:

>> Substance abuse

>> Risk to self

>> Risk to others

>> Domestic abuse

>> Child abuse

>> Sex crimes

>> Stalking

>> Threatening behavior

>> As a condition of probation or parole

>> Treatment in lieu of jail

These actions are not part of narcissism per se. However, narcissists are more likely than non-narcissists to engage in aggressive behavior. They are also at risk for substance abuse that increases their chances of escalation into more aggressive behavior. That's why judges sometimes send someone with narcissism to therapy. But what happens when they do? See the section later in this chapter, "Preparing for Pushback: Common Responses to Therapy," for more information.

Narcissistic injuries

A *narcissistic injury* occurs when there is a threat to a narcissist's ego or self-esteem. For example, a narcissist may experience profound rejection, defeat, or abandonment. When a narcissist feels injured, they are likely to react with anger, rage, or sometimes violence. They may hold onto these feelings for a long period of time, seeking revenge or ruminating on the injustice inflicted on them.

Narcissists, particularly the vulnerable type, are especially susceptible to narcissistic injuries because of their over-inflated, fragile, unstable sense of who they are. They can easily be injured by what others would consider mild rejection or loss. Therefore, an off-handed remark can lead to long-lasting distress.

Although most narcissists do not become depressed, those with a series of narcissistic injuries occasionally become despondent. They believe that they are victims when things do not go the way they want. This belief in their victimhood leads them to feel both rage and sadness. The distress associated with their moods may motivate them to seek psychological treatment.

Although some narcissists seek therapy, their goal may not be to change, but to make the case about how they have been harmed by others. They prefer exoneration over actual treatment.

Preparing for Pushback: Common Responses to Therapy

When narcissists make their first appointment with a mental health provider, they are often in some sort of trouble. These troubles are often interpersonal in nature. And they usually involve a loss, suffered either in the past or looming in the future. Narcissists hate to lose.

For most people, connecting with a psychotherapist offers a safe space to work on emotional, behavioral, or relationship problems. But many narcissists see psychotherapy as the place to plead their case before a judge. The therapist is put in the role of the judge and jury, and the narcissist is the star attorney presenting a case for their own defense.

This setup does not work well in therapy. One of the most important goals in the early stages of psychotherapy is the establishment of an authentic relationship between the therapist and the client. This bond, known as the *therapeutic alliance*, involves mutual respect, warmth, trust, and honesty. If the main goal of narcissistic clients is to win rather than develop and change, that will likely disrupt the developing alliance with the therapist. Thus, it requires a highly skilled therapist to achieve and maintain an effective alliance with a narcissist.

Limited research demonstrates that at least three types of therapy may help some people with narcissistic personality disorder. (You may recall that people with narcissistic personality disorder rarely agree to participate in research studies.) The therapies are called transference-focused psychotherapy (which is a form of psychodynamic therapy, see Chapter 19), cognitive behavioral therapy (see Chapter 20), and dialectical behavior therapy (see Chapter 21).

TIP

These therapeutic approaches may be even more helpful to those who have a modest mix of narcissistic traits but don't exhibit the more profound diagnosis of narcissistic personality disorder.

Managing manipulations

Narcissists tend to be master manipulators. But how do narcissists manipulate their treatment? The following list gives you a few ideas.

>> They often present themselves as reasonable and rational. However, they feel entitled to special treatment. For example, they may cancel at the last minute and demand a quick rescheduled appointment. They may show up late and try to extend their allotted time.

>> They ask for exceptions in scheduling to meet their own needs, which are always given priority. They subtlety suggest that they deserve these accommodations, and that the therapist is unreasonable if their wishes aren't granted.

>> Narcissists may try to win the therapist over to their side. They frequently do this by flattery. They may tell their therapist how much they appreciate them and compare former therapists unfavorably to the current one.

>> Like in other relationships, narcissists may use gaslighting to confuse the therapist about what's really going on. They lie about their actions in ways designed to create a favorable impression. They attempt to get the therapist to align with their side of events and to perceive things the way they see them.

>> Narcissists in therapy present themselves as the victim of actions by partners, family members, coworkers, or law-enforcement personnel. Striving for victimhood lets them off the hook. In no way do they assume responsibility for their difficulties.

Meet Adam. He goes to therapy after a particularly vicious altercation with his wife. She demands that he see a therapist for anger management, or she'll divorce him. The following dialogue occurs during his third session.

Therapist: So, Adam, have you had time to think about some of the strategies we talked about last week?

Adam: Yes, I found them extremely helpful. I started doing deep breathing when I found myself getting angry, and that worked for a little while. But I wanted to ask your opinion about my wife. She's always getting on my case about doing chores. I wish she'd just quit nagging and chill out.

Therapist: Well, nagging can be annoying. Have you talked to her about it?

Adam: Yes, I've told her to knock it off. But, at work, my boss seems to think I'm too much of a perfectionist. I think that's a good thing, don't you?

Therapist: Well, that sort of depends. Does your perfectionism get in the way of you completing your work?

Adam: Maybe, but by the way, I need to leave early today. Can you make next week's session a bit longer, so I don't lose money on my time?

Therapist: I'm afraid I have people scheduled all day next week.

Adam: That's okay. I really need to talk to you about my kids. They have been doing horribly in school because my wife won't help them with their homework.

Therapist: So, you feel like your wife isn't doing what she should to help the kids? Do you think maybe you should help them as well?

Adam: Maybe, but that's not the biggest problem. I just can't seem to feel happy or satisfied with my life right now. Everyone is blaming me for stuff I didn't do.

Therapist: Do you realize that you've brought up problems with your wife, your boss, length of your sessions, your kids, and how you feel blamed? And each time I ask a question to explore an issue further, you change the subject again. It feels to me like you brought in a large bag of marbles and threw them across the floor. You want me to run after each marble instead of focusing on the problems we agreed to work on.

Adam: I thought the whole point of therapy was to talk about my problems. I have more problems than most, so that's what I'm talking about.

Therapist: The point of therapy is to work on solutions to problems. We need to take on your problems one at a time and look for solutions.

Adam: Do you think you have the proper training to deal with my issues? I feel like you rejected me. I thought you were on my side, but I guess you're not, just like the others.

Adam is attempting to manipulate his therapist by jumping from topic to topic and avoiding grappling with any specific problem. When the therapist points out this pattern, Adam gets angry and tries to make the therapist feel bad.

How the therapist handles this type of challenge may determine the outcome of therapy. However, narcissists rarely change and often put up roadblocks at every turn. If the therapist pushes Adam too far, he's likely to quit therapy altogether. It can be a very delicate balance.

TIP

If your parent or partner is in therapy, I recommend a neutral to hands-off approach. Leave the therapy to the professional. You can help by listening, not judging, but not necessarily agreeing with your loved one's complaining. You don't want to take sides. That's another narcissistic manipulation.

For more information about treating narcissists in psychotherapy, see Chapters 19, 20, and 21.

Tempering potential breakthroughs

Since most narcissists don't believe that there is anything wrong with them, they tend to be difficult to treat. While in therapy, they can be resistant and defensive, blaming others for their situations. Do narcissists get better?

Narcissism is a deeply ingrained way of thinking, feeling, and behaving. Like most habits, narcissistic traits are quite hard to break. However, some people with narcissism are able to function better in their worlds by going to therapy.

Therapy involves learning new ways of thinking and behaving and applying those new skills to everyday life. Working successfully with narcissists takes an experienced, strong therapist. For any improvement to take place, considerable repetition and practice is required.

TIP

The relatively few narcissists who are motivated, intelligent, and especially able to reflect on their own behaviors may be better candidates for successful therapy than those with less motivation, intelligence, or self-awareness.

Giving Therapy a Chance

Perhaps you see yourself as special, unusually talented, and highly deserving. But life is not treating you as well as you feel entitled to. Numerous friends and family members have suggested that you get help for your issues, but you don't believe you have a problem.

On the other hand, maybe you have a relationship with a narcissist and feel stuck or unhappy. In both cases, therapy may help.

The following sections deal with making a decision about seeking therapy for yourself or someone you care about.

Considering the cost/benefit analysis

If you have a family member or someone you care about who you think would benefit from therapy, you might consider doing a cost/benefit analysis describing the pros and cons of getting some help. The cost/benefit analysis is a tool to help you or your loved one consider your options and possibly take action if it seems like the right thing to do. Ultimately, seeking therapy is a personal decision.

Vincent is 67 years old. His fourth wife left him a few months ago, and he's still boiling with anger. Yet, he's unable to acknowledge his role in his relationship problems. Instead, he's worried about his finances heading into retirement, losing his dashing good looks, and feeling more than a bit lonely and frustrated. His brother suggests that he might get some relief from the uncertainty and pain of dealing with his losses by finding a good therapist. Vincent argues with his brother that none of these problems were his fault and he doesn't need some shrink telling him what to do. Finally, the brothers agree to put the pros and cons for seeking therapy on paper. Table 18-1 shows what they came up with.

TABLE 18-1   **Vincent's Cost/Benefit Analysis of Seeking Therapy**

Potential Benefits	Potential Costs
I might feel less angry and frustrated.	I don't know how much, but it will cost money, at least a copay.
I could learn to control my temper better, so I don't get into trouble.	I don't really like people criticizing me, and a therapist might do that.
It might be nice to have someone understand how other people hurt me.	I don't have a lot of extra time in my schedule.
I can get my brother off my back about this whole mess.	I don't trust most people to be on my side.
My friends might be impressed that I would actually go to therapy.	People might see me as weak.
Women like men who go to therapy.	I don't like all of that touchy feely stuff.
I don't really have anything to lose other than time and a small copay.	

Vincent's reasons for considering psychotherapy all pretty much relate to his narcissism. However, they are enough to get him through the door. A highly skilled therapist may be able to help Vincent improve his interpersonal functioning and increase his ability to handle difficult emotions.

TIP

If you have a family member or someone you care about whom you think needs therapy, consider doing a cost/benefit analysis with them. It can help make sense of a difficult decision, especially for a narcissist.

Going with a pro: Why an experienced therapist matters and how to find one

If you interact frequently with someone who shows narcissistic traits, you probably know they've mastered an exquisitely well-developed method of pushing your buttons. That may be one of the reasons that you want your loved one to agree to therapy.

Therapists are not immune from getting their buttons pushed. Although all licensed mental health professionals have training and supervised experience prior to being licensed, some may not have had the seasoning that working with a narcissistic client requires. That's why it's important to do your homework prior to making that first therapy appointment.

You won't see billboards or advertisements touting the successes of any individual therapist. That's because it's unethical to share confidential information about clients. Instead, go to your state government website and search for licensing and regulation. You can access information about therapists' licenses, when they were obtained, and in many cases any disciplinary problems that they have had in the past. Additionally, ask your primary care provider, family, and friends for their recommendations.

Once you've made a potential decision, contact the therapist and ask for a call back. Then have a conversation about their experience with your particular problem and what training they have in the area of treating narcissism. Therapists are generally happy to talk to potential patients.

TIP

Even with preparation, it's possible that a patient and therapist fail to develop a good working relationship. When that occurs, first talk to the therapist and see if there are potential solutions. If issues cannot be resolved, try another therapist until you find a good fit.

Getting the help and support YOU need

If you are in a relationship with a narcissist, whether a close family member, parent, partner, or even a colleague, you may experience difficult emotions. Those emotions may interfere with your ability to carry on in your daily life. You may feel sad, anxious, angry, or confused. See Chapters 5, 6, and 7 for more information about relationships with narcissists.

If you need help sorting out these feelings, consider going to a therapist yourself. You may resist, thinking that you were perfectly fine before getting involved. The problems you are experiencing are not your fault. You may be right, but not all therapy involves going deeply into your past or solving long lasting severe emotional problems.

Many mentally healthy people get involved with narcissists. See Chapter 8 for examples of people who are attracted by narcissists. Therapists are generally good problem solvers. They can help you figure out how to handle or disentangle yourself from your relationship.

WARNING

On the other hand, some people suffer severe depression, debilitating anxiety, or trauma while in a relationship with a narcissist. If you feel overwhelmed with negative emotions, it's critical that you get help as soon as possible. Get a referral. And if you feel helpless, hopeless, or have thought of harming yourself, either go to an emergency room, call 911, or call the national Suicide and Crisis Lifeline by calling 988. Help is available 24/7.

The bottom line is that help is available. Don't be shy or embarrassed. Mental health professions go into the profession because they want to help others. You can benefit from an outside, neutral, knowledge-based perspective.

Chapter **19**

Taking the Psychodynamic Approach to Treating Narcissism

O verindulgent, permissive parenting in which a child is undisciplined and given favored status can lead to self-centered, spoiled children. These children grow into narcissistic adults who feel superior, entitled, and omnipotent. Often, there is a discrepancy between their beliefs of grandiosity and their actual ability to achieve greatness. This discrepancy may lead to failure, which if not easily blamed on others, can cause severe narcissistic injury. An injured narcissist may act out with rage or collapse into hopelessness. When feeling hopeless, a narcissist may be open to therapy.

This chapter deals with psychodynamic therapy, including a specific form known as transference-focused psychotherapy (TFP). These therapies are based on the principles that current behavior and emotional reactions generally originate from early childhood experiences, especially those that involved primary caregivers, and these early interactions from childhood still influence perceptions, feelings, and functioning today.

REMEMBER

The following pages provide you with important basic concepts, examples, and common terms used in TFP and other psychodynamic approaches. This chapter introduces you to some basic concepts, but it isn't meant to be a comprehensive overview of the approach. Instead, use this information to get a flavor of what this type of therapy is all about. That way, you can see if this therapy feels like it may be a good fit for someone you care about or yourself.

Exploring Important Concepts Related to Psychodynamic Therapy

The roots of psychodynamic therapy trace back to the late 1800s. Although it has changed over the years, the major principles originated with Sigmund Freud. His ideas about the composition and development of the human mind remain influential today. The following sections take a glance at some of the main concepts found in psychodynamic approaches to therapy.

The unconscious, preconscious, and conscious

The mind, according to psychodynamic theory, can be conceived of as having three parts. The largest part is the unconscious. The unconscious mind contains material such as instincts, deeply held beliefs, and urges. This part of the mind drives much of human behavior. For example, inappropriate sexual urges or violent tendencies likely reside in the unconscious. The unconscious mind represses this material to avoid feeling guilt, shame, and distress.

The conscious mind reflects what you are thinking about right now, in the present moment. It is an active part of everyday awareness. However, psychodynamic theory contends that the unconscious mind still influences the conscious mind.

The preconscious mind consists of things that you can remember just by focusing your attention or being prompted or cued to recall them. You don't consciously think about the alphabet, but if someone asked you to recite it, you probably could. That's because it exists in your preconscious mind, out of your awareness but easily recalled.

These theories, although used currently, remain unproven. Researchers agree that there is consciousness and that some remembered material is easily accessed; the unconscious mind can only be hypothesized. Nonetheless, common sense suggests that things long forgotten may still profoundly influence people's emotional lives.

People with narcissism may be unaware how their past and unconscious minds influence their present behavior. They believe that how they are feeling, thinking, and behaving in the moment is perfectly normal and have little insight into how their actions affect others. The following vignette illustrates this point.

Sebastian seeks therapy because he is unable to find a mate who meets his very high expectations. He has a long history of brief affairs followed by disappointment and ultimately his decision to break off the relationship. He's approaching the age of 40 and decides he wants to find out why women are failing to measure up.

He begins therapy complaining about his situation. His therapist asks him if possibly his expectations are out of reach for anyone. Sebastian denies that possibility. He's unaware of the influence of his childhood. His therapist begins to explore this unknown time in his life.

Sebastian talks about his early childhood. He's been told that his parents were both drug users and that he was seriously neglected. They rejected his frequent cries for attention and love. After multiple calls to the state about his care, he was placed with his grandmother when he was 4 years old. She spoiled him and treated him like a prince.

The therapist was able to guide him to see what was previously unconscious. Specifically, his first years did not give him the love and care he needed. Then his grandmother bombarded him with excessive praise and taught him that he was better than others. Thus, he expected others to do the same. Although Sebastian does not recall the neglect, he does remember his grandmother spoiling him. This pattern of neglect and overvaluation is common in the development of narcissism later in life.

After months of therapy, Sebastian came to realize that his early childhood set him up to, like his parents, reject anyone who wanted to get close to him. At the same time, he had excessive expectations of women that were impossible to achieve. This realization arose from understanding his grandmother's overindulgence. These insights brought material from his unconscious to his consciousness. With help from his therapist, he is able to change his now conscious thoughts and behaviors to more adaptive ones.

Free association and interpretation

One of the primary tools used by psychodynamically oriented therapists is known as free association. *Free association* involves instructing the client to say whatever comes to mind. There is no censorship during free association.

The assumption behind free association is that the process brings unconscious material to the conscious part of the mind. Once the material becomes conscious, it is more easily subject to change. Then, the therapist interprets the material that is produced by the client.

This technique may encourage a narcissist, who's reluctant to share or even admit weakness, to speak freely. For example, imagine the following free association from a narcissistic client who is having marital problems.

> My husband doesn't really care about me. I feel like I deserve more. I think about a long vacation from my life. I'm thinking about my father. He was a prince of a man. He adored me. I miss him. I'm not really sure what I am supposed to say right now. This is kind of boring. I know you want to hear meaningful stuff, but I just don't really care. This is sort of stupid. Do you like my outfit? Oh, can I ask a question? This is weird just talking about nothing of significance. I have a lot of important things to do with my day and this does feel like a waste of time. Are you sure this is going to help? Oh, another question. I am actually getting a bit tired of doing this. I have no more to say. Why am I here? I wish my husband was more like my father. Okay, I said something now, is that enough? Do I really have to keep going on and on? It makes me uncomfortable.

> An interpretation might go like this, "At the last session, you complained about a lack of attention from your husband. In today's free association I heard you repeat that theme. I wonder if your father thought you were special and entitled and gave you whatever you wanted? And now your husband is not paying you enough attention. Furthermore, it seems like you resent me for not being the therapist you want. Perhaps it feels like I'm not supportive enough for you, a bit like your husband. Is that possible?"

These interpretations may be correct and lead to a new understanding; however, there's no way to be sure one way or another. Some suggest that interpretations such as these can make the client feel or seem more dysfunctional or be completely off base.

TECHNICAL STUFF

Another free association technique involves the therapist reading a list of words and having the client respond with the first word that comes to mind. This method ostensibly brings forth unconscious or repressed material that the therapist can use to reveal problematic patterns. If a client pauses before each response, it may indicate resistance to opening up. However, if the pauses only occur in response to certain words, it may indicate discomfort or avoidance of a specific topic or issue.

Defense mechanisms

Defense mechanisms are strategies designed to avoid unpleasant feelings, urges, thoughts, impulses, or behaviors. These ways of avoiding, first proposed by

Sigmund Freud, are mainly unconscious processes, and people utilize them without awareness. Some of the most common defense mechanisms, their definitions, and an example for each can be found in Table 19-1.

TABLE 19-1   Common Defense Mechanisms

Defense Mechanism	Definition	Example
Denial	A rejection of reality, data, or events	A narcissist refuses to admit that they have a substance abuse problem and blames their partner for behaving in ways that make them drink.
Repression	Stuffing feelings, memories, or thoughts into the subconscious, where they remain outside of awareness	Narcissists refuse to believe that they have any flaws. They may repress feelings of guilt or shame when they do something wrong.
Projection	Disowning unacceptable urges or thoughts by transferring them to another person	Narcissists are notorious for using this defense mechanism. They may lie to get ahead but instead claim that someone else is actually lying.
Splitting	Extreme all-or-none thinking, designed to simplify and resolve conflicted feelings	Narcissists have difficulty seeing people as a mixture of traits. They view them as all good or all bad and sometimes flip between the two.
Rationalization	Making excuses for bad behavior or unacceptable emotions by coming up with alternative, more socially acceptable facts, or explanations	Someone with narcissistic traits engages in multiple affairs and justifies their behavior because they have special sexual needs that require multiple partners.
Intellectualization	Denying or blotting out all emotions and focusing on logic rather than uncomfortable feelings	Faced with major surgery, a person focuses on detailed planning regarding running the business or household rather than acknowledging intense anxiety or fear. Narcissists believe that expressing anxiety or fear shows weakness.
Compartmentalization	Concentrating on the parts of life or their personality that are manageable and blocking out those that are not.	A narcissist might claim to be pro-life but pay for someone else's abortion to escape the discomfort of taking responsibility.
Sublimation	Redirecting strong emotional responses to something that is socially acceptable.	A vulnerable narcissist who unconsciously feels shame could increase involvement in a charitable cause. That way, they ignore their feelings of shame and focus on their good work.

REMEMBER Defense mechanisms are all ways of avoiding unpleasant emotions, behaviors, urges, or thoughts. Most psychotherapies encourage directly dealing with the avoided material. That's because avoidance underlies most psychopathology.

Transference

Transference describes the process by which individuals direct their emotions and desires about one relationship to another person. In real life, you may be talking to someone who reminds you of your brother. You didn't really get along with your brother, and you find yourself arguing with this person but you're not sure why. You've experienced transference of your feelings for your brother to someone in your current life.

Transference can occur without you even realizing that it's happening. For example, you may take an instant liking to someone. You may later realize that the person reminds you of a favorite teacher.

In therapy, transference occurs when the client treats the therapist as if they were someone else, such as a father or mother figure. This transfer of identities onto the therapist can greatly impact therapy. The impact may be positive or negative.

For patients with narcissistic tendencies, the therapist may be thought of as the parent who always overvalued them. Therefore, they demand confirmation of their superiority and perfection from the therapist. Another possible narcissistic transference is when the patient wants to control and dominate the therapist. However, transference can show up in an infinite number of ways.

Consider the following example.

> Anna had a difficult relationship with her father. He was demanding and strict. She got attention only when she met his high expectations. She was a competitive gymnast, and he was harsh when she lost but happy when she won. When she quit gymnastics in high school, he didn't speak to her for months.
>
> Now, Anna is in therapy. She transfers her ambiguous feelings about her father to her therapist. Anna finds herself trying to please her therapist and is reluctant to open up and disclose her troubling insecurities because of her inner belief that she can't ever measure up.

In Anna's case, the transference interferes with the establishment of a good therapeutic alliance. The therapist must identify and explain the concept of transference and work with Anna to help her understand how it affects her.

Transference can also have neutral or beneficial effects. When the client transfers positive qualities of someone onto the therapist, it may make the connection easier to accomplish. Nevertheless, a therapist should be aware of how the relationship is influenced by transference. Indications of possible transference during therapy include:

>> A childlike voice tone with the therapist but not others

>> Inappropriate expressions of affection for the therapist

>> Excessive need for praise and affirmation

>> Extreme resistance to working on problems in therapy

>> Excessive emotional reactions to therapist's input or interpretations

>> What appears to be excessively rapid progress

>> Extreme dependent behavior with the therapist

>> Demanding special consideration and favors

TIP

Teaching clients about transference can help them understand the effects transference can have on other relationships in their lives.

The source of transference usually stems from important relationships. These relationships occur throughout life, but most sources of transference can be found in early childhood. Common types include:

>> **Maternal:** This transference happens when the client treats the therapist like their mother. Maternal transference can involve feelings of warmth, love, and caring, or anger, rage, and pain.

>> **Paternal:** In this case, the client transfers feelings about their father to the therapist. In some cases, these feelings can involve belief in the therapist's authority, power, and ability and desire to protect. In other cases, feelings of abandonment, cruelty, or dismissal may prevail.

>> **Sibling:** These relationships can cause an endless variety of emotional responses such as jealousy, love, anger, or despair. Transference of a sibling relationship in therapy reflects those various feelings.

>> **Other important relationships:** Best friends, an uncle or aunt, a special teacher, or a romantic relationship can serve as potential sources of transference.

Understanding transference and how it affects relationships is part of many different psychotherapies. It is also a good concept for you to be aware of in your daily life. Transference is the main focus in transference-focused psychotherapy (TFP) as described in the upcoming section.

Countertransference

Anyone can experience feelings derived from transference, including therapists. Countertransference occurs when therapists project their feelings onto clients. The process is much the same as transference — early or important relationships affect the way therapists relate to certain clients.

It's important for therapists to tune in and be aware of this process to be maximally effective. Otherwise, the therapist's earlier relationships can affect the way the therapist views and reacts to the client. Signs of countertransference include:

>> Unexplained or undeserved dislike of a client.

>> An excessive desire on the therapist's part to disclose personal information during therapy

>> A desire to have a relationship with a client outside of therapy

>> Strong physical reactions to a client, such as tension

>> Strong emotional reactions to a client

>> Feelings of unexplained distrust of a client

>> Difficulty staying focused or feeling bored during therapy

>> Dreading the next session with a client

When a therapist experiences countertransference, they often reach out to peers (other therapists) for feedback and advice. Most of the time, issues can be resolved. However, sometimes countertransference is so strong that a referral to another provider is required.

Gaining Awareness with Transference-Focused Psychotherapy

Transference-focused psychotherapy (TFP) is a type of psychodynamic therapy developed to work for people suffering from major personality disorders or problems such as narcissistic personality disorder (NPD) and borderline personality disorder (BPD). For more information about the latter, see *Borderline Personality Disorder For Dummies* (authored by Charles H. Elliott and myself and published by Wiley).

Narcissism at its core is an interpersonal problem. Narcissists struggle with obtaining satisfying, enduring, and reciprocal relationships. They are less likely than most clients to complain about feelings of anxiety or depression. A strength of psychodynamic therapy, including TFP, is that it emphasizes interpersonal relationships.

The emphasis on transference allows the therapist to clarify the nature of troubling interpersonal issues and how they originated. Greater understanding of these patterns can lead to improved interpersonal functioning.

TFP emphasizes understanding the reactions of the client to the therapist. Communication between the client and therapist often mirrors the earlier patterns between the client and their childhood caregivers. For more information see the earlier section "Transference."

TFP represents a refinement of psychodynamic therapy because it's laid out in a structured form, complete with a manual and a contract for therapy. This structure allows multiple researchers to follow a similar format, thus facilitating study of the technique. The contract outlines goals of therapy and addresses problematic behaviors that may interfere with therapy. Clients generally attend sessions twice a week.

Narcissistic clients sometimes resist TFP and its structure. The structure is seen as a loss of freedom and capitulation to an authority figure.

Clients are expected to be actively engaged in therapy. The therapist helps the client become more aware of how early patterns of behavior are carried out in current relationships.

REMEMBER

TFP goals are broad. The therapist focuses on bringing understanding to the client by increasing awareness of the nature of past relationship patterns and their influence on current emotional and interpersonal issues. See Chapters 4 and 6 for more information about early childhood experiences and narcissism.

Unfortunately, not enough research has been conducted specifically with a narcissistic population to verify the full value of TFP. However, case examples suggest that TFP helps narcissistic patients understand their problematic interactions and move toward change.

Chapter **20**

Changing Thoughts and Behaviors with Cognitive Behavioral Therapy

magine you are playing a friendly game of cards. You have very little invested in the outcome of the game; you're just trying to pass the time in a pleasant way. You happen to be a pretty good card player. So, you easily win the first match. You look up, smiling at your opponent.

Your opponent is definitely not smiling; in fact, they look angry. You tell them it's only a game. No, it's not. For someone with narcissism, the only option is winning. Losing is not okay. Not ever. Even at cards or something else that others might consider unimportant.

Sighing, you think it must be hard to be so uptight over a game of cards. You're right. Losing a game is so difficult for narcissists because they truly believe that losing anything is *horrible*. That thought is what leads to their anger. Any threat to their fragile self-esteem often causes fury. Nothing is worse for a narcissist than being called a *loser*.

Cognitive behavioral therapy (CBT) is based on the premise that what you think about something influences the way you feel. Because narcissists have thoughts, such as they are better than others and deserve special treatment, CBT may help a narcissistic client examine and rethink those thoughts. This chapter describes many of the techniques of CBT as it can be applied to a person with narcissistic traits or narcissistic personality disorder.

This chapter is not meant to describe all the techniques used by a CBT therapist. Rather, it gives you an idea of how this therapy is structured. That way you can tell if it is a good fit for you or someone you care about.

Research suggests that CBT may be an effective approach for people with narcissistic traits or narcissistic personality disorder. However, randomized controlled studies, the gold standard of research, are lacking. At the same time, many of the problems people with narcissism have, such as lack of empathy, anger, relationship problems, and poor impulse control, have been successfully addressed with CBT in controlled studies.

Taking a Collaborative Approach: The CBT Client/Therapist Partnership

All psychotherapy involves the establishment of a relationship between client and therapist. In the case of CBT, a collaborative relationship sets the stage for progress. The therapist and the client form a partnership to work on the problems at hand. A good working relationship involves openness, trust, and mutually agreed upon goals.

WARNING

This collaborative approach may be somewhat challenging to establish with a narcissist. Do you recall the old saying, "You can lead a horse to water, but you can't make them drink?" The same is true for a narcissist starting CBT. If you can lead a narcissist to water (or therapy), you're halfway there. However, getting narcissists to work on their issues is a slow, tedious, and difficult process. Many of them want to vent to a therapist on how they have not been sufficiently heard, adored, or validated by others.

Furthermore, the grandiose, narcissistic client may resist giving equal power to someone they perceive as a lowly therapist. CBT practitioners need to have thick skins, considerable patience, and good skills to find ways in which to work together collaboratively. Maintaining empathy can be difficult but is necessary for a good outcome.

Setting treatment goals together

An early step in forming a collaborative team involves setting goals for treatment. Because narcissists feel superior, special, and entitled, they are quite reluctant to admit that they have problems. If there are problems in their lives, they almost always have an excuse, and it's usually someone else's fault.

It's rare for a narcissist to confess to being a narcissist. But fortunately, therapy can be conducted without ever discussing a diagnosis. Most cognitive behavioral therapy emphasizes problematic behaviors and emotions more so than diagnoses. Treatment is geared toward helping improve day-to-day functioning.

The therapist may have to help the client see the need for specific changes. This may require the therapist to ask lots of questions about what behaviors are troubling to the client and what areas of life are difficult. Even with the narcissist's tendency to blame others, the therapist can usually identify a few specific problems. Skilled professionals keep the focus on problematic outcomes rather than the inappropriateness of the narcissistic client's attitudes and behaviors. That practical focus is important when working with narcissists because they rarely believe that there is any need for them to change.

Treatment goals need to address particular problems. So, instead of the global goal to decrease narcissism, targets may include:

>> Managing anger in a more productive way

>> Improving relationships with family members

>> Reducing negative feedback from others

>> Learning appropriate problem-solving skills to handle work frustrations

>> Understanding the connection between thoughts and feelings

>> Cultivating more supportive friendships

>> Discovering new ways to manage stress

Goals must be agreed upon by the therapist and the client. They need to be reasonably specific and add to the quality of the client's life. Throughout therapy, goals should be referred to and progress acknowledged.

Minding motivation

Given that narcissists think of themselves as perfect, superior, and entitled, why in the world would they want to change? They believe that whatever problems they may be experiencing are certainly the fault of others.

REMEMBER

Narcissists rarely come to therapy without outside pressures such as a partner threatening to break up, a business relationship going sour, or in a few cases, a legal entanglement. See Chapter 18 for more information on when and why narcissists may seek help.

So, how does a CBT therapist help the narcissistic client buy into setting goals and working on issues? Working collaboratively, the therapist needs to guide the client in identifying the benefits of change. In order to be collaborative, the therapist resists pushing clients too hard and avoids harsh confrontation. It's a balance between acceptance and change.

Specifically, the therapist shows the narcissistic client what they stand to gain from changing some thinking or behaving patterns. Referring back to the goals, the therapist can show the client how working through the issues will lead to improvement in their lives. This exercise increases their motivation for participating in therapy.

TIP

Even if a narcissistic client refuses to take responsibility for their problems, they can usually be convinced that therapy can help them change their interpersonal style or manipulate their situations so that they get better outcomes.

Establishing boundaries

Narcissists expect special treatment by everyone, including their therapists. Early in the process of establishing a collaborative relationship, it's imperative that therapists clearly state the rules of engagement.

These rules must be spelled out plainly and specifically, in advance. What happens to a session when the client is late, does not show up, or cancels at the last minute? How is communication between sessions handled? Are texts or phone calls okay? If so, for what purpose and during what hours? What are the hours of the practice?

Even when the rules are clear and the narcissistic client agrees, testing of the limits is to be expected. Boundaries will almost certainly be pushed. Because narcissists are entitled, they expect special treatment. Having the therapist enforce guidelines during therapy is a way to show the client how to see other perspectives. These guidelines, clearly discussed, can teach self-control and frustration tolerance, and encourage empathy for the rights of others.

Therapists use information about pushing boundaries to help the narcissistic client better understand how their behavior affects others. These boundary violations need to be explicitly explained to the client.

For example, take a look at the following therapist/client dialogue.

Client sends text: I need to cancel today's 10 a.m. appointment. I have to pick up some things at the store.

Therapist at next appointment: Although I fully understand that unexpected things come up, when you cancel an appointment without giving me notice, it means that I am unable to schedule any other client in that hour. So, instead of seeing other clients that would like to see me, I am unavailable.

Client: Sometimes other stuff comes up. I can't stop my life just because you might lose some money.

Therapist: Money is not the point. It's important for you to give me more notice. I realize important things come up, but by cancelling at the last moment, you are inconveniencing me and denying others of my services.

Client: You're really an uptight person. I thought therapists were supposed to be calm and supportive.

Therapist: Is there any chance that it annoys you that I am calling you out on this issue? Because my intention is only to help you see the effect of your behavior on others.

Client: Well, it does annoy me. I thought I was special to you. You seem to enjoy what I have to say.

Therapist: I do enjoy working with you, and all of my clients are special to me. I just need to have you hear the basic rules and boundaries. That way you learn that your actions have consequences for not just you, but others.

TIP

Dozens and dozens of interactions like this need to occur before any actual change occurs. Most narcissists have been pushing through boundaries most of their lives. The therapist helps affect change by planting a few seeds in a dry field, hoping that some will sprout.

Reinforcing the CBT model

A good portion of CBT involves teaching the client to recognize how they perceive themselves, the world, and the future. Then they are given ways to identify those thoughts and determine whether or not they may be distorted. This lesson is repeated throughout the therapy. A premise of CBT is that with practice and corrective thinking, clients eventually are able to become their own therapists.

The basic foundation of CBT is that the way you respond to certain situations is determined by how you think about them. People react to situations with perceptions that are not always accurate. Their thoughts or perceptions may be clouded by faulty thinking. These distorted perceptions lead to responses that are unhelpful. A situation occurs, and there is a perception that leads to a reaction. The reaction may include emotions, behaviors, and physical responses.

For example, narcissists may believe they are entitled to special treatment. When they don't receive special treatment, they become angry. In CBT, the therapist gradually questions those underlying beliefs and guides the client to more realistic beliefs. When the entitlement belief is scrutinized, some of the frustration and anger may decrease. See the section "Addressing Dysfunctional Thinking with CBT" later in this chapter for more information.

Using CBT to Change Problematic Behaviors

The "B" in CBT stands for behaviors. Problematic behaviors are those which interfere with getting along with others and handling the many challenges of life in general, work, and living a healthy life. Changing behavior is sometimes the most important part of therapy and can lead to improved functioning and more stable, positive emotions.

The first task of therapy with a narcissist who is exhibiting problematic behaviors is to get the client to agree that these behaviors cause trouble. What are problematic behaviors commonly found in people with narcissistic traits? Here are some:

>> Obnoxious bragging

>> Pushing others out of their way to get ahead

>> Demeaning or insulting others

>> Blaming others

>> Not taking responsibility (at work or home)

>> Unjustifiable anger and possible physical aggression

>> Excessive focus on their status

>> Disrespecting others

>> Hurting others with callous disregard

>> Stealing ideas and claiming credit

>> Blatant lying

>> Seeking revenge

>> Stalking

There are certainly other behaviors that I don't include on this list. Each person has different configurations. It would take many pages to cover all the possible behaviors. However, the first step in CBT remains the same: zeroing in on a few core behaviors that are particularly problematic in clients' lives.

Several techniques are commonly used in CBT to address these challenges. The following sections briefly describe a couple and give examples. Narcissists, even if they deny responsibility, can gain useful skills from CBT that lead them to more effective behaviors and even attitudes.

Developing new strategies for persistent problems

When a narcissist reports repeated problems of a specific nature, such as arguments at work, marital conflict, financial problems, or conflict with friends, problem solving may be called for. Even if a narcissist denies having a problem, this strategy may illuminate a troubling pattern.

TIP

Considerable research supports problem solving as an effective way to help people with emotional problems, especially depression. This technique is also used in many settings to solve problems or develop new strategies, such as business teams, academic departments, engineering, marketing, and many other technical fields. In addition, the technique can be quite beneficial for just about anyone dealing with a difficult problem or for complex decision making.

The problem-solving process in a nutshell

People with narcissistic traits usually believe that they have nothing to do with the daily problems they experience. They act impulsively without considering alternatives, other perspectives, or possible consequences. Teaching this technique to narcissistic clients can help them slow down and do some thinking.

There are four specific steps or strategies in problem solving. (*Note:* There are several similar models). The strategies should be followed sequentially for each problem. They are as follows:

1. **Identify the situation.**

Define all aspects of the problem. Speculate on what caused the problem. Consider emotional responses to the problem. Look for beliefs that may interfere with problem solving, such as thinking there is no solution or that the problem doesn't really have anything to do with you.

2. Explore options.

Brainstorm all the possible ways to solve the problem. Be creative and inclusive. Think about how each option might impact the problem, yourself, and others around you. What are the likely consequences?

3. Choose and implement the best option.

Run through each option in your mind and imagine how it turns out. Choose the option that seems to have the most promise, and then just do it.

4. Review the outcome.

After implementing the plan, step back and evaluate the success of your solution. Did it lead to a good or bad outcome? Did anything change? How do you feel? How did those around you react? Did they notice a difference? If the solution didn't work, start over with Step 1.

So that you can see how this process might work with a narcissist who denies having a problem, I present an example. Then I follow through the problem-solving steps with Crystal, a narcissistic client, in the sections that follow.

Crystal's adult daughter, Brenna, recently told her that she no longer wants any contact with her. Crystal was stunned. After considerable thought, she decided to start therapy to sort this out. Besides, Brenna told her that the only way she'd agree to see her was if she went to therapy and got help for her narcissism.

This estrangement had occurred after a huge argument during a holiday dinner. Brenna had worked all day to decorate and cook. She was a bit nervous because her mother traditionally hosted this dinner.

Crystal was late for dinner, her usual habit. After her arrival, she dominated the conversation, told the family that her cooking was much better than her daughter's, and criticized the place settings. She bragged about the praise and admiration she received from other friends and family about her skills at entertaining.

After the guests left, Brenna told Crystal that she was hurt by her criticism. Crystal told Brenna she needed to stop complaining and grow a thicker skin. This led to an argument that became filled with grievances from the past. When all was said and done, Brenna decided she needed to break off all contact from Crystal until and unless Crystal got professional help.

During the first therapy session, Crystal tells the therapist that she wants to reconcile with her daughter. She seems clueless as to why her daughter claims she's a narcissist and denies that she caused trouble at the family dinner.

The two agree that the main goal of therapy is to improve Crystal's relationship with her daughter, Brenna. Her narcissism is not a problem she's aware of or willing to work on. Later, other goals may be chosen for therapy. Crystal is quick to point out that she is innocent, but willing to try some different methods of relating.

Crystal shows adequate motivation and understands the basic model of CBT. The therapist and Crystal agree to use a problem-solving approach to see if they can come up with a plan to help Crystal in her relationship with Brenna.

Figuring out the situation

Through collaboration, the therapist and Crystal come up with the following core problem: Crystal says that her daughter gets upset when Crystal criticizes her, and this has resulted in Brenna saying that she wants her mother out of her life.

Notice that Crystal is still not really admitting fault, which is typical of a narcissist. However, by keeping the conversation focused on the situation, the therapist is able to guide Crystal into stating the obvious facts.

Laying out the options

This step is more difficult and may take another session. This is where Crystal's refusal to take any responsibility becomes a challenge. The therapist guides her by reminding her of her ultimate goal, to repair the relationship with her daughter.

Through much discussion and gentle questioning, Crystal is able to come up with several possible actions she could take. The therapist suggests that Crystal write down her thoughts on paper. Table 20-1 details possible solutions to Crystal's problem.

TABLE 20-1   **Crystal's Problem-Solving Options**

Option or Solution	Probable Consequence
I can leave it alone and not see her; she's bound to forget what she said eventually.	
I can pretend this never happened.	
I can tell her she's too sensitive, and maybe she'll agree.	
I can go over to her house and apologize.	
I can write her a letter of apology and explain to her that I'm working on myself in therapy.	

Choosing and implementing the solution

Crystal and her therapist discuss each option and decide which one is worth trying. Again, this requires a delicate give and take between the therapist and Crystal. Each possible solution must be given careful consideration and evaluation. The following Table 20-2 depicts the results.

TABLE 20-2 **Crystal's Problem-Solving Consequences**

Option or Solution	Probable Consequence
I can leave it alone and not see her; she's bound to forget what she said eventually.	This won't work. Brenna will not forget; she's made up her mind.
I can pretend this never happened.	I'd like to pick this one, and I might get away with showing up. But not for long — she'd nail me.
I can tell her she's too sensitive and maybe she'll agree.	This one also sounds good to me. Last time I saw her I told her she needed to get a thicker skin, but that didn't go so well.
I can go over to her house and apologize.	I'm not good at apologies, especially when I didn't really do anything wrong.
I can write her a letter of apology and explain to her that I'm working on myself in therapy.	I might be able to write a letter. But I think I may need your help. I can't really see that I have anything to apologize for.

Looks like Crystal needs a bit of help understanding the need to admit some fault and assume responsibility. Therapy takes several sessions to get to the point of Crystal being able to understand her daughter's perspective. After multiple sessions, Crystal agrees to write a letter of apology. She sends it in an email.

Reviewing the outcome

Crystal's daughter replies to the email telling her mother that she is delighted she is going to therapy. She praises her for her apology, remarking that in all these years, she's never heard Crystal apologize for anything. However, she still doesn't want to see Crystal until she's convinced that her mother has changed.

REMEMBER

Psychotherapy with someone who has narcissistic traits is not likely to be brief. These traits are habitual and deeply ingrained in the personality. But there is hope that change can come with hard work and patience.

Conducting behavioral experiments

A *behavioral experiment* is an opportunity to test out a person's beliefs, behaviors, and assumptions. Many times, a person fervently believes that certain behaviors are normal — or at least advantageous. However, those very behaviors are those that land a narcissist in trouble.

Behavioral experiments are planned activities devised so that the client can actually test out whether or not a certain belief is valid or true. These experiments are conducted in real life settings. After the conclusion of the experiment, the client and therapist re-examine the original belief in light of new evidence.

For example, narcissists may believe that they are wonderful conversationalists and that people hang on their every word. In fact, after a while, many people eventually find a narcissist loud, boring, and dominantly verbose.

Here's a behavioral experiment a therapist might propose to an overly talkative narcissistic client:

1. Identify a time when you are speaking with a small group of people.

It could be an afternoon break from work, a dinner out, or an evening out with friends.

2. Find a timer on your smart phone.

All phones are a bit different, so I suggest you search for "how to set up a timer on your specific phone". Most phones have various "Clock" apps, or you can download a free timer. Be sure to practice with it so you can discretely turn it on and off. Turn the sound off on your phone so it doesn't beep.

3. Time the conversation.

Take note of the time when a conversation begins. Hold the phone in your lap so that others don't notice what you are doing. Start the timer when you begin to talk. Stop the timer when someone else is talking. Start it up again each time you talk. After 30 minutes, stop timing.

4. Check out the time you spent talking.

Divide the number of minutes you talked by 30. That will give you the percentage of time you were talking.

5. Ask yourself how that compares to the rest of the group.

If your percentage is more than double the average for the rest of the individuals in the group, you may be talking too much.

6. **Test this out a few times; then consciously decrease the amount of time you are talking.**

Try to ask questions about what other people think or feel. Wait quietly and give them plenty of time to answer. While you are talking, make eye contact with the person to whom you are addressing your questions. Then ask follow-up questions.

7. **Time yourself again with this new approach.**

Don't count the time you are asking questions as time you are talking. Divide the time you talked by 30 minutes. Has your percentage decreased?

8. **Evaluate the results.**

How do you feel after attempting to change your habit of dominating the conversation? Have you noticed any changes in the people around you?

This experiment gives the narcissistic client direct, factual information about their conversational habits. The client may be able to see they normally dominate conversations. Decreasing the amount of time speaking may lead to improved relationships. This simple experiment would lead to much discussion during subsequent therapy sessions.

Other possible behavioral experiments could address different issues of narcissism. For instance, a therapist may suggest that a grandiose narcissist play around with role playing humility or minor self-deprecation. Check out the nearby sidebar, "Making an effort to be humble," for how that experiment might play out.

MAKING AN EFFORT TO BE HUMBLE

A narcissist may benefit from making an effort to decrease grandiose behaviors by committing to a goal like one of the following:

- Plan to compliment three people daily for a week without referring to yourself.

- Point out some minor flaw or weakness in yourself daily for a week. For example, you might say, "I'm not an expert in this. What's your thought?" or "I'm not coming up with anything brilliant. Do you have any ideas?"

- Practice random acts of kindness. You can make a list, or the therapist can help. Do one act each week.

At the end of this experiment, the narcissist should think about how the action taken made them feel. How did people respond to their efforts? Did it make them feel better or worse about themself?

There are countless ways to conduct behavioral experiments. Good therapists help by setting up appropriate experiments in real world conditions that are consistent with the goals of therapy. It's important for the client to notice how they feel and how those feelings change over time with practice.

Addressing Dysfunctional Thinking with CBT

Thoughts are a major driver of problematic behavior. Narcissists have thoughts that they should be first in line. They think that they are better or superior to other people. They casually hurt people without thinking it's wrong. They respond to perceived insult with thoughts of revenge. Therefore, they think that it is perfectly okay to attack someone verbally or physically when they feel threatened.

Since they believe that they are uniquely grand, they believe that their actions are completely justified because they must not be seen as weak. Thus, they act with impunity, walking over and using others as if they were only there to fulfil the narcissist's desires.

Working with narcissists to help them change dysfunctional thoughts and beliefs is more challenging than working with folks with other problems such as anxiety or depression. That's because by their nature, narcissists do not admit to having problems. And they may have a group of people around them who cater to them and keep them pumped up with positive feedback.

So, the first challenge in cognitive work is to convince narcissists that their behaviors and resulting problems are affected by their thoughts. And whatever brought them to therapy cannot be addressed without looking closely at their thinking.

Identifying unhelpful thoughts

The narcissistic mind distorts reality through a prism of grandiosity and entitlement. This view of the world can be challenging to others, and eventually, to narcissists themselves. This acknowledgment of a problem usually occurs when the narcissist loses important relationships, opportunities, or runs into trouble in other ways.

As challenging as it may be, CBT requires psychoeducation in how distorted thoughts influence feelings and behaviors. A therapist working with a narcissist must teach slowly and patiently and provide multiple examples.

Some of the major distortions in thinking include the following:

>> **Black-and-white thinking:** This distortion involves thinking that everything is good or bad, with nothing in-between. A narcissist might fall in love with someone, and then when that person doesn't meet their every need, decide to hate the same person who was recently loveable. This distortion can be quite confusing to those who go from good to bad in the eyes of a narcissist.

>> **Catastrophizing:** This is a major magnification of a small event into something horrible or unbearable. Narcissists may magnify the importance of not getting the right table at a restaurant or getting cold food. That common occurrence is annoying but trivial to most people. Narcissists, on the other hand, may react with fury. Many dramatic arguments in public stem from catastrophizing minor events.

>> **Dismissing or distorting evidence:** If evidence contradicts what a person believes, it is turned into something irrelevant, ignored, or explained away. For instance, if someone accuses a narcissist of lying or stealing, the narcissist might disregard the information or try and explain it away by accusing the accuser of lying. In other circumstances they blame someone else for the theft or lie. The denial of truth can lead to confusion and uncertainty (see section on gaslighting in Chapter 5).

>> **Overgeneralization:** This distortion of thinking involves looking at a single incident and, from that incident, believing that it is true in all cases. Narcissists may overgeneralize their expectations, based on their parents' spoiling and overindulgence in the world at large. They then believe that they deserve special treatment in all circumstances. Overgeneralization can increase frustration for both the narcissist and significant others.

>> **Mind reading:** This belief occurs when people think that others should somehow know what they are thinking or want. It also happens when someone believes that they know what others are thinking. This happens automatically, with no exchange of words. Narcissists may believe that those around them will and should know what they want at all times. They also believe that other people value and worship them, even though they don't. Incorrect mind reading is the fuel of multiple disagreements and fights.

>> **Emotional reasoning:** Emotional reasoning occurs when someone has a feeling or emotion and assumes that it is grounded in facts. This distortion is quite common. For example, someone with social anxiety may feel frightened about going to a gathering and conclude that there is a high likelihood of rejection even though it's a friendly crowd. A narcissist is angry and concludes that someone must be out to get them. For example, say a narcissist receives a positive but not perfect evaluation at work. The narcissist reacts with fury and assumes the boss must be picking on them because they feel rageful. Emotional reasoning, like mind reading, occurs automatically, and causes much misery.

In CBT, clients are taught to look for distortions in thinking in their everyday lives. If this technique is rejected by a client, distortions can usually be picked out by the therapist as the client describes challenging situations during therapy.

TIP

You don't have to have emotional problems to engage in distorted thinking. How many times have you catastrophized about an incident in your life and then found out that it was no big deal? Or have you ever felt really anxious for no reason at all? Try to catch yourself when you distort thoughts. The next section gives tips on how to challenge those distorted thoughts with more realistic thinking.

Challenging unhelpful thoughts

Once a client starts to recognize distorted thinking, the task begins to discover more adaptive ways of thinking. This in turn can lead to better overall functioning.

There are multiple ways of challenging thoughts in CBT. Here, I'll describe a few of them.

Checking evidence

When the narcissist or therapist recognizes a distorted thought or one that makes the narcissist feel miserable, the idea is to check for evidence that the thought is true or false. In this way, they can better understand the nuances of their thinking and see whether there are alternative ways to think. Here are some questions narcissists may ask themselves to determine whether a thought is true, distorted, or uninformed:

>> Do I have any experiences from my own life that would contradict my thought?

>> Have I ever had this thought and it didn't come true?

>> Am I catastrophizing or exaggerating in my thinking?

>> Is this thought distorted in any way?

>> Am I not considering other evidence that might contradict my thoughts?

>> Is my thought realistic and based on facts, or am I impulsively jumping to conclusions?

To illustrate how this technique pertains to narcissistic thinking, here's an example of Landon, who has narcissistic traits.

Landon's best friend, Felix, invites him to lunch. Landon arrives 20 minutes after the agreed upon time. After eating, Felix tells Landon that he needs to talk to him.

Felix then pulls out his phone and opens his to-do list so that he can remember what he planned to say.

"This is hard to do, bro," Felix says. "I've been thinking about this for a long time, but I just didn't have the nerve. I really care about you, but you need to know how excruciating it is to be your friend. I just can't do it anymore."

Landon exclaims, "What the hell are you talking about, we've been friends for 15 years!"

Felix replies, "Look, today is just a small example. You're always late when we meet. And sometimes you cancel at the last minute. That's just plain rude and inconsiderate. Most of the time we're talking about you, your job, and your conquests. Basically, it's all about you. I love your stories, man, but I hardly get a chance to talk."

"You're full of it, man," Landon says, his voice getting louder. "Remember the time your mom died? I went to the service and held you when you wept."

"I'm not saying that you're never there, but you take advantage of me. I buy most of the lunches, and it's like you expect it. I could go on and on, but I won't. I just needed to tell you how I feel."

Landon throws down his napkin and leaves the table — without paying his share of the bill.

This has happened to Landon before, with friends, coworkers, and multiple romantic relationships. He's feeling like people don't appreciate him at all. He happens to be seeing a therapist because of his latest breakup and describes what happened to her. Together, they deal with the following possibilities.

The therapist asks Landon whether other people have complained about his lateness. Landon agrees he's often late but excuses it because he is a busy man. The therapist recalls that she discussed this issue with him during the first session. Landon has been distorting the information coming through to him from others: That is, he is rude when he routinely shows up late to appointments.

They identify the potentially distorted thought and then check the evidence. See what they came up with in Table 20-3.

Clearly Landon and his therapist have made a start, but they have lots of work to do. Landon barely grasps that he has a problem, but he does show some fragments of insight.

REMEMBER

Therapy with people who have narcissistic traits takes time. Instant therapeutic breakthroughs are rare. But with lots of repetition and a constant stream of empathy, successful outcomes are possible.

TABLE 20-3 **Checking the Evidence of Landon's Thought: "I'm a busy person; there's nothing wrong with being late."**

Questions	Answers
Do I have any experiences from my own life that would contradict my thoughts?	I do have to admit, I get annoyed when people are late when I'm on time.
Is this thought distorted in any way?	I don't think so; I am busy, and I have important work to do.
Am I not considering other evidence that might contradict my thoughts?	I guess other people are busy too, but I'm not sure if they are as important as I am.

Pausing to gain a better perspective

Many narcissists act impulsively. They speak without reflection and react quickly, especially when frustrated. Anger management is often an identified goal of CBT with narcissistic individuals. Therapists often suggest these three simple techniques to prevent some impulsive, angry reactions. Briefly, they are:

>> **Be quiet.** Clamp your mouth shut. Don't speak. Breathe deeply. Breathe in and out slowly ten times. Your odds of saying something useful are about a million to one.

>> **Be patient.** Grandiose narcissists talk a lot. And they respond to threats with words, often aggressive words. Many times, those words add to the fire of anger. A simple way to quiet your mind includes counting to 100 or, better yet, starting with 100 and subtracting 7 until you get to 30 or less.

>> **Crush a piece of candy.** Pop a mint or piece of hard candy in your mouth and suck, don't chew. It mimics the sucking reflex of a baby and can give you a moment. Savor the candy for a few minutes and slow down your response.

These are only a few brief, easily learned strategies for managing anger. CBT offers many more that target distorted and unhelpful thinking. See my book *Anger Management For Dummies* (Wiley) for more insights about controlling anger.

REMEMBER

Habits of responding are hard for your loved one to break. Take one day or experiment at a time.

Replacing distorted thoughts

Once a client has begun to recognize distorted thoughts, they can move on to finding ways to replace those thoughts with something more logical and reasonable.

REMEMBER

With someone like a narcissist, who may have deeply ingrained thinking patterns, replacing distorted thoughts takes your patience and their persistence. You can help support your loved one by noticing and validating their attempts at change.

Some common distorted thoughts and replacements for them can be seen in Table 20-4.

TABLE 20-4   **Identifying and Replacing Distorted Narcissistic Thoughts**

Distorted Narcissistic Thought	Replacement Thought
I am better than other people.	I am highly skilled, but that doesn't make me superior.
I demand that others give me respect and admiration at all times.	While that might be nice, lots of people won't do it. I need to be okay with that.
I always deserve special treatment.	I think I should get special treatment, but in reality, that won't happen all the time. I just need to chill out.
It's okay to step on other peoples' toes to get ahead.	Even if it's okay, it can come back to bite me when others get mad at me.
I want more than everyone else around me has. I hate it when someone I know gets something better than mine.	I may want these things, but envy and jealousy don't feel good. And most of the stuff I buy just gets tossed eventually.

These are just samples, but note they may take a long time to develop and be incorporated in a narcissistic person. The CBT therapist works with their client in a gentle, playful manner, gradually guiding the client to come up with thoughts that, over time, become more adaptive.

Tracking Your Loved One's Progress

Expect your loved one's progress to go slowly and unevenly. In other words, two steps forward, one step back. This pattern will vary. Sometimes the narcissist will move forward in one area and back in another. Progress looks more like the stock market than a gradual, smooth move upward.

Tracking progress should focus on the original treatment goals that were laid out in the early stages of therapy. For example, the narcissistic client should

>> Keep track of the number of arguments had each day.

>> Monitor moods over time. Expect feelings of uneasiness for a while.

>> Rate relationships with people they are close to once a month.

Unfortunately, not every narcissist will benefit from any kind of therapy. But the hope is that some positive changes in behaviors will make life better, both for narcissists and those that care about them.

If your loved one is making sincere efforts at change, support them with smiles of encouragement and gratitude for their efforts. Be quick to forgive and keep a positive, optimistic attitude. Change is always difficult, especially for someone with narcissistic traits.

Chapter **21**

Coping Skills for Narcissists: Dialectical Behavior Therapy

This morning, my puppy brought in a large multi-branch piece of sage brush from my backyard. The house had been thoroughly cleaned yesterday. About a million leaves littered the house before I noticed the mess. Then, my daughter called to chat, and my husband groused about his mouse not working, all while I was supposedly writing this chapter. With all the interruptions, I was feeling distressed and frustrated. I felt like saying something I might regret. Instead, I made myself an iced coffee, picked up a few pieces of sage brush, took a few slow, calming breaths, and decided to write about my own distress.

The point is that everyone suffers from distress from time to time. It's part of being human. It's perfectly normal to react with frustration. And sometimes people say things they regret later, but most people handle day-to-day distress without getting overwhelmed by negative emotions.

However, other people experience similar frustrations and feel as if they are about to explode. They rage during traffic, yell at salespeople, snap at family members, harshly punish their pets, scream at their kids, slam doors, berate waiters . . .

you get the idea. Some of those people who lose control when frustrated are narcissists.

Dialectical behavior therapy, or DBT, assumes that people often act out because they lack specific skills. DBT focuses on improving emotional and interpersonal functioning by teaching the following skills:

>> **Distress tolerance:** Helping people accept and get through frustrating situations without acting out.

>> **Mindfulness:** By learning the skills of mindfulness, including acceptance and meditation, people are able to put their problems into perspective without feeling quite as overwhelmed.

>> **Emotional regulation:** This skill involves helping to understand emotions and develop skills to keep emotional responses in balance with the current situation.

>> **Interpersonal effectiveness:** This portion of DBT helps people learn effective ways of communicating, including handling conflict, and developing better boundaries.

DBT, originally developed to treat borderline personality disorder, is now used to help thousands of people with a wide range of emotional or behavioral problems.

Research is scant on what treatment works best for narcissistic personality disorder. However, there are a few reasons to consider DBT for narcissism. First, narcissism and borderline personality disorder sometimes occur together. Second, narcissists often have difficulty controlling and regulating their emotions, a problem that DBT addresses quite well. Finally, narcissists have difficult, conflicted relationships. DBT teaches interpersonal effectiveness.

This chapter outlines relevant premises of DBT so that you can see whether or not this approach may benefit you or someone you care about. This chapter is by no means comprehensive. For more information about the approach, check out *DBT For Dummies* (written by Gillian Galen and Blaise Aguirre and published by Wiley).

TECHNICAL STUFF

DBT weaves concepts from cognitive behavioral therapy (CBT) and mindfulness. In its pure form, DBT consists of individual therapy, phone consultations, group therapy, and a team for therapists who gather to receive support and consultation from each other. Some professional practices are able to utilize this intense program, but the costs are significant and waiting lists are often long. Another option is to find a therapist that has training in DBT even though they do not offer the full program.

Tolerating Distress

Narcissists want their own way. They feel entitled to special treatment. They crave attention and admiration. And they don't react well when someone or something gets in the way of them getting what they want.

When their expectations are not met, narcissists can get extremely angry and sometimes aggressive. DBT teaches how to handle distressing situations without succumbing to rage. Two strategies offered by DBT are learning to delay or distract when strong, negative emotions get out of hand.

Delaying impulsive responses

Narcissists who are presented with this strategy may dismiss it as too simple. However, a skilled therapist suggests ways that narcissists can benefit from controlling their emotions, especially if they have gotten negative feedback from others. These tactics can be presented as ways narcissists can get what they want by acting in a more socially acceptable way.

WHAT THE HECK IS DIALECTIC?

I really wish there was another name for Dialectical Behavior Therapy (DBT). Dialectic is not a word that most people throw around or routinely use in everyday conversation. I'm betting the founder of DBT, Marsha Linehan, Ph.D., did not realize her treatment would become widely popular throughout the world. Maybe if she had known, she might have chosen a more understandable name.

Dialectics is the process of reasoning in which two opposite or contradictory points of view are considered in order to make sense of them and come to some sort of conclusion. It synthesizes or blends what would seem to be incompatible ideas and resolves their disharmony by accepting and working with parts of both.

A couple of examples of a dialectic would be how you can love and hate a person at the same time or crave a cigarette when you desperately don't want to smoke. Another example might be that you want to stay calm yet are overwhelmed with anger. People are faced with dialectics all the time.

In DBT, the dialectic or opposite ideas that are the basis of the practice are the balance between acceptance of the status quo and change. During therapy, there are times when pausing efforts to change and accepting "what is" makes sense, and other times call for active efforts to change. Both acceptance and change are acknowledged and blended in a way that benefits the client.

Delaying does nothing to solve a problem, especially long-term challenges. But when someone feels overwhelmed by their current situation, they're not in a good position to think and figure out what to do. Delaying is a DBT strategy that gives a person time and relief and allows them to settle down. It's a way to chill out so that an impulsive response doesn't make things worse. Most stress is fleeting. If it is chronic, there may need to be another game plan. See Chapter 20 for ways to solve major, chronic problems.

The therapist helps the narcissist client stop before acting out by asking themselves the following questions:

>> Is this really so important that I need to respond right now?

>> How will I feel if I express my feelings tomorrow?

>> What about next week?

>> How about in a year?

>> How do things usually turn out when I act impulsively?

>> How will I feel if I resist and don't react at all?

Just by asking these questions, they're likely to compose themselves and act in a more rational, socially acceptable way. Most of what is distressing resolves after a while. For example, if your dog brings in a sage brush branch, it only takes a few minutes to pick up the big pieces and vacuum the rug. Is it worth getting furious or miserable about it? I suspect most people would say no.

TIP

Other strategies that postpone an impulsive reaction include counting, deep breathing, or just stopping and thinking about all the possible consequences of acting impulsively when distressed.

Distracting the mind from a stressful situation

If a client with narcissistic traits agrees that acting impulsively when frustrated or distressed hasn't worked out for them, they are likely to agree on another technique to handle distress called distraction.

Simply put, when a person feels overwhelmed, DBT teaches distraction by doing something different. Distraction is a DBT strategy that helps move someone's mind off the present stressful situation by engaging in another attention-getting activity.

TIP

A therapist would help a narcissistic client plan some activities ahead of time that can fill their mind. They should make a list and keep it handy. In case of frequent, overwhelming urges to act out, having a list on their phone is a good idea. The following are some possible ideas:

>> Take a walk, jog, or do jumping jacks for a while.

>> Decide to take an hour off to watch a show.

>> Play a game on your computer or phone.

>> Scroll through social media.

>> Read a good book.

>> Text or call a good friend.

>> Have a cup of tea (or iced coffee).

>> Listen to your favorite music.

Everyone's list is different and likely evolves over time. The therapist and client would continue to explore ideas and activities that help keep the client from ruminating about their current situation.

Practicing Mindfulness

In order to understand how mindfulness is used in DBT, a narcissistic client could be asked to consider the following scenario:

Imagine you are with a group of friends. You're having lunch at a great restaurant. You're savoring your dessert, enjoying every bite. You notice something out of the corner of your eye. You take a furtive glance — oh no, it's your ex. You had a nasty breakup, and thoughts come racing back through your mind. You regret that you got together in the first place, you really should have gotten more in the settlement, they ruined your finances, and on and on. You put down your fork; suddenly, nothing tastes good.

Now imagine another lunch. Again, your dessert is delicious; each bite seems better than the first. One of your friends asks you how work is going. You say fine, but you start thinking about all the undone tasks piled on your desk, the upcoming meeting with your bosses, an audit you're supposed to complete by next Friday, and what could happen if you're not prepared. How are you going to get off work early to pick up the kids? You put down your fork; suddenly, nothing tastes good.

The therapist would then explain the following to the narcissistic client:

> In the first instance, your mind makes you miserable by going to the past. In that past you have regrets, guilt, and resentment. In the second scenario, your mind takes you to the future, full of worries, stress, and what ifs. Both take your attention away from the scrumptious dessert you were enjoying.

The therapist would then describe that mindfulness is the practice of staying in the present moment. The narcissist would be guided to become aware of their current state, thoughts, feelings, and bodily sensations. In addition, they would be directed to pay attention to their feelings, right now, with *acceptance*. Awareness comes without judgment.

WARNING

The practice of mindfulness can help decrease or prevent narcissistic anger and rage. However, some narcissists may misuse mindfulness and turn it into something that adds to their superiority. Instead of being humble, they use their special status as a highly mindful human with the goal of showing off.

Mindfulness is an essential skill in the DBT tool kit. Therapy sessions often begin with mindful meditation. Learning mindfulness takes time and practice, so the following sections offer a few major components of mindfulness within the scope of DBT.

Accepting the present moment

The dictionary explains that acceptance means to agree to receive something tangible or intangible or take on a particular task. Acceptance can also mean being allowed into a position, such as accepting a job, or accepting a new member in a group.

In psychology, especially as it relates to mindfulness, acceptance is the act of taking on and *tolerating* the present moment. Acceptance includes acknowledging positive or negative experiences or emotions.

Teaching acceptance to a narcissist can be quite challenging. A narcissist may resist acknowledging negative emotions without expressing them. They tend to be quite intolerant and hold grudges. Living in the present and accepting reality can be quite frustrating to a narcissist with little empathy and a need to have their own way. Nevertheless, if a narcissist is open to exploring acceptance, they may benefit from this technique.

When a person accepts negative emotions as they are, they don't pile anger and resentment on top. For example, if they accept that they're angry when the feeling arises, then they can recover and move forward. But if they can't stand being angry, and being angry makes them even madder, things only get worse.

REMEMBER

Acceptance means allowing all emotions to be felt, whether good or bad. Narcissists are taught to hold onto and welcome their present experience. They are encouraged to give the feeling time. *All strong feelings lessen eventually.*

Acceptance requires a stance of openness to all that is present reality. Acceptance of self and others, feelings, and conditions leads to tolerance of the good and the bad. Those who learn to embrace the present, acquire the possibility of changing.

Giving up judgment

Acceptance accompanies a non-judgmental frame of mind. When a person accepts their current reality, they learn to embrace without evaluation. Their mind then allows all emotions, negative or positive to live in each moment.

People who suffer emotional distress are often quite judgmental. They may label themselves or others as good, bad, silly, unpleasant, upbeat, and so on. Those judgments tend to stick and can cause considerable suffering for all concerned. Narcissists are especially judgmental. They believe that they are usually right and others wrong. End of story.

Calming down through controlled breathing

Focused breathing is a way to calm down when people are upset. Therefore, breathing exercises are recommended for stress management, anger management, anxiety, and as a way to curb impulsive behavior. Sometimes the breaths are a way to clean out current stirred-up emotions; therefore, they are called *cleansing breaths.*

Since narcissists are frequently upset, angry, or frustrated, breathing techniques may be a particularly good skill to teach in therapy. Narcissistic clients may welcome a technique that makes them feel better without dealing with any of their problematic thoughts, beliefs, or behaviors. There are dozens of specific ways to engage in breathing techniques, but most involve teaching the client the following basic steps:

1. **Breathe in very slowly through your nose until you feel full of air.**

2. **Hold the breath for a few seconds.**

3. **Breathe out (through either your nose or mouth), again as slowly as you can.**

4. **Repeat this way of breathing for a certain time period. Some recommend ten breaths, others a minute or more.**

    Practice a couple of times and choose whatever works best. Daily practice is encouraged so that it becomes a habitual way to handle stress.

TIP

The basic idea of slow breathing is to focus attention on breaths rather than the current pressing urge, impulse, or emotion.

Meditating to focus the mind

Meditation, a part of mindfulness, is another DBT strategy. Its known benefits make it a good choice for narcissists and the people who care about them. However, narcissists may resist meditation because it doesn't offer them instant gratification or adoration.

Meditation has been practiced for thousands of years. It has become increasingly popular over time because of the many benefits that regular meditation delivers. For example, engaging in a meditation practice has the following effects:

>> Reduces stress hormones

>> Improves sleep

>> Reduces high blood pressure

>> Alleviates some of the suffering from chronic pain

>> Improves immune function

>> Reduces anger

>> Decreases digestive problems

>> Reduces impulsiveness

>> Helps with addiction

>> Reduces rumination (thinking negative thoughts in a continuous loop)

>> Improves attention

That's a pretty impressive list of benefits. Someone can meditate briefly; even a few minutes a day is helpful. Meditation should be practiced regularly to obtain and enjoy major benefits.

TIP

No equipment is needed to meditate. A quiet place without distractions is preferable, but not required. Detailed explanations of each type of meditation can be found by searching on the internet.

Some people meditate using apps. If your narcissistic partner or loved one decides to use an app, take advantage of the free trial most offer and make sure they like the voice and style of the meditation before buying. Expect the cost to be reasonable.

WARNING

Some meditation promoters make outlandish claims. They promise that their specific type of meditation will absolutely change lives. By the way, a person may only pay $199 for the basic training, but after completing that, they are offered the opportunity to become a "certified" expert and pyramid their way to the top. More often than not, these claims are based on someone making money. And it's not you or your loved one. Beware: Some meditation gurus are narcissists too.

There are many techniques and strategies for meditation. The following briefly describes a few of the most common forms of meditation that may be taught to a client:

>> **Breathing meditation:** In this form, attention is focused on the breath. Concentrate on what every part of your body is feeling as you slowly breathe in and out. Sometimes people count the breaths, either consecutively or from one to ten repeatedly. This practice can be done for a minute or more.

>> **Mantra meditation:** Sounds, words, or phrases are repeated rhythmically during the meditation. When the mind wanders, simply bring it back to focusing on the mantra.

>> **Body scan:** The body scan can be used to relax or as a way to manage chronic pain. Attention is paid to each section of the body. Often body scans start at the feet and go up, but it really doesn't make any difference. As you move through the scan, each part of the body is accepted as is.

>> **Moving meditations:** These include walking meditation, tai chi, and various yoga practices. The focus is on the movement as well as the breath.

>> **Loving-kindness meditation:** In your mind, you send messages of love, peace, and goodwill. This type of meditation, while often directed to others, can also be directed at yourself. Loving-kindness meditation will likely feel quite strange to a narcissist. They may resist, but the other types of meditation may feel more comfortable for them.

TIP

When your loved one meditates, expect focusing for them to be difficult at first. Their minds will fill with distracting thoughts. They may have a sudden unrelenting itch somewhere on their body. They might cough, sneeze, or even have a cramp. Their phone may beep. Good therapists teach clients to expect distractions and to simply return their focus to the present meditation. As they practice meditation, they will find that it becomes easier to focus and distractions lessen.

Emotional Regulation: How it Works

Emotions are signals that alert people to what is happening. Sometimes emotions are obvious and a result of something that actually occurs. Someone wins the lottery and they're happy. A beloved dog dies, and the owner is sad. Someone is insulted and feels angry. When a person can't find their keys, they're frustrated. Someone finds a buried treasure and becomes excited.

At other times, the source of an emotion is less clear. A person may feel sad, but they're not sure why. Or someone may get angry and can't seem to think of anything that's currently making them frustrated. A person feels anxious in a situation that is normally comfortable. In those cases, other factors such as hunger, fatigue, or lingering grief or trauma may be the origin.

Emotional regulation is the ability to display emotions in a way that matches what is currently happening. It involves skills to choose how and when to express emotions. In other words, emotional regulation includes discretion. It also requires the capacity to be aware of one's own emotions and the emotions of others.

For example, if a person is pulled over in a traffic stop, for no reason at all, they are likely to have a mixture of fear and anger. If the officer is polite, most people settle down. However, a few officers sometimes act belligerent and rude. What does someone do? If a person has good emotional regulation, they inhibit their outrage and answer as politely as possible. It's not usually a good idea to yell or become aggressive with a police officer. Narcissists don't always get this essential principle.

Those who don't have the capacity to regulate their emotions face a life of continuous conflict and chaos. The good news is that emotional regulation can be improved.

Emotional regulation and narcissism

Narcissists have trouble identifying their own feeling states. They may have a disconnect between the physical feeling and the expression of emotions. Narcissists especially deny feelings such as anxiety or fear. They repress and deny anything that could suggest weakness.

They yell, insult, criticize, reject, and seek revenge, but deny their anger. Lacking empathy, they are also unaware of many of the feelings of others. Therefore, they don't understand their effect on those around them.

Narcissists have difficulty regulating their emotions when faced with a threat to their self-esteem. They are fragile when it comes to the possibility of humiliation. When their sense of superiority is threatened, they may callously and impulsively react with aggression and even violence. See Chapter 11 for more information about types of narcissists and aggression.

Differentiating primary and secondary emotions

DBT teaches narcissistic clients how to recognize their emotions when they occur in order to help regulate them. Emotions communicate how a person feels about the situation in which they find themselves. Emotions emerge from thoughts and physical sensations. Sometimes the body communicates a few seconds before the mind. Other times the mind reacts before the body.

For example, if a person sees something thin, squiggly, and long while walking through a field, their body instantly goes into fight, flight, or freeze mode. But then their mind kicks in and realizes it's not a snake, just part of an old hose. They settle down. The process works the same for all people, narcissistic or not.

Emotions can also be sparked by remembering things from the past or anticipating future events. Recalling pleasant happenings brings joy, happiness, and contentment. Remembering terrible experiences causes anger, pain, shame, or guilt. Looking forward to a vacation may bring feelings of happiness or excitement. Looking forward to a long jail sentence (as narcissists sometimes experience) can cause grief, anger, and fear.

Primary emotions

The emotions people feel just after experiencing an event are called primary emotions. People experience these emotions immediately, without thinking. Primary emotions are often transient and show up in physical responses. When people are happy, they smile; when disgusted, they scrunch up their lips and nose. These emotional experiences are felt to some degree by people all over the world. Lists vary, but primary emotions include these:

>> Anger
>> Contempt
>> Disgust
>> Fear
>> Guilt

- » Joy
- » Sadness
- » Shame
- » Shyness
- » Surprise

Primary emotions arrive and depart quickly. They are replaced by the emotional response that happens as the mind kicks into gear and starts ruminating.

Secondary emotions

After the thinking brain starts working, another set of emotions may appear. Secondary emotions refer to how people think, interpret, and feel about their primary emotions. For example, when someone gets into an argument with their partner about taking out the trash. They're angry. Words are said that are over-the-top and cruel. Later driving to work, they feel regret about their fight. They wish they had handled it better; they feel guilty. Pride, envy, regret, jealousy, and frustration are also common secondary emotions.

These secondary emotions occur frequently among people with narcissistic traits. For example, a vulnerable narcissist may act superior and special, but underneath, harbor shame, guilt, and self-loathing. These secondary emotions may seem confusing to a person with narcissistic personality disorder. Therapy can help them uncover underlying emotions.

WARNING

Secondary emotions sometimes lead people to feel worse about the event than the original primary emotion. A chain of emotional responses can emerge from the primary source.

TIP

Emotional regulation calls for recognizing emotions and taking a stance of non-judgment of any emotional experience. Clients are taught to allow emotions to flow in and accept them as they are without fighting, judging, just allowing.

Taking care of basic needs

When a person is hungry or tired, they're more likely to get emotional. Therefore, one part of emotional regulation consists of taking care of the body. Emotions bubble up when the body is not taken care of. Some issues, when not addressed in a healthy manner, may increase emotional volatility. These include sleep, diet, exercise, and addiction.

In DBT, the therapist works with the client to clear obstacles such as poor sleep, lack of exercise, or poor eating habits, that may get in the way of good emotional regulation. Narcissistic clients may be able to accept this guidance because it does not threaten their egos.

Sleep

Sleep refreshes and invigorates. Most adults need seven or eight hours of sleep. Sleep deprivation decreases the ability to pay attention, depletes memory, increases irritability, suppresses immune functioning, and makes it more difficult to regulate emotions.

The following are a few tips on falling and staying asleep that may be part of a DBT treatment plan for clients presenting with a variety of concerns, including narcissism:

>> Associate bed with sleep and sex. Other activities such as eating or working should not be conducted in bed. People want their bodies to know that when they pull up the covers, it's time to sleep.

>> Darken the bedroom as much as possible and turn the temperature down. Adding blankets when cold is better than keeping a warm room for sleep.

>> Consider a sound machine. Either buy one or download one of many free apps.

>> Make sure that the mattress is comfortable. If pillows are older than a year or so, consider replacing them.

>> Don't eat or drink too much before bed. A glass of wine is probably okay, but decaffeinated tea is better. Alcohol can interfere with sleep cycles.

>> If not asleep after 20 minutes or so in bed, get up. Do something boring. And remember, lots of people have gone through many days without a long sleep.

TIP

These sleep suggestions represent a small sampling of ideas. For more information, see *Anxiety For Dummies* (authored by Charles H. Elliott and myself, and published by Wiley).

Diet

There are simply too many diet plans to review each one. Some suggest no fat or low fat; others call for lots of certain kinds of fat. So the therapist may suggest that your loved one keep a few general principles in mind and talk to their primary care provider or a nutritionist for recommendations about diet.

Anyway, this is a book about narcissism and the chapter is about DBT. However, you should know that DBT stresses taking care of the body. That's because a healthy diet allows people to regulate their emotions more easily. And a poor diet leads to anxiety, irritability, and stress. Here are some basic diet suggestions:

>> Enjoy nonprocessed foods such as fruits, vegetables, nuts, whole grains, and beans. Minimize processed foods like chips, sugary cereal, soft drinks, frozen pizza, and deli meats.

>> Cut back on sugar. Everyone knows how to do that. Doing it is always more difficult.

>> Use only healthy fats such as olive oil, avocado oil, certain fish, nuts, and seeds.

>> When eating out, split a meal. If that's not possible, ask the waiter to box up half of the meal before it is served.

>> Eat slowly and chew each bite. Consider using smaller plates and fill up a plate one time only.

You get the idea. You can find so much more about specific diets such as Mediterranean, DASH, keto, plant-based, and low carb in the *For Dummies* series (Wiley).

Exercise

Like dieting, there are many ways to exercise. Any exercise regimen should include endurance (aerobic), strength training (or resistance training), stretching or flexibility, and balance. Most adults and active seniors should be getting about 30 minutes every day of moderate exercise.

Regular exercise has many health benefits such as lowering blood pressure, protecting against most heart disease, and preventing or managing type 2 diabetes. In addition, vigorous exercise helps to calm emotional upset. When exercising, the body releases endorphins, which are natural pain killers. Endorphins also decrease stress and lead to a sense of well-being. Most DBT therapists strongly encourage exercise.

Exercise is a good tonic for most emotional disorders. Exercise leads to less depression and anxiety. In addition, it is a wonderful tool for anger. Vigorous exercise quickly dissipates anger, which is often a problem for people with narcissistic traits.

Addictions

People turn to substances to make them feel good, better, numb, or increase their focus. They use them because of curiosity or pressure from their friends. In the beginning, drug use usually feels pretty good. And early on, people falsely believe that they can control their personal use of addictive substances.

People with narcissism have a higher-than-average problem with drugs and alcohol. Because they believe they have superior power, they also believe that they can control their use of addictive substances. However, narcissists are human and have human genetics. They are certainly not immune to addiction.

Most addictions begin with recreational use of a substance such as nicotine, alcohol, stimulants, marijuana, opioids, barbiturates, benzodiazepine, hypnotics, inhalants, hallucinogens, or synthetic drugs.

An addiction is a chronic brain disease. Once addicted, a person tends to engage in addictive behavior more often and obtain less benefit. People who are addicted crave their drugs or the experiences those drugs provide and have a diminished ability to recognize the costs to themselves and others due to their continued use.

Narcissists like to feel good. In fact, they feel entitled to special privileges and believe they are impervious to negative consequences of their behaviors. They are willing to put themselves at physical and legal risks to feel better than others. And addictions aren't limited to substance abuse. Other possible addictions that may seduce narcissists include

>> Compulsive shopping

>> Excessive gambling beyond their means

>> Compulsive sexual behavior

>> Excessive focus on bodybuilding and appearance

At the end of the day, narcissists want to feel good and have little tolerance or the self-control needed to participate in recovery treatment programs. That may, in part, be because they fear looking weak in front of others. For more information on addiction, see *Addiction & Recovery For Dummies* by Paul Ritvo, Jane Irvine, and Brian F. Shaw (Wiley).

Opposite actions: Countering common emotional responses

Did you ever wonder what Mona Lisa is smiling about? Scholars debate to this day on that smile's significance. One thought is that she is both happy and sad. Others speculate that the smile is disingenuous. Both happy and sad can apply to the next DBT skill, *opposite actions*.

Opposite actions refer to digging down deep to engage in an action that runs counter to a person's feelings. Feelings are messengers that tell the brain to act in a certain way. When people act differently than what their brain tells them to, it opens up unexpected possibilities for change.

When an emotion or belief is triggered, narcissistic clients usually have a habitual response. For instance, when they feel angry, they lash out. When they feel fear, they cower and avoid. DBT therapists suggest trying a different — actually, opposite — path. When someone feels angry, instead of lashing out, DBT suggests taking a moment to find calmness. Or when someone feels afraid, instead of hiding or avoiding, the recommendation is to take steps toward what is feared.

Although narcissists may have difficulty with this exercise, they may become convinced to try them as simple experiments. See Table 21-1 for examples of how common narcissistic feelings and beliefs can be countered by opposite actions.

TABLE 21-1   ## Taking the Opposite Path

Belief or Emotion	Habitual Response	Opposite Path
Entitlement: I should always get what I want.	If I don't get everything I want, I am furious and shout about the failure of others to meet my needs.	I will engage in deep breathing, smiling, and showing gratitude for what I have.
Uniqueness: I am different and superior to others. I am perfect.	I must be perfect. If I'm not, I blame others, collapse into despair, or explode in anger.	When I make a mistake, I will take several deep breaths and be happy that I had an opportunity to grow and learn something new.
Lack of empathy: Other people are objects for me to exploit.	If I meet someone new, I size them up for how they can be useful to me. I don't mind stepping on a few toes when I need to.	I am going to pick two or three of my acquaintances and then compliment them, do something nice, and ask how I can be a better friend.
Rage: I feel extreme anger when people get in my way.	I fly into a rage, yelling, screaming, and throwing papers. Others deserve what I dish out.	Next time I feel anger stirred up, I'm going to take five deep breaths, put on a Mona Lisa smile, and think of how lucky I am to have this opportunity to practice a new skill in emotional regulation.
Demanding approval: I expect praise. When I don't get it, I get angry.	When I complete a project, I need recognition and praise. If I don't get it, why bother? I may rip up the whole thing.	Next project I complete, I will not tell anyone that I have finished. I'll just put it out there. I might consider pointing out how other people helped me.

TIP

If you've been accused of being a narcissist and are reading this book to get your partner, friends, family, or workmates off your back, you're in the right place. You may think that these techniques are easy or below your superior skill level, but think of them as thought experiments and give some of them a try. I suspect that you may find them both difficult and surprisingly beneficial.

Improving Interpersonal Skills with DBT

Getting along with others is a skill. Some people are better at it than others. Everyone knows people who are extroverted and make good first impressions. Similarly, narcissists often make excellent first impressions.

However, narcissistic traits get in the way of long-term, deep relationships. Narcissists talk too much without listening. They are always right and don't take kindly to any form of criticism even when it's intended to be constructive.

DBT teaches interpersonal skills without assigning blame. It assumes that everyone wants to get what they want, improve relationships, and maintain self-respect.

Paying attention

When someone with narcissistic traits enters a conversation, the topic often veers and becomes personally relevant to the narcissist. No matter what the conversation was prior to their entrance, narcissists like the spotlight turned entirely on them. This habit may work well at parties and large social functions; however, desiring all the attention can wreak havoc on close relationships.

If almost all the attention is focused on one person, the relationship suffers. People with narcissism do not wake up one morning and decide to become narcissists. They can change. Not easily, but they can.

In order to train those with narcissism to be better at one-on-one conversations, some of the skills discussed earlier in this chapter, such as mindfulness and acceptance, are necessary. Skill-building exercises increase the ability to focus attention on something other than oneself, to ask questions, and to balance the conversation.

Examining conflict

Narcissists find themselves in regular conflict with others. Often, they come to therapy because important people are insisting that they do so. It's a great opportunity to discover a few tactics to de-escalate rather than escalate conflicts.

Among other things, DBT teaches interpersonal skills to narcissistic clients, including the following:

>> They should stick to the facts. Describe the situation completely without using expletives or extreme language. Make descriptions akin to a science report to minimize intense emotions.

>> Narcissists should listen carefully to both sides. There are no right or wrong feelings.

>> They should strive to take the time to be nice and remain calm and open to new ideas even if they don't feel like it. In addition, they should respect both themselves and the person they are engaged with, even if they don't want to.

>> They can learn to show other people that they understand the other person's message by repeating it and asking if they got it right.

>> They should try to find something to agree with, even if it's small. This technique can be surprisingly powerful and helpful.

REMEMBER

The client should practice these skills with their therapist, partner, and others — even in front of a mirror. These responses to conflict will slowly become second nature. Expect the practice to take significant time. The results may be more substantial than expected.

6

The Part of Tens

Discover some quick ways to defuse a narcissist.

Find ways to safely leave a narcissistic relationship.

Chapter **22**

Ten Quick Ways to Diffuse Narcissistic Behavior

I magine you are attending a holiday celebration for a large group of people. As you're mingling, you happen to start a conversation with someone who seems receptive but quickly begins arguing with you, no matter what you say. You don't really know the person, and you certainly don't want a confrontation, but they're getting louder and more argumentative by the minute. What should you do?

Now, I'm in no way suggesting that you can spot narcissists by having a casual conversation with them. However, if you find yourself in an unexpectedly loud, self-serving, and argumentative exchange that you just want to leave, this chapter gives you tips for defusing the tense situation. These tips aren't meant to solve any big problems with a narcissist, but they are handy when you want to keep the peace in public.

WARNING

Narcissists love to be the center of attention, and escalating an argument is one of their tools to get the spotlight. Narcissists can increase the volume, constantly repeat themselves, and occasionally even use physical aggression when they feel challenged. It's not worth risking a fight (see Chapter 11 for more information about narcissists and aggression).

Don't Let Your Ego Get in the Way

Conversations with narcissists have nothing to do with you. Don't forget this essential point. Actually, narcissists rarely have real conversations; they lecture without listening. They simply want to hear themselves talk. Because narcissists only view their side of an argument as correct, no amount of logic or evidence will change their mind. Put your ego safely high up on a shelf in your mind. This has nothing to do with your worth as a human being.

Excuse Yourself and Walk Away

Sometimes you just need to excuse yourself before things get too heated. Remember that narcissists love attention and conflict. I'm not advocating harmful lying, just a gracious way to leave the scene so the narcissist can save face and find someone else to bother.

Here are some things you can say to get out of the situation:

>> "Excuse me, I have to use the restroom."

>> "It's been great talking with you, but I see a friend over there I desperately need to talk to."

>> "Oh, I just got a notification from my [fill in the blank — kid, babysitter, partner, boss, or the like]. I need to check and see if they're okay."

>> "I was having such a good time that I didn't realize what time it is. I've got to get going. Great talking to you."

Appeal to Their Uniqueness

Narcissists believe that they are unique and special. Use that. When things go sideways, highlight their uniqueness. You might say, "I hate to interrupt, but I just love your jacket!" (or purse, or whatever else stands out). Or you can tell them that they have a unique and creative perspective on things. Say, "Wow, I never thought of it that way. That's interesting."

You're not really agreeing with them; you're just trying to shut down a situation that could possibly escalate.

Puff Up Their Superiority

Narcissists believe themselves to be superior to others. Use that knowledge to de-escalate a heated situation. Here are some ideas of things to say:

>> Tell them it's clear they've put quite a bit of thought into the matter.

>> Ask if they were previously on a debate team.

>> Inquire as to whether they went to law school (try to do it without sarcasm).

>> Tell them they sure have lots of passion and interest.

Again, this technique doesn't advocate blatant lying; it's just a way to calm down the situation so you can safely move on.

Appear Engaged

Remember that you can never win an argument with a true narcissist. You simply want to minimize harm and avoid an argument. Turn your mind to neutral. Pretend that the narcissist across from you is your 2-year-old toddler, who is telling you an incomprehensible story about preschool.

Smile and say:

>> "Oh, really"

>> "Umm"

>> "Sure"

>> "Yup"

>> "Aha"

Then nod your head as if you agree, but just stop listening. After all, the argument, just like your 2-year-old's rendition of preschool, is incomprehensible.

Apologize for Small Stuff

Your goal is not to completely give in to a narcissist. However, you don't want to engage in an argument with someone whose opinion you don't care about. Try to find something to apologize for and then change the subject or, better yet, make your exit. It doesn't need to even make sense.

Here are some examples:

» "I'm sorry, I'm having trouble hearing you in this room. Perhaps we can talk later when it's quieter."

» "I'm sorry if I misunderstood you."

» "I'm afraid I'm not able to follow the complexity of this conversation. Please excuse me."

» "I wish I had expertise in this topic. I'm sorry, I'm in way over my head."

Partially Agree

It's harder to argue with someone who partially agrees with you than someone who outright disagrees. Let the narcissist make their point and then find some piece of it to agree with. For example:

» "Sometimes that's probably true."

» "You could be right on that" (Note the use of the word *could*.)

» "You could have a point there."

» "That's an interesting perspective."

Lose the Battle but Win the War

Don't try to win an argument with a narcissist. The battle is unwinnable and simply not worth it. Instead, keep your sights on staying out of a situation that could potentially escalate into aggression and occasionally even violence. The goal of your war is to live a peaceful, meaningful life. Engaging with a narcissist in an argument will not give you fulfillment.

Even in the situation in which a narcissist is saying something obnoxious, inappropriate, vile, or even loathsome, getting involved won't solve anything.

Encourage others to back off as well. No need to make a point with someone who will never concede that point or change. Consider them impaired; you can't challenge a drunk or high person and expect a reasonable response.

REMEMBER

If you feel that you have to say something, you can simply say, "I can't agree with that" and remove yourself from the conversation. If you feel a moral imperative to state your opposition, you do have the option of expressing that opinion and then walking away. Just do so calmly, without anger or blame. Even knowing your opinion isn't likely to truly be heard, you may feel better expressing it. Just don't let the situation escalate; there's no point. (To make a quick exit, see the earlier section "Excuse Yourself and Walk Away.")

Don't Get Mad

Anger leads to more anger. You are faced with someone who actually enjoys getting into arguments, but you don't have to engage. If you feel your emotions are beginning to get the best of you, pause and try the following:

>> Take a few slow, deep breaths.

>> Count from 10 to 1 backwards, slowly.

>> Ask yourself if this is worth taking a stand that won't be listened to.

>> Appreciate the strength of calmness in the face of battle.

>> Be silent; there's strength in that as well.

Drop the Rope

Imagine that you are standing on a precipice overlooking the Grand Canyon. On the other side of the canyon is the Hulk. You are both holding an end of the same rope. The Hulk challenges you to a tug of war. You like contests and challenges, and you find it almost irresistible.

But your logical mind checks in. Obviously, the Hulk is a superpower, and you are human. Can you win? No.

However, there is one and only one way to win. You realize that your options are limited. You can't overpower a superhero. But you can drop your end of the rope. Game over, you won.

Chapter 23

Ten Tips for Leaving a Narcissistic Relationship

Some people can tolerate a relationship with a narcissist. Probably more cannot. If you are considering a rupture in your connection, plan ahead. That's because narcissists don't like to be left. It's a blow to their egos, and they don't like losing control.

This chapter gives you some general tips on leaving a narcissistic relationship. They apply to narcissistic partners, parents, and even casual friends. However, these suggestions are not comprehensive. For lots more information about leaving a relationship with a narcissist, refer to Part 2.

If domestic violence or abuse is involved, call the National Domestic Violence Hotline at 800-799-SAFE (7233).

Consider Getting Professional Mental Health Support

Sometimes you need someone on the outside to help you see clearly what is right in front of you. However, friends and family may be too biased to see things accurately. In addition, it's always hard to leave someone that you once cared about.

Consider finding a mental health professional who has experience with narcissism to help you develop a plan that will keep you emotionally and physically safe. You don't need to commit to months of psychotherapy; just a few sessions may be all you need.

Copy Documents and Protect Privacy

Before you leave a narcissistic relationship, realize that potential trouble may be ahead. Be sure to start changing your passwords and get your documents in order. Consider buying a disposable or burner phone to make calls to your lawyer, mediator, financial planner, or other people who are helping you.

WARNING

Don't take these suggestions as legal advice. Especially if you are married, you will want to get help from a divorce attorney or mediator.

Check your credit rating and that of your partner's if possible. If you have only joint credit cards, start to open a few in your own name. Then start calling the number on the back of your old, jointly owned credit cards to see whether your name can be taken off. Some will allow it; others will need you both to sign off, especially when there is a balance.

Open a bank account in your own name. Make copies of any documents that you need to have in your possession, such as previous years' taxes, medical records, and children's school records. Also make copies of any insurance plans. Again, how you handle joint finances may require legal intervention.

Establish Financial Independence

Understand what it takes to live independently. You are likely going to have a change in income if you were previously living with someone. The first thing to do is take a look at the potential costs of living on your own. Look at the costs of housing, utilities, insurance, car payments, and so on. If you have children, you need to consider all the costs of childcare and necessities. Add them up. Consider how you will manage them.

If you don't have the resources to make it on your own, consult with an attorney to see what to expect. Consider talking to a community college career counselor to see how you might prepare yourself by taking some classes or earning a certificate that could help you get a better-paying job or advance in your current field. Do not depend on your ex to support you financially unless you obtain a court order for child support or alimony. Realize if you do depend on them, in some cases, you'll remain partially under their control.

Make a Clean Break

Once you decide to end a relationship with a narcissist, it's important to end it as completely as possible. Obviously, if you have children, leaving becomes more complicated (see Chapter 9 for more information).

The point is to stop engaging in the normal give and take of a relationship. You need to find the strength to become independent. Further interactions with a narcissist will certainly interfere with your new freedom.

Resist Being Sucked Back In

Narcissists are unable to love unconditionally. Strings are always attached, and many of those strings involve being in total control. So when you leave, they feel enraged and anxious at the same time.

Hoovering, an expression meaning to suck you back in (so-called after the Hoover vacuum maker), is a common strategy of narcissists. That behavior was what got you into the relationship in the first place — don't be surprised to see it resume when you attempt to leave.

A narcissist will promise better behavior, more commitment, and caring, all the while bombing you with flattery, attention, and gifts. Don't fall for it again; it is simply a way to control you.

Know Setbacks Are Normal

Things rarely go up in a straight line. There are usually ups and downs. But as long as the trajectory is trending up, you will succeed. Prepare for setbacks; the narcissist will pull out all stops to take you back under their control. Be kind to yourself if you succumb temporarily; it will get better. Be strong, get outside support, and continue to grow as a person.

Discard Mementos

This may seem rather silly, but it is important. Discard the photos, souvenirs, or gifts that remind you of your past relationship. Take the photos of the two of you off of your phone.

If you can't stand to do that with gifts or printed photos, put them away in a cupboard. Narcissists often trap their prey with gifts and pleasurable adventures. But remember, all is not well. You need a fresh start!

You want to get on with your life — looking at the past will keep you there. Of course, if your narcissist bought you a new car, consider trading it in.

Keep Clear of Narcissists' Allies

Early on, a narcissist will often try to isolate you from your friends. This isolation may continue throughout the relationship. When you are ready to leave, you may reach out to your former friends.

Incredibly, they may be cold and unresponsive. A clever ploy a narcissist uses is to poison your relationships and form alliances with those you were once close to. Narcissists may tell your friends lies about you and accuse you of exactly what narcissists were doing themselves. The damage may be irreparable or may take significant time to undo.

Watch Out for the Narcissistic Storm

When you leave narcissists, it is a severe blow to their often-fragile egos. They may react with rage that seems excessive and scary, even if you've had a relatively poor relationship for years or a superficial relationship that you believed wasn't really that important.

The anger and aggression narcissists display often exceeds the actual experience. This anger explodes with intensity that may surprise you. Stay away; it isn't worth trying to figure out their unreasonable reaction.

Give Yourself Time to Grieve

The loss of any important relationship, no matter how tumultuous, can cause feelings of grief. You may also be quite relieved that you no longer have to put up with excessive demands or abuse. However you feel at first, a twinge of sadness for what you thought the relationship could and should have become may creep in. In the beginning, you were optimistic and hopeful; now you are sad and depleted. Give yourself some time to come to terms with the loss.

Index

A

abandonment, 93, 100
abused children, 53
acceptance, 290–291
actors, 210
Addiction & Recovery For Dummies (Ritvo/Irvine/Shaw), 299
addictions, 298–299
adolescence, 92–93
aerobic exercise, 298
ageism, 232
aggression, narcissistic
   after breakups, 314
   bullying, 166–169
   coping with, 176–177
   emotional abuse, 170–171
   example of, 164–165
   forms of, 166–174
   in groups, 14
   mass shootings and, 173
   overview, 163
   passive, 169–170
   pets and domestic violence, 170–171
   physical violence and, 172–173
   proactive, 166
   reactive, 165–166
   self-esteem and, 170
   threatened egos and, 164–166
aggressive driving, 236–237
aging narcissists, 174
agoraphobia, 199
Aguirre, Blaise (author), 286
air-rage, 235–236
alcohol abuse, 299
American Psychiatric Society, 20
Americans with Disabilities Act (ADA), 245
anger, 74, 295, 298, 309, 314
animal cruelty, 171–172
anonymity, 220, 234
anorexia nervosa, 201, 232

anti-Semitism, 41
antisocial personality disorder, 174, 194–195
anxiety
   in children of narcissistic parents, 100
   reducing with exercise, 298
   social media's impact on youth, 223
anxiety disorders, 199–200
Anxiety For Dummies (Elliott and Smith), 198, 297
anxious attachment, 86
apologies, 55, 308
approval
   demand for, 22–23, 300
   habitual response, 300
   opposite actions, 300
argument
   avoiding, 307
   backing off from, 308–309
arrogance, 27–28
arrogant pride, 159–160
assumptions, in this book, 2
astrosurfing, 220
attachment
   anxious, 86
   avoidant, 87
   disorganized, 87
   infancy to early childhood, 86–87
   secure, 86
   styles, 86–87
attention
   demand for, 22–23
   paying, 301
attorneys, 142, 144, 312
attractiveness
   ageism and, 232
   benefits of, 230–231
   characteristics of, 231
attribution, 155–156
authentic pride, 159–160
authority, 209
autocrats, 207

burner phones, buying, 312
Bushman, Brad, 236–237
business leaders, narcissistic, 203–204

C

calls, blocking, 143
canceling plans, 72–73
caregiving, 88–89, 129–130
catastrophizing, 278
CBT (cognitive behavioral therapy)
  behavioral experiments, 275–277
  boundaries, establishing, 268–269
  client/therapist partnership in, 266–270
  dialogue (example), 269
  for dysfunctional thinking, 277–282
  model, reinforcing, 269–270
  motivation in, 267–268
  overview, 265–266
  problematic behaviors to change using, 270–271
  problem-solving process in, 271–273
  strategies for persistent problems, 271–274
  tracking loved one's progress in, 282–283
  treatment goals, setting, 267
Centers for Disease Control and Prevention (CDC), 11
charitable narcissists, 187–189
cheating
  academic, 52
  chronic, 136
  by narcissistic partners, 72–73
  signs of possible infidelity, 72–73
Cheat Sheet (web site), 3
child abuse, 53
child maltreatment, 51
children
  anxiety in, 223
  depression in, 223
  duck syndrome and, 223
  emotions, 92
  focus from family to friends, 92
  healthy self-esteem in, 53–55
  identity formation, 92
  loneliness in, 222–223
  narcissistic parents and, 220–223
  neglecting, 51–52
  opinions, 92–93

overvaluation of, 47–49
permissive parenting effects on, 49–50
questioning and challenging narcissistic parents, 93
social media's impact on, 220–223
suicide, 223
turning cold shoulder to, 52
children of narcissistic parents
  adult children of narcissists, 121–122
  anxiety in, 100
  avoidant, 100–101
  being empathic to concerns of, 144–145
  cost of narcissism, 13
  daughters, 94–95, 97
  disagreeable, 100–101
  fear of abandonment in, 100
  learned narcissism in, 101
  pleasers, 99
  repeating themes from childhood, 123
  self-doubt in, 99–100
  sons, 95–96, 98
  as targets of narcissistic abuse, 122–123
chronic diseases, avoiding, 148
civility
  definition of, 234
  enforcing in schools and workplace, 240
  reciprocity and, 239–240
  teaching children about, 240
Civility in America poll, 237
cleansing breaths, 291
clickbait, 220
cognitive behavioral therapy (CBT)
  behavioral experiments, 275–277
  boundaries, establishing, 268–269
  client/therapist partnership in, 266–270
  dialectical behavioral therapy and, 286
  dialogue (example), 269
  for dysfunctional thinking, 277–282
  model, reinforcing, 269–270
  motivation in, 267–268
  overview, 265–266
  problematic behaviors to change using, 270–271
  problem-solving process in, 271–273
  strategies for persistent problems, 271–274
  tracking loved one's progress in, 282–283
  treatment goals, setting, 267

diffusing narcissistic behavior *(continued)*
  overview, 305
  partially agree, 308
  pretending engagement, 307
  puffing up their superiority, 306
disagreeability, 100–101
disgust, 295
dismissing or distorting evidence, 278
disorganized attachment, 87
disposable phone, buying, 312
dissonance, 132
distraction, 288–289
distress tolerance
  delaying impulsive responses in, 287–288
  in dialectical behavioral therapy, 286
  distraction from stressful situation, 288–289
  questions asked by therapist, 288
divorce, 66
divorce attorney, 312
documents, copying, 312
domestic violence, 171–172
doxing, 169. *See also* cyberbullying
driving, aggressive, 236–237
duck syndrome, 223
dysfunctional thinking
  black-and-white thinking, 278
  catastrophizing, 278
  challenging unhelpful thoughts, 279–283
  checking evidence of, 279–281
  cognitive behavioral therapy for, 277–282
  dismissing or distorting evidence, 278
  emotional reasoning, 278
  example of, 279–280
  identifying unhelpful thoughts, 277–279
  mind reading, 278
  overgeneralization, 278
  pausing to gain better perspective, 281
  replacing distorted thoughts, 281–282
dysthymia, 198

E

Eastern cultures, 10
eating disorders, 201
economic instability, 125

egos, 164–166, 306
Elliott, Charles H.
  Anxiety For Dummies, 199, 297
  Bipolar Disorder For Dummies, 199
  Borderline Personality Disorder For Dummies, 262
  Depression For Dummies, 198
  Obsessive-Compulsive Disorder For Dummies, 200
email addresses, 9
embezzlement, 182
emotional abuse
  effects of, 77–79
  feeling of helplessness and hopelessness in, 78
  isolation from family and friends as, 75
  loss of self-esteem in, 77
  red flags of, 170–171
  sacrificing yourself and, 78
emotional disorders, 202
emotional neglect, 51
emotional reasoning, 278
emotional regulation
  addictions and, 298–299
  basic needs and, 296
  definition of, 294
  in dialectical behavioral therapy, 286
  diet and, 297–298
  example of, 294
  exercise and, 298
  narcissism and, 294–295
  opposite actions, 299–300
  sleep and, 297
emotions
  primary, 295–296
  secondary, 296
empathetic people, 128–130
empathy
  lack of, 25–26, 75–76
  teaching, 53–54
employee assistance programs, 245
engagement, pretending, 307
enmeshment, 94
entitlement
  definition of, 46
  in everyday life, 183
  example of, 22
  habitual response, 300

vlogging, 211
volunteering, 83
vulnerable narcissists
anxiety in, 223
child abuse and, 53
depression, 223
described, 29–30
neglect and, 52
reporting to or working for, 117
social media and, 67

W

war, 14
warning signs
friends, narcissistic, 111–112
neighbors, narcissistic, 108–109
workplace narcissists, 113–114
weight, maintaining healthy, 148
Western cultures, 10
white-collar crimes, 182
whites of eyes, 231
work conflicts, 13
workplace narcissists
boundaries, setting, 115
counterproductive work behaviors, 182
dealing with, 115
documenting violations of company policy by, 115

entitlement and, 180–182
gaslighting and, 114–115
gossips and, 114–115
overview, 113
therapy for, 245
warning signs, 113–114
work-related problems, 245

X

xenophobia, 37

Y

young people
anxiety in, 223
depression in, 223
duck syndrome and, 223
emotions, 92
focus from family to friends, 92
identity formation, 92
loneliness in, 222–223
narcissistic parents and, 220–223
opinions, 92–93
questioning and challenging narcissistic parents, 93
social media's impact on, 220–223
suicide, 223
youth, as attractiveness characteristic, 231

About the Author

Laura L. Smith, PhD, is a clinical psychologist and a past president of the New Mexico Psychological Association. She has considerable experience in school, hospital, and clinical settings dealing with children and adults who presented with anxiety, depression, anger, and personality disorders including narcissistic personality disorder. She has also worked with many patients who come to therapy for help dealing with the devastating effects of having a toxic relationship with a narcissist.

Dr. Smith first became fascinated with the topic of narcissism about 20 years ago while working as a school psychologist in the Albuquerque Juvenile Detention Center. Part of her job was to evaluate juveniles who were detained after their arrests. She administered a variety of psychological tests, including a test measuring self-esteem. Surprisingly, the vast majority of detained children and teens demonstrated high or even excessively high self-esteem on those measures. Those findings led her to research the literature regarding aggression and high self-esteem. A resulting book, *Hollow Kids: Recapturing the Soul of a Generation Lost to the Self-Esteem Myth* was coauthored with her husband Dr. Charles Elliott. Her interest in narcissistic self-absorption and psychopathology is reflected in many of her other works.

Dr. Smith has presented workshops on cognitive therapy and mental health issues to national and international audiences. She recently completed *Anxiety & Depression For Dummies Workbook,* 2nd Edition; *Anger Management For Dummies,* 3rd Edition; and *Obsessive-Compulsive Disorder For Dummies,* 2nd Edition.

Dr. Smith has worked on numerous publications together with Charles Elliott, PhD, who is now retired. They are coauthors of *Anxiety For Dummies,* 3rd Edition; *Depression For Dummies,* 2nd Edition; *Quitting Smoking & Vaping For Dummies;* *Borderline Personality Disorder For Dummies,* 2nd Edition; *Child Psychology & Development For Dummies;* and *Seasonal Affective Disorder For Dummies* (all published by Wiley).

Author's Acknowledgments

First, I'd like to thank the wonderful team at Wiley who've supported my work through many projects. Tracy Boggier, senior acquisitions editor, has been a consistent guide in developing the early concepts. Vicki Adang also contributed important ideas to the initial concept. Alissa Schwipps, development editor, guided me through the writing process and helped tighten the organization and conceptualization of the project. A special thank you to Martha Fiedler, PhD, who served as an exceptionally insightful technical editor and mentor throughout.

Finally, copy editor Christy Pingleton made sure the i's were dotted and the t's were crossed, among other critical clean-ups of the text.

As always, my family has sustained me throughout this time with goodwill, tolerance, and cheerleading. My editor in chief, Charles Elliott, encouraged and lifted me up when life got challenging. I am forever changed and grateful for the life we have lived.

Publisher's Acknowledgments

Senior Acquisitions Editor: Tracy Boggier
Development Editor: Alissa Schwipps
Copy Editor: Christy Pingleton
Technical Editor: Martha Fiedler, PhD

Senior Managing Editor: Kristie Pyles
Production Editor: Tamilmani Varadharaj
Cover Image: © Viktor Aheiev/Getty Images

Leverage the power

Dummies is the global leader in the reference category and one of the most trusted and highly regarded brands in the world. No longer just focused on books, customers now have access to the dummies content they need in the format they want. Together we'll craft a solution that engages your customers, stands out from the competition, and helps you meet your goals.

Advertising & Sponsorships

Connect with an engaged audience on a powerful multimedia site, and position your message alongside expert how-to content. Dummies.com is a one-stop shop for free, online information and know-how curated by a team of experts.

- Targeted ads
- Video
- Email Marketing

- Microsites
- Sweepstakes sponsorship

20 MILLION PAGE VIEWS EVERY SINGLE MONTH

15 MILLION UNIQUE VISITORS PER MONTH

43% OF ALL VISITORS ACCESS THE SITE VIA THEIR MOBILE DEVICES

700,000 NEWSLETTER SUBSCRIPTIONS TO THE INBOXES OF *300,000* UNIQUE INDIVIDUALS EVERY WEEK

# of dummies

Custom Publishing

Reach a global audience in any language by creating a solution that will differentiate you from competitors, amplify your message, and encourage customers to make a buying decision.

- Apps
- Books
- eBooks
- Video
- Audio
- Webinars

Brand Licensing & Content

Leverage the strength of the world's most popular reference brand to reach new audiences and channels of distribution.

For more information, visit **dummies.com/biz**

PERSONAL ENRICHMENT

9781119187790
USA $26.00
CAN $31.99
UK £19.99

9781119179030
USA $21.99
CAN $25.99
UK £16.99

9781119293354
USA $24.99
CAN $29.99
UK £17.99

9781119293347
USA $22.99
CAN $27.99
UK £16.99

9781119310068
USA $22.99
CAN $27.99
UK £16.99

9781119235606
USA $24.99
CAN $29.99
UK £17.99

9781119251163
USA $24.99
CAN $29.99
UK £17.99

9781119235491
USA $26.99
CAN $31.99
UK £19.99

9781119279952
USA $24.99
CAN $29.99
UK £17.99

9781119283133
USA $24.99
CAN $29.99
UK £17.99

9781119287117
USA $24.99
CAN $29.99
UK £16.99

9781119130246
USA $22.99
CAN $27.99
UK £16.99

PROFESSIONAL DEVELOPMENT

9781119311041
USA $24.99
CAN $29.99
UK £17.99

9781119255796
USA $39.99
CAN $47.99
UK £27.99

9781119293439
USA $26.99
CAN $31.99
UK £19.99

9781119281467
USA $26.99
CAN $31.99
UK £19.99

9781119280651
USA $29.99
CAN $35.99
UK £21.99

9781119251132
USA $24.99
CAN $29.99
UK £17.99

9781119310563
USA $34.00
CAN $41.99
UK £24.99

9781119181705
USA $29.99
CAN $35.99
UK £21.99

9781119263593
USA $26.99
CAN $31.99
UK £19.99

9781119257769
USA $29.99
CAN $35.99
UK £21.99

9781119293477
USA $26.99
CAN $31.99
UK £19.99

9781119265313
USA $24.99
CAN $29.99
UK £17.99

9781119239314
USA $29.99
CAN $35.99
UK £21.99

9781119293323
USA $29.99
CAN $35.99
UK £21.99

dummies.com

dummies
A Wiley Brand